Democracy by Bullets and Teargas: Essays and Short Stories by Dwayne Wong (Omowale)

Dwayne Wong (Omowale)

ISBN: 9798485091774

Contents

1

DEMOCRACY BY BULLETS AND TEARGAS

I first became aware of the struggle against dictatorship in Togo when I came across information about Tavio Amorin, who was a political activist and the leader of the Pan-African Socialist Party in Togo. Tavio was murdered on July 23, 1992, at the age of 34. Tavio was living in exile in France, but returned to Togo in 1991, hoping to help restore democracy in the country. Tavio declared, "We will fight so that the memory of victims of the struggle for democracy will be respected." Sadly, Tavio himself would become one of the victims of the struggle for democracy.

Tavio's murder was condemned by the French government, but no action was taken by France or by Togo. Joseph Koffigoh, who was the Prime Minister of Togo at the time, made it known that a bag was discovered not far from the scene of the shooting. The bag contained the identity cards of two police officers. This would indicate that security forces were involved in the assassination, but no one had been arrested. When Jacques Chirac decided to visit Togo in 1999, Pierre Sané, who was serving as the Secretary General of Amnesty International, wrote an open letter to him informing him that Tavio's killers had not been brought to justice. The letter went on to document a number of abuses which have been carried out in Togo. This included the Bé lagoon massacre in 1991, in which 28 demonstrators were killed by the army and an attack against the Lomé Peace March in which 20 people were killed by the army.

In 1999, Amnesty International published a report titled "Togo: Rule of Terror". The report noted:

Human rights and international law have seen significant progress in the past 12 months. Last July in Rome, the statutes of the International Criminal Court were adopted, in October 1998 in London, General Pinochet was arrested and a procedure started for his extradition, recently the International Criminal Tribunal for the former Yugoslavia decided to indict Slobodan

Milosevic; these steps reflect the determination of an international community committed to end human rights violations and impunity across the world.

However, many Africans have the impression that this determination is lacking when it comes to protecting their people against abuse of power, systematic human rights violations and abuses by armed opposition groups. Africa is today ravaged by violent conflicts which are the result of systematic human rights violations, persistent impunity and inaction by the international community. In turn, these conflicts lead to the serious violations which we all observe in Sierra Leone, Congo, Sudan and elsewhere.

The fact is that this determination to protect human rights and to ensure democracy in Africa has been lacking on the part of the international community, particularly on the part of Western nations. The report by Amnesty International noted: "This inertia on the part of the Togolese authorities can only lead to the conclusion that such practices have become completely commonplace. Furthermore, the fact that detainees with swollen faces are sometimes shown on Togolese television indicates that torture and ill-treatment are used to discourage not only breaches of common law but also political dissent." That abuses in Togo have been so widespread has not prevented Western nations from continuing to support the regime in Togo. In fact, the report by Amnesty International was denounced by certain French politicians, including Chirac who suggested that the report might "be an exercise in manipulation." The reaction was likely due to the fact that Amnesty's report criticized France's role in Togo.

As I stated, I first became aware of the history of dictatorship in Togo when I read about Tavio Amorin, who was assassinated for daring to advocate for change in Togo. My own involvement in Togo's struggle began in 2017, when the people of Togo rose up in protest to demand change. The Gnassingbé regime had been fifty years old by this point. Gnassingbé Eyadéma came to power following a coup in 1967. When he died in 2005, his son Faure Gnassingbé took over. In 2017, the people of Togo were demanding the removal of Faure. They were demanding "Faure Must Go." This was not merely just a slogan. Faure Must Go was a movement which was organized by Togolese activists who were fighting for change in Togo.

One of the things that caught my attention about the protests in 2017 was that the protesters fought back against the government's force. The Togolese people confronted the military. There was a video taken of Togolese civilians holding down one of the soldiers to wrestle his gun from him. Protesters also chased away soldiers by pelting items at the soldiers. Following the arrest of a popular imam in Togo, the people responded by burning down government buildings and the houses of political leaders. The message of the Togolese people was clear. No amount of violent force from the government would deter them in their effort to overthrow the regime.

I was optimistic about change in Togo when I saw the protests in 2017, but also aware of the potential challenges that faced the Togolese people once Faure was removed. In 2014, Blaise Compaoré was toppled after mass protests in Burkina Faso. This was a situation in which the army and the protests clashed. The military began firing at protesters, but this did not quell the uprising. The protests forced Compaoré to resign as president. The military moved in to take control of the situation, which sparked even more protests. The army once again used violent force against the protesters. The lessons of the revolution in Burkina Faso were clear. Once the dictator had been toppled, the next concern would be how the military would react. Would the military rush in to seize power?

The military in many African nations has been an institution which has been used to exploit and oppress the masses. Thomas Sankara's revolution in Burkina Faso is one exception to this. What made Sankara's government different was that he did not view the military as being exploiters of the masses. In his view, the military had to serve the masses. He explained that he did not want the army to be an aristocracy which was above the masses. Instead, he held the view that the army must participate in agricultural production. During Sankara's presidency, the military was an institution which served the masses. This has not been the case in Togo. The military in Togo has been trained to oppress the masses in service of the brutal regime.

Eyadéma was not only a very brutal dictator, but he was a man who thought very highly of himself. In Togo, people were made to line up to clap for Eyadéma whenever he went to or left his presidential office. Those who were caught not clapping for the dictator were arrested. Civil servants were also made to wear uniforms with Eyadéma's image and to dance for him. There was also a comic book, which was made to honor Eyadéma, as well as watches with his face on it. This was the type of personality cult which Eyadéma fostered for himself.

The Togolese artist Ras Ly provided a description of the struggles that the people of Togo have endured under the Gnassingbé regime in his song "Boro d'Afrique." In his song, he described how the youth in Togo suffer due to the greed of the ruling class. The youth are made to go to overcrowded amphitheaters with no sound system and after graduating the students use their degrees to perform jobs such as being a motorcycle taxi driver or a dock worker. Ras Ly also sang about the suppression of freedom of press as journalists are incarcerated and tortured.

Another example of the poor infrastructure in Togo is how the government charges citizens a large tax simply to make phone calls. What is worse is that despite having to pay so much, Togolese citizens still must deal with poor phone service. The government took huge loans from international banks to improve the communication network in Togo, but still nothing was done. Togolese activist Farida Nabourema decided to address this problem by calling on Togolese to call Cina Lawson, who headed the Ministry of Posts and Telecommunications in Togo.

Despite the numerous problems in Togo, the regime wastes a lot of money to bolster its international image. For instance, the government of Togo invested a great deal of money in an African Union conference which Togo decided to host. Not only was money spent to host the conference, but money was also spent to develop the airport, build a five-star hotel, and improve roads. This was all done in an effort to present a favorable image of Togo to the international community. Nabourema called on international journalists to visit Lomé for themselves to see the poor conditions which the government of Togo has been trying to cover up.

The struggle to liberate Togo from dictatorship has been a decades long struggle. The aspect of this struggle which I have been dealing with is the issue of how the international community treats Togo. The coup which brought Eyadéma to power was supported by France. Over the years France has continued to support the regime in Togo. An example of this was when Togo held elections in 2010. France provided military equipment such as teargas, guns, and police cars. The intention was obviously to help arm the government of Togo to suppress protests following the election. France anticipated that there would be unrest in Togo.

France has been the biggest international supporter of the regime in Togo, but other Western nations have supported the regime in Togo as well, including the United States. This support for the government of Togo was very apparent during Barack Obama's presidency. Hillary Clinton went to Togo to help legitimize the dictatorship of Faure. At the time, Clinton was serving as the Secretary of State for Obama's administration. The Obama administration helped to provide international legitimacy for the dictatorship in Togo. By the time that the protests began in 2017, the Democratic Party offered no support for the people of Togo. Hillary Clinton found the time to express her support for the people of Iran when they rose in protest in 2017, but Togo was of no concern for her.

Following America's intervention in Libya to help topple Muammar Gaddafi, who was another dictator who was supported by the United States at some point, Libya was plunged into instability. The consequence of this instability would result in four State Department employees who were stationed in Libya being killed, including Ambassador J. Christopher Stevens. In the remarks which Obama delivered to honor Stevens and others who were killed, Obama stated that "we hold our head high, knowing that because of these patriots, because of you, this country that we love will always shine as a light unto the world." These were nice sentiments which expressed a very idealistic view of America, but Obama's sentiments were simply at odds with the reality of America's policies in the rest of the world. I would argue that the sentiments expressed by Obama are part of the problem.

American leaders like Obama seem to view America as a shining light for the rest of the world and this sense of self-righteousness leads to actions such as the intervention in Libya. Obama explained that he felt intervening in Libya was the right thing to do, but he also admitted that the worst failure of his presidency was failing to plan for the aftermath of the intervention. Why would one intervene in a nation for the purpose of helping to topple a leader who had been in power for decades without preparing for the possibility that doing so could lead to instability? This failure to plan is especially astonishing when one considers that the safety of American citizens such as Stevens depended on Libya being stable. A destabilized Libya is not only a threat to the people of Libya, but to the Americans who are in Libya.

A point that must be understood about the American intervention in Libya is that although Gaddafi had a strained relationship with the United States in the past, prior to the intervention which overthrow Gaddafi, Gaddafi's relationship with the United States was such that the American Central Intelligence Agency (CIA) was assisting Gaddafi with capturing and torturing dissidents. If the American intervention in Libya was indeed the correct thing to do, America only did so after doing the wrong thing by supporting Gaddafi. In his presidential debate with Mitt Romney, President Obama declared that Gaddafi had more American blood on his hands than any individual other than Osama bin Laden. What Obama did not inform the audience was the fact that the United States was supporting Gaddafi prior to the intervention. Secretary Clinton's conduct was even worse. She joked and laughed about Gaddafi's death. The situation was not so funny when Gaddafi's murder was being investigated as a war crime and it became even less of a joke when Stevens was killed in Libya. Gaddafi is not the only example of the United States having to intervene to oppose a leader or a nation which it once supported. This seems to be a common trend with American foreign policy as it relates to Muslim countries.

Prior to going to war against Iraq, Saddam Hussein had been an American ally. The United States not only supported Saddam Hussein during the war between Iraq and Iran in the 1980s, but Saddam's rise to power in Iraq was one which was assisted by the United States, which was eager to remove Abdel Karim Kassem from power.

From 1958 to 1960, Dwight Eisenhower's administration had aided Kassem against Iran. By 1961, Kassem had grown more assertive. This included seeking arms, quarreling with Kuwait, and threatening Western oil interests. Kassem came to be viewed as a regional threat that needed to be removed. In 1963, Britain and Israel supported an American intervention in Iraq. Kassem stepped down following a coup. He was executed and replaced by the Baath Party. Saddam was a member of this party. Saddam had previously been forced to flee from Iraq after he was involved in a failed assassination attempt against Kassem in 1958, with Kassem out of power, the Baathists began to systematically eliminate Iraq's educated elite. Hundreds of doctors, teachers, technicians, and lawyers were murdered. This did not seem to concern the United States, which sent arms to the new regime in Iraq. The United States would later find itself invading Iraq and toppling Saddam, the very dictator that America had supported in the past.

In an interview with Fox News, Hillary Clinton noted that the United States contributed to the problem in Afghanistan. The United States armed the mujahadeen forces against the Soviet Union in Afghanistan. This effort was successful, as the Soviet Union was driven out of Afghanistan, but years later the United States would return to Afghanistan to fight some of the very people which they had supported against the Soviet Union.

The CIA created the term "blowback," which refers to the unintended consequences of American foreign policy and intervention. This not only happened in Libya, Iraq, and Afghanistan, but also in Iran as well. President Eisenhower approved of a coup against Prime Minister Mohammad Mossadegh. Mossadegh's goal was to modernize and democratize Iran, which put him at odds with the nation's monarch, Mohammad Reza (the Shah). Mossadegh also wanted to nationalize Iran's oil fields. This outraged BP and the British government so much so that they determined that Mossadegh had to be removed. Together the United States and Britain plotted the overthrow of Mossadegh. The plot involved bribing journalists, editors, Islamic preachers, and others to enhance public hostility and distrust of Mossadegh. Thugs were also hired to carry out staged attacks against religious leaders to make it appear as though Mossadegh had ordered these attacks. On the day of the coup, thousands of paid demonstrators converged on parliament to demand that Mossadegh be dismissed. The plan was a success.

With Mossadegh removed, the Shah was returned to the throne. Shah Reza was a pro-American leader who established a repressive regime. This included the creation of the Savak, which were a secret police force which were known for their brutality. These abuses did not concern America, which was very eager to arm the government of Iran. Iran became America's single largest arms purchaser.

In 1979, Iran experienced a revolution. Protesters took to the street to cry "Death to the American Shah." These uprisings were led by an Islamic cleric named Ayatollah Ruhollah Khomeini. Unlike the pro-American shah, Khomeini held a very hostile view towards the West. The 1979 revolution overthrew a pro-American dictatorship and replaced it with a regime which was hostile towards America. This hostility was displayed when students in Iran broke into the American embassy and took 52 Americans as hostages. It would take 444 days before the hostages were released.

It was mentioned before that the United States supported Saddam Hussein. In 1980, Hussein decided to invade Iran. The United States intervened in this war by providing intelligence to Iraq, as well as arms. During the war, Hussein used chemical weapons against Iranians. The United States was aware of this, but supported Hussein in the war, nevertheless.

The United States was making deals with Iran as well. Iran made a secret request to buy weapons from the United States. The United States entered talks with Iran and struck a deal. Iran would help with the release of American hostages who were being held in Lebanon in return for the weapons. America overcharged the Iranians for the weapons and used the surplus to fund the Contras who were trying to overthrow the government of Nicaragua.

Given these foreign policy blunders—as well as other military interventions which have produced disastrous consequences such as the Vietnam War—it is very apparent that America simply is not the shining light which Obama spoke of. This applies to Togo as well, where America has continued to ignore the abuses of the

Togolese regime under the leadership of Faure Gnassingbé. Even when the people of Togo protest against the dictatorship, the very American political leaders who praise democracy in Togo have nothing to say in support of the Togolese people. There is not even so much as a hint of fake concern about democracy in Togo.

The American interventions in the Muslim world are also relevant in this discussion not only because it demonstrates the folly of American foreign policy, but also because the war on terror which was declared by President George W. Bush in 2001 has helped to provide cover for Faure's government. Faure has been able to gain support from the American government by claiming to be fighting terrorism in Togo. The reality is that it is the government of Togo which has been terrorizing its citizens, but Western governments have been willing to ignore the abuses which have been committed by Faure.

Apart from the struggle being waged against the regime itself inside of Togo, there is a larger international component to the struggle as well, which is putting an end to the foreign support that the regime in Togo continues to receive. This support not only comes in the form of the military equipment which the government of Togo receives from foreign donors, but also the fact that when the government of Togo unleashes its violence against ordinary citizens the government faces no consequences for doing so.

We live under a global system which not only systematically exploits us and neglects us. The United States government will offer support for the brutal regime in Togo while neglecting African American citizens. This demonstrates the importance of building Pan-African organizations which recognize the global nature of the struggle that African people face. Malcolm X spoke to the importance of Pan-Africanism at a 1964 speech at the Audubon. Malcolm explained: "I, for one, would like to impress, especially upon those who call themselves leaders, the importance of realizing the direct connection between the struggle of the Afro-American in this country and the struggle of our people all over the world. As long as we think—as one of my good brothers mentioned out of the side of his mouth here a couple of Sundays ago—that we should get Mississippi straightened out before we worry about the Congo, you'll never get Mississippi straightened out. Not until you start realizing your connection with the Congo."

Malcolm was very much concerned about the struggle which was taking place in the Congo. It was something which he spoke about often. Malcolm recognized that there was a connection between the struggle in Africa and the struggles of African Americans. Remember that the 1960s was a period when the civil rights movement was taking place in the United States as African nations were struggling against colonialism.

Malcolm also recognized that what was being done to Africans in the Congo could also be done to Africans in the United States. He stated, "they're able to take these hired killers, put them in American planes, with American bombs, and drop them on African villages, blowing to bits black men, black women, black children, black babies, and you black people sitting over here cool like it doesn't even involve you. You're a fool. They'll do it to them today, and do it to you tomorrow." Malcolm was correct. In 1985, a black commune known as MOVE had a bomb dropped on it. The United States was dropping bombs on Africans in the Congo in the 1960s and in the 1980s it dropped a bomb on Africans in Philadelphia.

My effort to support the liberation struggle in Togo coincided with the struggle over land ownership in Barbuda. In 2017, Barbuda was devastated by a hurricane which destroyed most of the structures on the island. As if this was not bad enough, there were concerns on the part of the residents of Barbuda that the government was using the repair efforts as an opportunity to undermine the Barbudian people by overturning the island's tradition of communal land ownership. I wrote several articles in an attempt to raise attention and support for the struggle being waged in Barbuda. The January 1, 2018, edition of *Kaieteur News* ran a story with the headline, "Guyanese author documents Barbudians land ownership struggles." That was a very proud moment for me not only because it demonstrated that my efforts at publicizing the struggles of the Barbudian people was effective, but also because I caught the attention of one of the major news outlets in Guyana.

The report itself covered an article I wrote which detailed the historical struggle over land rights in the Caribbean, beginning with the fact that after Columbus arrived in the Caribbean in 1492, the European settlers stole the land from the native people of the Caribbean. This involved a campaign of genocidal violence against the native people. With the native population removed, the land in the Caribbean was controlled by a small class of wealthy white property owners. Jean-Jacques Dessalines recognized the importance of land ownership, which is why one of the provisions that he put in place after declaring Haiti's independence was that foreigners would not be allowed to own property in Haiti. I noted that for many of the Caribbean countries that have gained their independence after Haiti, retaining local control of the land has not been a priority. Some Caribbean leaders have freely given away ownership and control of their land.

Caribbean artists have often complained about this very situation, which is something which I referenced in my article. I listed some songs "which have been aimed at exposing and criticizing these policies." I gave examples of Lord Kitchener in Trinidad and Tobago complaining the natives of Tobago being arrested for using their own beaches or Gabby's hit song "Jack", which was in response to a policy put forward by Jack Dear, the chairman of the Tourist Board, who suggested allowing hotels to privatize beach land. I also mentioned that Mutabaruka had complained in one of his songs about the all-exclusive hotels, which would make tourists believe that Negril is a separate island apart from Jamaica.

The history of Barbuda is unique. The island was leased to Christopher Codrington by the British monarchy in 1685. Codrington sent his slaves to Barbuda to grow food and raise livestock to supply the people of Antigua. Products such as meat, fish, and cocoplum were sent to Antigua from Barbuda. Barbuda had a population of 500 slaves and one white manager. Given that there were not many white people in Barbuda, the island was left underdeveloped. The Codrington family continued to run Barbuda this way until their lease ended. By this point slavery had been abolished, so the people of Barbuda were virtually left alone on the island. This meant that they were free to develop their own system of land ownership. Rather than private land ownership, the people of Barbuda developed a system in which all land was owned in common. Land in Barbuda was not bought or sold. It was instead rented to foreigners. The Barbuda Council approved or rejected any development projects on the island. This system was formalized in 2007 following the passage of the Barbuda Land Act. Prime Minister Gaston Browne dismissed the collective land ownership in Barbuda as a myth and that the 2007 act was unconstitutional. Browne's plan was to get rid of Barbuda's system of land ownership to transform the island into a vacation spot. In the view of some Barbadians, Browne's plan is to steal the land.

I recognized one significant parallel between Togo and the political history of Antigua, which was the existence of a dynasty which dominated the nation's politics and ruled in a corrupt manner. Antigua's first prime minister was Vere Bird, who was succeeded by his son Lester Bird. The difference was that the Birds were democratically elected in Antigua and Barbuda, but this to me simply demonstrated the fact that democratic elections alone are not enough to ensure true democratic representation. The Birds in Antigua and Barbuda were very corrupt and behaved as if the country was their personal property. The Bird administration in Antigua and Barbuda was also a very scandal filled one. A Canadian company known as Space Research owned by Gerald V. Bull was permitted to test howitzers in Antigua. Space Research withdrew when a local newspaper exposed that Space Research was supplying weapons to the government in South Africa. Bull was in the news again in 1990 when he was shot to death in Belgium, where he was reported to have been working on making weapons for Saddam Hussein.

The situation concerning Bull was just one of the many scandals that the Bird administration in Antigua found itself caught up in. It was revealed in 1990 that an Israeli officer had illegally shipped weapons to Vere Bird, Jr. in order to have the weapons shipped to members of a drug cartel in Colombia. When this scandal was exposed, Antiguans responded by protesting, with some holding placards which stated, "The Birds Must Go." Bird Jr. resigned as the Minister of Public Works, but no charges were filed against him. There was yet another scandal in 1995 when Ivor Bird, another one of Vere's sons, was fined $75,000 after being caught with a twenty-five pound shipment of cocaine as he boarded a plane. Ivor was a former cabinet member and also directed the family owned radio station.

In my view, these issues are all interconnected. The racial oppression which African Americans endure is connected to the struggles in Togo, Barbuda, and wherever else African people are located in the world. This is part of the historical legacy of the assault on African societies which was carried out by European colonial powers. Amilcar Cabral explained: "The principal characteristic, common to every kind of imperialist domination, is the denial of the historical process of the dominated people by means of violent usurpation of freedom of the process of development of the productive forces." This is precisely what has happened to African people. We have been struggling with the denial of our historical process of development. We are struggling with the disruption caused by the slave trade and by colonialism.

This disruption was caused in Togo as well. The struggle against dictatorship in Togo is merely an aspect of the ongoing struggle against European colonial domination in Togo. The resistance to colonial rule on the part of Africans in Togo manifested itself in different forms. Joseph Udimal Kachim noted that "almost all African societies employed both collaboration and resistance at different times to deal with the threat of losing their sovereignty." One advantage which Europeans had was that they did not face a unified resistance among African people. Just as African states could be turned against each other during the slave trade, during the period of colonial conquest in Africa, African states often fought against each other. In doing so, African states believed that they were struggling for their own self-interest by aligning with a particular European power, but in the long-run these internal struggles among African states benefited the invading European powers.

Some Africans in Togo entered into alliances with the Germans in Togoland. Others resisted. The Dagomba people were among those who resisted. The Dagomba people first acquired firearms from the Asante people after the Asante people invaded and captured the Dagomba king, Na Gariba. The Asante had imposed a restriction on distributing firearms to the northern states, but this ban was eventually lifted, and the Asante people established Kambose (gunmen) as an arm of the Dagomba army. The Dagomba were armed, but they were not properly trained in the usage of firearms, which contributed to their defeat. The commander of the Dagomba army was said to have wielded two guns and a sword. He fired the two guns, but he could not reload and began to use his sword. He was among the 500 who were killed in the battle.

The resistance of the Konkomba people was much more successful. Kachim explained: "The Konkomba knew that they could not win pitched battles against an enemy who was far more powerful and better armed than they were and therefore they resorted to guerilla warfare which was the best tactic under the circumstance. Since each village resisted independently there was no identifiable army to be defeated and this enabled the Konkomba to resist the German occupation for a much longer time than their centralized neighbours. After the Konkomba had frustrated the Germans by the guerilla warfare, the latter resorted to the strategies of capturing hostages and appointing chiefs among the former, which they used as bargaining chips to avoid 'guerrilla warfare'". The Germans entered into a military alliance with the Kotokoli in the south and the Chakosi in the north in their attempt to conquer the Konkomba people. After nearly five years of resistance, the Germans were able to conquer the Konkomba with the help of their African allies.

Despite the resistance which the people of Togo put up against European invasion, Togo was eventually colonized by the Germans. Togoland later became a British and French protectorate. British Togoland subsequently became part of Ghana and French Togoland became the Togolese Republic. The struggle against Faure is, in my view, a continuation of the struggle against colonial domination. Colonial domination robbed the Togolese people of their sovereignty and so long as Togo remains under the control of an oppressive military dictatorship, the people of Togo can never be truly sovereign.

In the first place, the only democratically elected president of Togo was Sylvanus Olympio, who was also Togo's first president. He was assassinated. The government of Togo has been one which outwardly presents itself as a democracy because it holds elections.

Of course, it took years of struggle before the dictatorship in Togo would even allow for a multi-party state in which opposition parties could contest elections. For much of Eyadéma's reign Togo was a one-party state, but this changed in 1992 when multi-party democracy was restored in Togo. The brutalities and abuse continued, however. Opposition parties were free to organize and contest elections, but opposition leaders were still subjected to being abused and murdered by the state. Tavio Amorin's assassination was a clear example of this. Eyadéma also altered the constitution of Togo to allow himself to run for a third term, demonstrating that Eyadéma was not constrained by the limits of the constitutional reforms in 1992. When Eyadéma died in 2005, the military installed his son into power. This was yet another violation of the 1992 constitution. An election was held that same year, which resulted in hundreds of Togolese being killed.

It was apparent that Eyadéma was grooming his sons to take power after he was gone. There was talk about Faure being Eyadéma's successor before Eyadéma died. There was also Ernest, who was another son of Eyadéma. Ernest, who was a lieutenant colonel, was also viewed as a possible successor. Yet another son, Kpatcha, held an influential position at the Autonomous Port of Lomé. Apart from putting a family dynasty in place to rule Togo, Eyadéma also filled the army largely with recruits from his own Kabyé ethnic group.

Liberating Togo from this dictatorial regime is no easy task. I would argue that the dictatorship in Togo has proven to be more stubbornly entrenched than other dictators in Africa, such as Blaise Compaoré, Yayha Jammeh, and Omar al-Bashir who were all removed due to mobilization on the part of the masses. The masses in Togo mobilized as well, but the protests which began in 2017 did not succeed in removing the regime from power. The protests did manage to strike a blow at the regime, however. This blow will prove to be very useful moving forward in the struggle to liberate Togo.

One of the tools which has been utilized by the people of Togo has been digital activism. Digital activism allowed activists to reach a global audience, which is especially important when fighting a regime which tries to present a false image of itself to the international community. The effectiveness of this digital activism can be demonstrated by the lengths that the government of Togo has gone to suppress digital activism. In 2017, the government of Togo shut down the internet in the country. This actually worked to the favor of the activists. The shutdown brought more attention to the situation in Togo and because of the shutdown the only way for international journalists to get information about what was happening in Togo was through the opposition. The government of Togo also resorted to spying on the online activities of activists in Togo. Some of these activists have been arrested and imprisoned for their online activities.

Faure himself expressed his concern about the use of social media in 2018 when he complained: "Today, those who intoxicate, those who lie, have found allies in technology and can turn a righteous thing, or a simple man like me into a bloody dictator. But sooner or later, the truth shall triumph." Faure was obviously concerned about the fact that technology has helped to expose the true nature of his regime to the world. I would argue that this was the greatest achievement of the protests in Togo in 2017 and 2018. The protests during this period exposed the regime in Togo in a way that it had not been exposed before. Faure obviously would not admit to being a bloody dictator, but his deeds were on display for the world to see.

Faure referring to himself as a "simple man" was not merely an expression of delusion on his part. Whereas his father depicted himself as a supernatural military strongman, Faure's public persona has been much less grandiose. Faure has been very careful about the type of public image which he has crafted for himself. He has also received support from individuals such as Mohamed Ibn Chambas who served as the head of the United Nations Office for West Africa and the Sahel (UNOWAS). Chambas is also an individual who was known to have taken money from the regime in Togo to help protect its image. It is very critical in the battle against dictatorship in Togo that the dictator be exposed for who he truly is. The protests in 2017 have helped to accomplish this task.

I think the protests could have succeeded had it not been for two critical factors. The first is the role of the international community.

By this I am not only referring to the support which Faure received from Western countries which have continued to provide weapons and diplomatic support for Faure. Ghana's president, Nana Akufo-Addo, stepped in as a mediator between the government and the opposition parties. It was apparent that President Akufo-Addo intervened to assist Faure. By this point there should have been nothing to discuss. The Togolese people wanted Faure gone. Faure's reaction to the protests—sending the military to kill protesters and shutting down the internet—should have been enough for other African leaders in the region to pressure Faure to step down as well, sending the message that such conduct was unacceptable in the region. Instead, President Akufo-Addo intervened to hold a dialogue between the dictatorship and the opposition.

The protests which began were demanding that Faure step down as president, yet one of the issues raised in the dialogue was the reinstatement of the 1992 constitution. It was demonstrated already that the Gnassingbé has been willing to violate the constitution of Togo whenever it wanted, so it is not clear why this talk about reinstating the 1992 constitution was brought forward during the dialogue, rather than having the talks center around Faure stepping down from power. The dialogue was bound to fail because the central demand of the Togolese people, which was that Faure needs to leave office, was not what was being discussed at the dialogue. The dialogue only served to resolve the unrest in Togo in the favor of Faure, who never had any intention of stepping down.

The other factor are the political parties which were united against Faure, but ultimately were unable to sustain a united front. This coalition of fourteen political parties began bickering among themselves, which in turn significantly weakened the protest movement against Faure.

The failed dialogue—which the opposition parties opted to participate in—and the subsequent infighting among the opposition parties helped to derail the momentum of the protests which began in 2017. These factors combined with the continued violent repression of protests in Togo ultimately led to suppression of the mass mobilization against dictatorship in Togo which began in

2017.

The fight against dictatorship in Togo has been hindered by a weak and divided opposition. This was an issue in the 1990s. At the time Eyadéma was facing both domestic and international pressure to implement political reforms in Togo. There was a march and rioting on October 5, 1990 by intellectuals and students who were demanding the release of two imprisoned activists. Eyadéma was also experiencing pressure from France. In 1990, the president of France declared that future French aid would be linked to the democratization of France's former African colonies. The opposition united to form the Collective for the Democratic Opposition, but the opposition remained divided. The division of the opposition forces was one of the reasons why Eyadéma was able to withstand the pressure which he faced in the 1990s.

The protests which began in 2017 were very encouraging and it seemed that Togo would have been the next African nation to put an end to a decades old dictatorship. Though the protests in 2017 and 2018 failed to remove Faure, there are some lessons which can be drawn from the uprising. That uprising demonstrated the importance of social media as a tool to combat the dictatorship. The uprising also demonstrated the need for a genuine people's revolution which is not led by political leaders who are willing to dialogue with the dictatorship.

Selected References:

Amilcar Cabral, *Unity and Struggle: Speeches and Writings*

Amnesty International, "Togo: Rule of Terror," May 4, 1999.

Andrew Manley, "Togo: After Eyadéma," 2003.

Bradley Klapper, "US promotes democracy with suddenly important Togo," *Associated Press*, January 17, 2012.

Cody Morgan, "U.S.-Iran Relations: A History of Covert Action and a Promising Future," *The Cohen Journal*, Vol. 2: Issue no. 1, 2015.

"Guyanese author documents Barbudians land ownership struggles," *Kaieteur News*, January 1, 2018.

Howard W. French, "Island's Hushed Scandals, Unhushed," *New York Times*, June 16, 1960.

Ismail Akwei, "'They used technology to turn me into a bloody dictator' – Togo's president," *Africa News*, Sept. 31, 2017.

Joseph Udimal Kachim, "African Resistance to Colonial Conquest: The Case of Konkomba Resistance to German Occupation of Northern Togoland, 1896-1901," *Asian Journal of Humanities and Social Studies* (ISSN: 2321 – 2799) Volume 01– Issue 03, August 2013.

Malcolm X, *Malcolm X Speaks*

Peter Baker, David D. Kirkpatrick, and Suliman Ali Zway, "Diplomats' Bodies Return to U.S., and Libyan Guards Recount Deadly Riot," *New York Times*, September 14, 2012.

Pierre Sané, "Open Letter to Mr Jacques Chirac, President of the French Republic," July 15, 1999.

Roger Morris, "A Tyrant 40 Years in the Making," *New York Times*, March 14, 2003.

Jean-Claude Chanel and Jean-Philippe Rapp, *Sacrifices pour une Révolution* (1984).

2

THE TRAGIC DECLINE OF FREDDIE KISSOON: A DEFENSE OF EUSI KWAYANA

The election which was held in Guyana in 2020 was a very contentious one. Both the People's Progressive Party (PPP) and A Partnership for National Unity plus the Alliance for Change (APNU+AFC) parties claimed victory. A recount was necessary to determine a winner. This recount showed a victory for the PPP, but some in the APNU+AFC government refused to accept these results. Rather than concede defeat, the incumbent government took the position that the election was a fraudulent one. The coalition made unsubstantiated allegations of fraud against the PPP. Some within the coalition government even suggested that there was an attempt to install the PPP into power by launching a political coup in Guyana. It would take several months for the political impasse to finally come to an end in Guyana.

One of the most unfortunate developments which followed the 2020 election in Guyana was the exchange between Freddie Kissoon and Eusi Kwayana. I state that this was an unfortunate development because Freddie Kissoon was an individual that I respected for some of the positions which he has taken in the past, but I found his treatment of Eusi Kwayana following the election to be disrespectful. It also exposed a level of racism and malice which I had never detected before. Here I repeat the sentiments of Kwayana who stated in a June 7, 2020, letter that Kissoon was displaying a tendency to malice that Kwayana had never detected before.

The issue stems from the fact that Eusi Kwayana did not rush to condemn Claudette Singh, who was the Chairperson of the Guyana Elections Commission (GECOM). In Kissoon's view, this meant that Kwayana was trying to justify election rigging in Guyana. The problem is that Kissoon was too quick to judge Claudette Singh. Whereas Kwayana was very cautious about commenting on the events that were unfolding regarding the election, Kissoon concluded, with very little evidence, that Claudette Singh was part of the attempt to improperly influence the election results to secure a victory for the APNU+AFC.

Given the sort of things that Kissoon has stated about Kwayana in his writings, I would have to agree with Kwayana that Kissoon has displayed a tendency to malice. It is not so much that he criticized Kwayana over Kwayana's position on the election, but the manner in which Kissoon did so. Kissoon even tried to bring Walter Rodney into the situation. He wrote: "I say unapologetically, Kwayana's positive words on Singh is a betrayal of everything Walter Rodney stood for. Kwayana, perhaps like all his colleagues in and out of Guyana, in the Walter Rodney movement (I chose that appellation instead of Working People's Alliance, a name that is now leprous), has denigrated the beauty of Walter Rodney."

To bring Rodney's name into his dispute with Kwayana was unnecessary. Frankly, I found it to be disrespectful to Rodney. Take for example the previously cited quote from Kissoon. How could Kwayana's actions ever denigrate the beauty of Walter Rodney? Kwayana is Kwayana and Rodney is Rodney. The two men worked together as members of the WPA. They shared similar visions, political views, and ideologies. Both men were Pan-Africanists who opposed the People's National Congress (PNC) government which was led by Linden Forbes Burnham at the time. The two men expressed a great deal of respect for each other as well, but they were separate individuals who came from different generations. Rodney should be judged on his own merit and the same is true for Kwayana.

Kissoon goes even further by creating a fictional exchange between Rodney and Desmond Trotman, a member of the APNU+AFC government. I would argue that Kissoon is the one who has demonstrated a complete lack of respect for Rodney by creating a fictional exchange between Rodney and Trotman. Kissoon has Rodney say, "rigged elections were the cause of my death." Kissoon reduces Rodney's struggle against the PNC as a struggle against rigged elections when it was so much more than that. Rodney's struggle was a struggle for people's power, as he explained in "People's Power, No Dictator." Election rigging was certainly one aspect of Burnham's government which Rodney had denounced, but rigged elections alone were not the cause of Rodney's death. Furthermore, given the brutal manner in which Rodney was assassinated, I find it despicable that Kissoon would invoke Rodney's death to express Kissoon's own displeasure with election rigging in 2020.

Kissoon has Rodney conclude by saying: "I am turning in my grave knowing what you, Eusi, Clive, Bonita, Westmaas, Moses Bhagwan, Maurice Odle, David Hinds, Ogunseye and the rest I struggled with have become. Don't do this to my legacy." Not only is it disrespectful for Kissoon to speak for Rodney, but it is also disrespectful and self-serving to conclude that Rodney would feel the same way about Kwayana's position on the elections as Kissoon does. Kissoon could not possibly know what Rodney's position on Kwayana's behavior would have been, but I am certain that Rodney might have been more sensitive to the racial division in Guyana than Kissoon was. I hold the view that Rodney would not contribute to the racial division in the manner that Kissoon insisted on doing. And I would also imagine that Rodney would not be as concerned about his legacy as Kissoon suggests that Rodney would have been. Based on Rodney's speeches and writings, whatever concerns he would have expressed about the WPA's conduct during the election would have most likely been framed in terms of what is in the best interest of the Guyanese masses, not what is in the best interest of Rodney's legacy.

Why invoke Rodney at all? Why does Rodney's name need to be dragged into an exchange between Kwayana and Kissoon? As I stated, I found Kissoon's decision to do so to be very disrespectful to Rodney. I am certain that Rodney would have expressed concerns about the WPA's role within the APNU+AFC coalition. I was disappointed with the WPA's role in the coalition. I understood that the WPA joined in a coalition with the People's National Congress—the same party responsible for killing Rodney—to remove the PPP, which had been in power for over twenty years at that point. The corruption and racism of the PPP was too much, so the PPP needed to go, but I was also skeptical of the coalition given that it was being led by the PNC. I watched to see if the PNC had truly been reformed and I was not surprised to find that the PNC had in fact not been significantly reformed from the days of Burnham's leadership. I admired the fact that David Hinds and others in the WPA spoke out against corruption and the misuse of funds on the part of the APNU+AFC government, but the WPA was not really serving any purpose in the coalition. Instead, it remained in a coalition led by people who demonstrated a very blatant disregard for working people in Guyana. This was not an ideal situation for the WPA. The members of the party knew this and recognized the frustration of some of their own supporters who wished that the WPA had left the coalition altogether.

By the time that the WPA joined the APNU coalition with the PNC, Kwayana was no longer active in the WPA and was not involved in the decision to form a coalition with the PNC. One cannot know if Rodney would have remained active in the WPA or what his position on a coalition with the PNC would have been. I was disappointed with how the WPA was treated while in the coalition government, but I never felt that the actions of David Hinds and others were denigrating the legacy of Walter Rodney. As I stated, I admired that the WPA criticized certain actions on the part of the coalition government, but I did not understand why the WPA opted to remain in the coalition even after receiving backlash for its criticisms, such as when David Hinds was terminated from the government owned newspaper.

Kissoon's issue with Kwayana began over their differing opinions on Claudette Singh. Kissoon stated: "What Singh is doing to this country is so evil that those who support her support her evil." These are very strong words against Singh and those who support her. Kissoon continued to state that Singh "is one of the most unacceptable citizens this world has produced." He also suggested that "Singh wants to take away the right of Guyanese to have their vote counted."

Kissoon then addressed Kwayana, writing: "I have known Kwayana for more than 45 years and the position he took on the rigged election process that is unfolding cannot be defended." What was Kwayana's position? Kissoon quoted Kwayana as follows: "I for one, consider it unhelpful to prattle about facts I do not have…the impressions I am getting are not founded on facts that may pass my own test…I cannot pretend to be unaffected by the statement of (Singh) that she intended to deliver to the public a valid election. I have often wondered to what extent those who appealed to her public spiritedness…have taken the necessary steps to support her [stated] aspirations." This one statement from Kwayana seemed to have formed the basis for Kissoon's public attacks on Kwayana. It is worth noting that nowhere in the passage by Kwayana which Kissoon quoted does Kwayana express support for Singh or endorse her actions. What Kwayana expressed support for were Singh's stated aspirations, which were to deliver to the public a valid election. Kissoon deliberately misrepresents Kwayana's remark to mean that Kwayana supports Singh, whom Kissoon alleges was part of the effort to rig the election in favor of the incumbent government. The reality is that Kwayana's remarks express the view that he favors a valid election.

Kissoon wrote that "Eusi Kwayana has undermined a lifetime of work for his unashamed support for Singh." Kissoon tries to present Kwayana's refusal to rush to judgement to mean that Kwayana supports Singh. Kissoon also then presents this alleged support of Singh as support for rigged elections because Singh is supposedly part of this plot to rig the elections, even though she refused to accept the figures presented by Keith Lowenfield and instead decided to abide by the recount numbers which showed a victory for the PPP. Kissoon boldly predicted that Claudette Singh would accept Lowenfield's numbers and declare that the election was improper, but this did not happen, which only validated Kwayan's unwillingness to condemn Singh without seeing any wrongdoing on her part.

In a letter in which Rohit Kanhai called on Kissoon to apologise for his attacks on Kwayana, Kanhai explained: "It is noteworthy that Kissoon's attack on Kwayana, that he was condoning the behavior of Justice Claudette Singh in aiding and abetting the rigging of the elections, has proven to be false. Kwayana is an 'institutionalist', who does not prejudge official judgments until it is rendered from the official source. In this respect, Kissoon should apologise to Kwayana. It is his arrogance at being proven wrong that has forced him to launch this attack upon Kwayana." Kissoon was indeed proven wrong, but rather than apologise or recant, Kissoon continued to maintain his incorrect position.

In Kissoon's response to Rohit Kanhai, he predicted that Singh would vote to declare that the 2020 election was irregular, improper, and fraudulent. This never happened. Instead, Singh ordered Keith Lowenfield to submit his report on the accurate results of the recount and warned that if he refused to do so, he would be removed from his function as Chief Elections Officer. Kissoon was wrong, but his reasoning for suggesting why Singh would have voted to declare that the 2020 election was fraudulent was simply racist. He stated that "Singh considers herself an African Guyanese sympathetic to the PNC." Why mention Singh's race as a relevant fact? He continued to explain that Singh "embraces the doctrine that the PPP's state power is equivalent to loss of power by African Guyanese." Where is the basis for this belief? Kissoon has none, as demonstrated by the fact that his prediction was wrong.

In the same column, Kissoon expressed his belief—and he refers to his belief because he has no factual evidence—that Kwayana knew Sing is opposed to the PPP which is why "she"— Kissoon apparently confuses Kwayana and Sing here by incorrectly referring to Kwayana as she—"shamelessly endorsed her action even though it has damaged his iconic status and ruined his Rodneyite standing." Which action did Kwayana endorse? Kissoon could not say because in the end Singh herself did not engage in the action which Kissoon accused her of engaging in. Kissoon could have salvaged his reputation had he admitted that he was wrong, and apologise as Kanhai suggested, but Kissoon did not do so.

Rather than chastise Claudette Singh over her handling of the election, Kwayana took the opportunity to comment on remarks made by the former Attorney-General Anil Nandlall. Nandlall had declared that the PPP's lead over the APNU+AFC was the triumph of good over evil. Kwayana stated that Nandlall was falling back "on a well-known binary division of humanity that has seldom led to an uplifting experience for the quality of life." Kissoon himself was falling into this binary by trying to depict himself as being good and depicting Kwayana as being a racist simply because Kwayana took a more neutral position on the election.

Kit Nascimento wrote a letter in which he stated: "The

Chairman of the Elections Commission, former Justice Claudette Singh, has not been exemplary in the conduct of her responsibility of the events subsequent to the Elections which have led us into a Recount." Nascimento continued to state: "Nevertheless, she has kept her undertaking given to the Chief Justice, before the Granger/Jagdeo Agreement, that she would facilitate a Recount 'should there be discrepancies in the Statements of Poll as called by the Returning Officer', which she told the Court was 'bolstered' by the President and the Leader of the Opposition inviting CARICOM to observe a Recount."

I cite Nascimento's letter here to demonstrate that though he was critical of Singh's handling of the election, he recognized she did do what was expected of her by facilitating a recount. He did not rush to conclude that Singh would vote that the 2020 election was improper. He also did not invoke her racial identity to attack her character. Nascimento instead concluded: "We must now expect that GECOM, under her leadership, will move to declare the result of the Elections in accordance with the tabulated Recount of the ballots, for the swearing in of the Presidential Candidate of the People's Progressive Party/Civic, Dr. Mohamed Irfaan Ali." This is precisely what happened.

Being proven wrong about Singh should have ended Kissoon's dispute with Kwayana, but it did not. On August 27, 2021, *Kaieteur News* published yet another one of these vicious attacks in which Kissoon suggested that Kwayana is the type of man who supports ethnic genocide in Guyana. Kissoon wrote: "The present opposition leader and his party leader went up to Region Five just after the PPP came to power in August 2020 to stop the machinery of government. They incited people that resulted in violent attacks on Indo-Guyanese. The violence didn't spread nation-wide maybe because Kwayana was not able to return to Guyana to become Sydney King once more." The implication that Kissoon makes is that if Kwayana was in Guyana he would have incited more violence. This implication is baseless. In the first place, Kwayana was among those who condemned the violence against Indo-Guyanese which began in 2001. To those who were committing acts of violence against Indians, Kwayana wrote: "Indians were not responsible for the enslavement of Africans. Get that straight." He also told the gunmen of Buxton that "the Indian Guyanese, whether they have guns or not, have shown better behaviour, yes, better religion, yes better civilisation than we have shown. And I am very jealous of African civilisation and its values."

The implication of what Kissoon wrote also expresses a negative view of Africans in Guyana because he seems to think that stirring Africans into nation-wide violence against Indians would be as simple as Kwayana returning to Guyana to become "Sydney King." According to Kissoon, Sydney King (as Kwayana was previously known) "preached the sermons of race, perpetuated race narratives, advocated racial galvanization and participated in behavioural manifestation that had violent, racial overtones." One is not sure what "participated in behavioural manifestation" means, but it is notable that Kissoon does not directly connect Sydney King to any actual acts of violence or calls for violence against Indians. If Sydney King was such a racist man, surely Kissoon could reference a specific anti-Indian quote or anti-Indian action undertaken by King, but Kissoon provided nothing.

Kwayana himself noted that those who had accused him of being involved in racial violence in the past were unable to find evidence against him. Kwayana wrote: "During the 1980 election campaign boycotted by WPA, Mrs. Janet Jagan told an election meeting at Leonora, a village where WPA was very active, 'ask Sidney King what he did at Wismar in 1964.' It should be noted that a report of the PPP appointed Commission into the Wismar Disturbances disclosed no involvement by me in the events reported." He continued: "I state here for interested readers that there is no document, photograph, report or even rumour surrounding the 1962 disturbances implicating me as a reading of the Wynn Parry Commission report will easily establish."

Kissoon concluded his column by writing: "I suspect we will receive many more letters like the one last Wednesday from Kwayana and I will keep replying to educate the youth of my country about those who wanted to turn Guyana into Rwanda." It caught my attention that of all of the nations in the world that have experienced genocides, Kissoon would pick an African nation to make his point.

I was rather surprised to see the type of racism which Kissoon expressed not only towards Eusi Kwayana, but also at Claudette Singh when he implied that she would side with the PNC because of her racial identity. This accusation was proven false, but as I noted, Kissoon has persisted in his accusations against Singh and his attacks against Kwayana. I am not suggesting that Kissoon should not express disagreement with Kwayana, but the hateful and disingenuous manner in which Kissoon did so would suggest to me that Kissoon's issues with Kwayana were deeper than a mere disagreement with Kwayana over the election. These attacks have taken on a very personal nature which goes beyond critiquing Kwayana's position on the election. This is coming from Kissoon, a man who once admired Kwayana. By Kissoon's own admission, Kwayana paid for Kissoon to be able to go to Barbados to study abroad and earn a university degree.

That Kissoon would denounce Kwayana as being a racist who advocates for racial violence against Indians is at odds with a remark which Kissoon made on a tribute show to Kwayana. Kissoon stated: "But it is important that Indians tells other East Indians that this is a man if you got to know him you would see that though he felt that as an African he should address the wrongs of Africans, that this man was essentially, quintessentially, and most biologically a human being that loved people and that when it comes to struggle, when it comes to human rights, there was no man with an African name, there was no Africanist by the name of Eusi Kwayana. This is a Guyanese man who would go out into a crowd and tell a group of African people that you are doing a wrong to the Amerindian race, that you are doing a wrong to the European race, and that is what is so important about Eusi Kwayana."

I do not understand why Kissoon's anger that Kwayana did not agree with Kissoon's views on Singh would cause Kissoon to try to smear Kwayana in the manner that he has been doing. Kwayana himself wrote: "I do not think there is any doubt about what the Region 4 count is revealing or confirming allegations against a much discussed figure in the process but I do not regard it as my responsibility to rush to support Freddie Kissoon or any other person present in Guyana with allegations they feel empowered to make." Why should supporting Kissoon's allegations be Kwayana's responsibility and why is Kwayana now being accused of being a racist by Kissoon simply because Kwayana did not decide to support the allegations which Kissoon made—allegations which turned out to be false?

In his attempts to smear Kwayana, Kissoon wrote: "When my mother and mother-in-law were older people and I was younger, they both spent decades asking me what I was doing in politics with someone like Eusi Kwayana." He continued to note that he did not listen to his mother and mother-in-law because he "was young, stupid, naïve and drowning in idealism and the little philosophy I read from books." What I find curious about these remarks is what Kissoon does not say. He did not specifically state why it was that his mother and mother-in-law disliked Kwayana. He stated: "My two old folks knew him and always showed me his true colours." What were Kwayana's true colours? What specifically did Kwayana do that caused Kissoon's mother and mother-in-law to dislike him? Kissoon merely states that his "mother never liked Kwayana because she knew inherently Kwayana was all about race." One asks again, how did she know this? Did she know Kwayana personally?

I raise this question because of the fact that Kissoon stated that if Indians got to know Kwayana they would understand that he was not a racist. Did Kissoon's mother and mother-in-law know Kwayana or were they influenced by the accusations being spread about Kwayana being a racist? As was noted previously, Janet Jagan mentioned Kwayana's name in reference to racial disturbances in Guyana, but the PPP's own investigation could not conclude that Kwayana was involved. For Kissoon to convince readers that his past views on Kwayana were wrong, it would be helpful if he could establish a strong case to demonstrate Kwayana's racism, particularly if Kissoon is implying that Kwayana is someone who wanted to turn Guyana into Rwanda. I would conclude that either Kissoon was being dishonest when he praised Kwayana on the tribute show or he was being dishonest in his column because I have a hard time understanding how Kissoon's views on Kwayana could have changed so dramatically. Kissoon went from praising Kwayana as an activist who defended people of all races to accusing Kwayana of being a genocidal racist.

By Kissoon's own admission, Kwayana was a significant influence on him. Kissoon's explanations for why his view of Kwayana has changed so dramatically do not seem satisfactory. One struggles to understand why it is that Kissoon could have such admiration for Kwayana, only to utter such harsh denouncements of a man whom Kissoon admired. In the past, Kissoon has spoken about the influence that Kwayana's activism has had on him. Kissoon explained that Kwayana is the reason why he never ran as a candidate in an election and has never been interested in being a minister in the government. This was a testament to the type of influence that Kwayana has had on Kissoon's own activism. This commitment to justice and human rights is precisely why Kissoon felt so compelled to speak out against what he recognized as an attempt by the incumbent government of Guyana to remain in power by undermining Guyana's democracy. In taking this position, Kissoon was correct.

In defending Eusi Kwayana, I wish to make it clear that I am not defending the conduct of the APNU+AFC during the 2020 election. The APNU+AFC should have conceded defeat gracefully. Instead, the APNU+AFC's position alienated the party from the international community. Prime Minister Ralph Gonsalves of St. Vincent and the Grenadines, who was at the time the incoming Chair of the Caribbean Community (CARICOM), stated that "the loser of the elections must take his licks like a man", which incited a very defensive response from President David Granger of Guyana, who stated: "I'm not going to accept that type of language. CARICOM as a community of sovereign states has never used that sort of language to describe the Government of Guyana, and I would not describe my invitation or my participation in the agreement for CARICOM to come here which was consensual, it wasn't unilateral, as being one of interference. It was lawful, in the laws of Guyana, and that's why they are here." Ellen Johnson Sirleaf, a former president of Liberia, also commented on the election, expressing the view that the PPP was the victor.

There were those in the APNU+AFC who claimed that the election results were not credible. Among those voices were Prime Minister Moses Nagamootoo and Joseph Harmon. President

Granger himself claimed that he would accept any declarations made by GECOM, although the party later released a statement claiming: "Any results emanating from this process cannot be considered credible because of the high incidence of fraud." This suggested that within the APNU+AFC there was no consensus about how to handle the situation. Granger was saying one thing, but the party was claiming something else. Then there was Lowenfield, who was Guyana's Chief Elections Officer. He decided to present a report to the Elections Commission in which he invalidated over 115,000 votes. His report would have granted a victory to the APNU+AFC. Lowenfield's report was later invalidated by the Caribbean Court of Justice (CCJ). Granger expressed support for Lowenfield's report.

There was also an apparent lack of transparency on the part of the government. Granger held a press conference in which media houses which had been critical during the electoral proceeding were excluded from attendance. *Kaieteur News* reported that it had sought clarity on certain issues. These questions were directed to Granger via his Director of Public Information Service, Ariana Gordon. Gordon did not respond to the questions on the day which they were sent. Gordon responded to the questions the next day, but the statement which was issued by President Granger failed to address the questions posed by *Kaieteur News.*

The electoral impasse in Guyana was one which damaged the international reputation of President Granger. John Beale, who was the former Barbadian ambassador to the United States, stated: "Numerous opportunities have been given to the President of Guyana, David Granger to come clean and while he gives the impression that he supports free and fair elections, his actions do not. Indeed, he is being described in Caribbean political circles as a 'Sanctimonious Gangster'".

I would also add that I do not think that some of the remarks which David Hinds made in response to the electoral impasse were helpful either. Hinds wrote that any "claim of jurisdiction by the CCJ would be a political act with clear political intentions. It would be a clear attempt to install a party in power against the wishes [of] half of [the] population and in defiance of constitutional check." He described such an act as being "nothing short of a political coup." The CCJ was not trying to install the PPP into power. There was a recount in Guyana which CARICOM oversaw. The CARICOM team overseeing the election was invited by President Granger himself. The results of the recount demonstrated a victory for the PPP. In response to this, Lowenfield attempted to throw out a large number of votes which would give the victory to the APNU+AFC coalition. In Hinds' view the CCJ was trying to install a new government into power, but the reality of the situation was much more complicated. There was no basis for Lowenfield to try to throw out more than 115,000 votes and one could not have expected the CCJ to support such conduct. Had the CCJ supported the APNU+AFC's position, there is little doubt that PPP supporters would have similarly complained about the attempt to install the APNU+AFC against the will of half the country. The simplest way to resolve the situation was going by the recount numbers which gave a victory to the PPP. Hinds may have viewed this as a political coup, but what was the CCJ supposed to have done? There was no way that the CCJ could have ruled in a manner that would have been satisfactory to all Guyanese.

The refusal of the APNU+AFC coalition to accept the election results in 2020 was not much different than the conduct of the PPP in 2015 when President Donald Ramotar called for a recount. The international observers who were invited to oversee the election expressed the view that the election was free and fair, but Ramotar did not agree with the conclusions of the international observers. He was convinced that the election was rigged. Ramotar also claimed that the 2011 election was rigged as well. In 2011, the PPP retained control of the government, but became a minority government. This placed Ramotar in a very difficult situation and he was forced to prorogue parliament to avoid a vote of no confidence against him. The APNU+AFC's defeat was not the result of a political coup, as Hinds suggested. The APNU+AFC lost the election but refused to accept defeat. This is no different than how the PPP behaved when it lost power in 2015. Hinds seemed to have been engaging in the same type of behavior by suggesting that the defeat of the APNU+AFC was the result of the CCJ intervening in Guyana's election to engage in a political coup to overthrow one party in favor of another.

I agree with Rohit Kanhai when he wrote: "Some of Kissoon's attacks on the WPA over the years, on occasions, were justified. To a large extent, the WPA has had missteps, and should be criticized. Nevertheless, to personalize political problems as the failure of individuals, is another matter." It is Kissoon's decision to personalize his attacks on Kwayana that troubled me. In doing so, I think Kissoon has not only ruined his own credibility but has also contributed to the racial division in Guyana by framing his criticisms of Kwayana and Singh in racial terms, such as invoking Singh's race when doing so was unnecessary.

Whereas Kissoon used his disagreement with Kwayana as an opportunity to diminish Kwayana's legacy, I will not indulge in the same treatment of Kissoon by trying to diminish everything that he has done and stood for as an activist and columnist in Guyana. Kissoon's articles on Kwayana were disappointing to me because Kissoon is someone that I respected for the work that he has done as an activist in Guyana. I will mention here that Kissoon was the same man who was sued for libel by former president of Guyana, Bharrat Jagdeo, because Kissoon accused Jagdeo of engaging in racism during his tenure as president of Guyana. I recognize that Kisssoon was someone who was willing to decry racism on the part of the Guyanese government and suffered the consequences for doing so, which is why it was disappointing to see Kissoon contributing to the racial division in Guyana.

It is difficult to determine what caused this change in Kissoon. One explanation that I would offer is that Kissoon was disappointed with the conduct of the WPA. David Hinds and Kissoon stood together as activists who were confronting the PPP when the PPP was in power. When Kissoon was brought to court by Jagdeo, Hinds testified in defense of Kissoon. In 2020, it was noticeable that the two men stood on opposite sides. Kissoon denounced the electoral rigging on the part of the APNU+AFC, whereas Hinds concerned himself with what he regarded as a conspiracy to organize a coup against the APNU+AFC. Kissoon may have noticed that his associates in the WPA were not as vocal about the election rigging as he would have liked and was especially disappointed given that the WPA struggled against election rigging under the PNC in the past. Hinds was even imprisoned for his activism during the reign of the PNC government. Kissoon assumed that Kwayana's unwillingness to speak out about the situation meant that Kwayana approved of what was happening, but this was an improper assumption on Kissoon's part. One can certainly sympathize with Kissoon being disappointed with the conduct of the WPA, especially since the WPA was Walter Rodney's party, but there was no need to smear Eusi Kwayana and there was no need to drag Walter Rodney's legacy into the exchange. Doing so merely hurt Kissoon's credibility and undermined whatever legitimate criticisms of the WPA he may have had.

By trying to diminish Kwayana's legacy, Kissoon only damaged his own status as an activist who has denounced racism in Guyana in the past. It is particularly unfortunate that Kissoon would choose to engage in such racially divisive rhetoric during a period when Guyana was experiencing a contentious election. As if elections in Guyana are not divisive enough, Kissoon used this to spread more division and hate. Kissoon was correct in his assessment that after the election certain individuals would never be seen the same way again. This is how I feel about Kissoon. I recognize the fact that Kissoon was someone who stood against racism and injustice in Guyana. I respect Kissoon for doing so. I am also forced to recognize that in his conduct during the 2020 election, Kissoon revealed himself to be an individual who has a hard time expressing respectful disagreements, an individual who is too quick to condemn and judge others, and an individual who is not above unnecessarily injecting racist remarks to insult those whom he has disagreements with.

List of *Kaieteur News* articles referenced:

Clement J. Rohee, "When all is said and done, it is clear that the APNU+ AFC is fighting a losing battle," July 10, 2020.

"Coalition tells GECOM it cannot declare election results," June 8, 2020.

Eusi Kwayana, "Anil Nandlall has already reverted to a binary perspective on humanity," June 12, 2020.

___ "Mr. Kissoon is revealing a tendency to malice that I never detected before," June 7, 2020.

Freddie Kissoon, "After this, we will never see some Guyanese the same way again," May 10, 2020.

___ "Conversation between Walter Rodney and Desmond Trotman," July 10, 2020.

___ "Claudette Singh will declare the election improper," June 15, 2020.

___ "Eusi Kwayana, my mother and mother-in-law," August 27, 2021.

___ "Kwayana's [sic] is revealing a tendency to malice, never before seen," June 8, 2020.

"Incoming CARICOM Chair tells election loser 'take your licks like a man,'" June 12, 2020.

"Granger excludes critical media houses from press conference," June 15, 2020.

Kemol King, "Claudette Singh orders Lowenfield to submit recount figures by 2pm today," July 10, 2020.

Kit Nascimento, "It is expected that Claudette Singh will declare elections in keeping with the recount results," June 12, 2020

Mikalia Prince, "Granger says language of incoming CARICOM Chair unacceptable," June 15, 2020.

"Pres. Granger refuses to commit to recount declaration," June 7,

2020.

"PPP wins recount," June 8, 2020.

"Put country above party-Ex Liberia President, Ellen Johnson Sirleaf," July 10, 2020.

Rohit Kanhai, "Freddie Kissoon should apologise for his attacks on Eusi Kwayana," June 12, 2020.

Shikema Dey, "Granger backs Lowenfield's report-says he did a 'remarkable job,'" June 15, 2020.

3

THE REVOLUTION CAME

It was a quiet and usual day. Then the revolution came.

There were mass protests all over Africa. Every dictator and corrupt politician across Africa watched the revolution in fear. The security forces and soldiers which had killed, tortured, and brutalized the population in defense of these dictators decided that they would no longer take up their guns against their own civilians. They pointed their guns instead at the corrupt politicians. One by one, public officials were tracked down and arrested. Some were dragged out of their own homes to be charged in the people's court where they were convicted for treason against those whom they swore to serve.

Some leaders managed to escape by running to Europe, the land of their colonial masters because they no longer found refuge anywhere in Africa. Being of no more use to their European masters, these European states turned on them by extraditing them back to Africa where they were left to face justice at the hands of the people's revolution.

The justice of the people's court was not the justice of the colonial system. Those found guilty of treason did not have to face the inhumane prison cells, the beatings, the tortures, and executions which they inflicted on their citizens. Instead, the people's court put the convicted in service of the rebuilding. Presidents who once held exalted positions were put to assist in the rebuilding process.

No longer were presidents able to run to Britain or France for medical care. Hospitals were renovated. They were equipped with the latest technology. Some of the health ministers who left these hospitals in a state of neglect and disrepair were tasked with installing some of these renovations. No longer were surgeries conducted in dimly lit operating rooms. No longer were women made to give birth to their children on hospital floors. To address the shortage of doctors, scholarships were given out to anyone who was interested in going to medical school to become a doctor.

These programs were fully paid for by the state. Pharmaceutical factors were built all throughout Africa to address the shortage of drugs.

New governmental systems were developed all over Africa. Under these new systems, leaders were elected to their position by the masses in fair and free elections. No longer were elections in Africa rigged in favor of the incumbent government. Complete transparency was enforced throughout Africa for the purpose of keeping these newly elected leaders honest. Those who were exposed to have abused their power or engaged in corruption were dismissed from their positions and arrested to be taken before the people's courts.

Freedom of press was encouraged throughout Africa. No longer were journalists harassed, intimidated, imprisoned, or killed for exposing the truth. Artists were also free to publicly express disagreements with the ruling government through their music.

All of the assets of the corrupt political leaders, along with the assets of their friends and family members, were seized and placed into the treasury. This included assets from foreign property, such as mansions in Europe and America, as well as monies stashed in foreign banks. With the influx of the wealth, which was previously hoarded by the political leadership, new infrastructure projects were implemented. Citizens no longer had to worry about driving on poorly paved or unpaved roads. Access to clean water and electricity was established in every city, town, and village across Africa.

Rebels and warlords put down their weapons. Civil wars and conflicts all over Africa came to an end. Tribunals were established to resolve these disputes in a manner which was fair and just to all the parties involved. Angry and violent rebel soldiers who had taken up arms to attack and kill civilians were rehabilitated. These former rebel soldiers now formed the new revolutionary defense force which served and protected the masses. Strict discipline was demanded among members of the defense force, for these men and women formed an important cornerstone of the revolution.

The borders which were implemented by the European colonial powers were dissolved. No longer would Africans be harassed by officials at the borders. No longer would Africans be required to get a visa to travel to another African country. No longer would members of the same family be separated by the borders which the colonizers created.

African Americans, recognizing themselves as a separate nation within the borders of the United States, began organizing into semi-autonomous communities. These communities were built and sustained through a collective effort. Mayors, senators, representatives, and others who held public office no longer represented the interests of the Democratic Party or the Republican Party. These political leaders now served the interests of these newly formed communities.

The National Football League went out of business as brothers decided that no longer would they risk their own well-being for the enrichment of wealthy team owners and for the entertainment of football fans. These brothers put their physical abilities in service of the revolution. Those who made a fortune playing for the National Football League put together their money and formed a community task force which they led. The task force served the community in a variety of ways from construction projects, community farming, community defense, and community fitness programs to keep members of the community healthy. The brothers in the National Basketball Association followed this example by organizing a task force of their own.

Rappers and other musical artists used their musical talent in service of the revolution. They used their music to promote messages of revolutionary transformation, political consciousness, and self-determination. They ceased using their music to promote self-destructive behaviors. No longer would rappers glorify materialism, promote violence, or objectify women. These artists can be seen performing at community rallies, political events, and fundraising events.

Gang members were rehabilitated in training institutions which not only provided them with proper political and ideological training, but also provided them with the therapy and mental health counseling needed to address the lingering traumas caused by the hardships which they had faced in life. Every gang on the streets called a lasting truce. The guns which they had used to brutally murder and maim each other became instruments of self-defense and instruments to protect their communities from outside threats. The gangs ceased to peddle drugs to their own. The gangs joined different community task forces such as the community defense force and the community agriculturalists. Some would go on to become prominent political leaders.

The establishment of independent accredited law schools which were tuition free and financed by the community meant that law students could pursue legal training without being concerned about massive amounts of debt once they graduated. Funds from the community also went to employing community lawyers to ensure that anyone from the community who was arrested would have legal representation. No longer would indigent defenders have to rely on an underfunded and overburdened public defender system to represent them in court.

Community defense forces in which individuals from the community were trained to protect their communities were developed in every community. Self-defense training was taught in schools, so that everyone in the community was trained to defend themselves when necessary.

Community gardens were implemented to address food insecurity in African American communities across the nation. The gardens were controlled and operated by community farmers and agriculturalists. The food grown in these gardens were distributed throughout the community.

African Americans ceased voting for the Republicans and the Democrats until both parties were willing to meet the agenda put forward by the revolutionary movement. The agenda called for an end to American militarism abroad, an end to tax cuts for the wealthy, the cancelling of all student loan debt, for all public colleges to be tuition free, and for universal healthcare for all. The agenda also called for the establishment of a green economy in which fossil fuels were phased out in favor of more environmentally friendly sources of energy. Until these and other demands were met, African Americans had decided that they would no longer vote for either party.

The revolution arose in the Caribbean as well. Citizens from throughout the region rose up in protest. Some countries sent the police out to try to subdue the protesters. The attempt to stop the protests turned violent as some of the protesters were injured and even killed, but the protesters were not deterred. The protesters eventually overwhelmed the police forces. Governments across the region collapsed. Some leaders resigned. Others fled the region and went into exile in the United States. They were unwilling to stay to confront the wrath of the people whom they had neglected for decades.

Every politician who worked in the previous neo-colonial system came before an integrity commission which was established in each country. Those who were found guilty of corruption were summarily dismissed from their position. Interim governments were established until a new constitution could be finalized. The new political system which was established abolished all political parties in the region. No longer would citizens of the Caribbean argue with each other or even kill each other over political differences. The British parliamentary system was replaced with a new system which ensured true representation and democracy.

Freedom of press was supported throughout the region, as political leaders were no longer above criticism. Journalists no longer worried about being harassed or sued for reporting on the events in the country. Musical artists were no longer censored or punished for using their art to voice their displeasure at the state of affairs.

New jobs and opportunities were created throughout the region. The increase in opportunities led to a reduction in crime. Young men who had previously taken up guns to rob and steal for survival put away their guns. They became scholars, lawyers, doctors, scientists, engineers, farmers, artisans, and business owners. Eventually the unemployment rate dropped to zero, as every able-bodied adult in the region was given some form of meaningful employment which allowed them to earn a living, while also contributing to the building of new societies.

Free housing, education, and healthcare were available to all citizens in the region. As part of the program to implement infrastructure repairs, access to clean water was provided in every household.

The Caribbean region has been one which has been vulnerable to hurricanes and other natural disasters. To address these problems, new homes were constructed. These homes were fortified and strong enough to withstand hurricane force winds, yet also flexible enough and shock absorbent enough to also withstand the impact of earthquakes.

The Caribbean Community (CARICOM) was redeveloped to produce a meaningful Caribbean unity. From now on, all citizens of CARICOM member states were regarded as CARICOM citizens. This allowed for freedom of movement throughout the region without being mistreated or harassed by immigration officials. Jamaicans were no longer deported from Barbados. Guyanese were no longer deported from Trinidad. Haitians were no longer deported from the Dominican Republic. Haiti and the Dominican Republic came together to become a united island once more.

Puerto Rico joined the newly configured CARICOM as a member state after obtaining its independence from the United States. The U.S. Virgin Islands declared independence as well and joined CARICOM. Martinique, Guadeloupe, and Guyane declared independence from France and joined CARICOM as well.

In Brazil, revolution spread as well. The African masses rose up and overthrew the government overnight. The military police forces which had for so many years murdered and terrorized African people in Brazil were powerless to stop the swift, massive uprising. Some of the corrupt political leaders in Brazil escaped to neighboring countries. Those who were unable to escape were captured and placed on trial. Those who were found to be guilty were dismissed from their position and banished.

The police force was dismantled and replaced with a new security force. No longer did the police force harass and murder citizens. This new security force was one which served the community and protected the community from crime, although crime decreased sharply with the massive increase in employment opportunities.

No longer were Brazilian citizens made to live in slums and shacks. Adequate housing facilities were provided for everyone, free of charge. Medical treatment for citizens became free as well. This was financed in part by money which was seized from the oligarchy which held power in Brazil. The new revolutionary government of Brazil also implemented a community fund. These were funds which were specifically allocated for the purpose of benefiting the community. No longer could political leaders in Brazil enrich themselves at the expense of the masses.

Brazil's indigenous and African roots were promoted throughout the nation. A new revolutionary culture emerged. Artists used their skills to promote the message and the values of the revolution. Carnival now became a celebration of Brazil's new revolutionary culture. Football too became yet another method of promoting the values of the revolution. Football players became global ambassadors for the values of the revolution. They also became members of the various task forces which were created in Brazil such as the task forces for construction projects, farming, national defense, and national fitness programs.

The new revolutionary government of Brazil ceased the destruction of the Amazon rainforest. The new government worked in collaboration with the indigenous people of Brazil to ensure that significant parts of the rainforest were restored. In addition to restoring the Amazon rainforest, the African scientists in Brazil designed a machine to absorb a large volume of carbon dioxide and other greenhouse gases, thereby helping to reverse the global heating caused by the massive emission of greenhouse gases into the environment. Brazil became a nation which led the way in working to reverse the effects of climate change.

These new revolutionary societies around the world established industries and trade among themselves. The Western corporations which had benefited from the exploitation of African resources were driven out and replaced by companies which were owned and operated by the African citizens and citizens from the Diaspora, who used the resources for the benefit of the people of all African people. Worker cooperatives were established to manage these new companies.

The revolution also created new attitudes and a new culture among African people the world over. Strangers became brothers and sisters. Every adult male became a father to every child in the community and every adult female became a mother to every child in the community. The Western nuclear family was replaced with the African extended family.

Capitalist values were replaced by communal values. No longer would the wealthy hoard more wealth and resources than they needed. Wealth and resources were freely shared. No longer could an individual be arrested for stealing food, for satisfying one's hunger was no longer regarded as a crime. The values of the old European colonial system crumbled. In its place came a new system which upheld the humanity and dignity of all African people.

All over the African world, monuments which were dedicated to European colonizers were torn down and replaced with monuments to honor those who fought for the liberation of African people. In every school across the African world, African language classes were offered so that African students became proficient in at least one African language. Curriculum which centered the history and culture of the colonizer was replaced with a curriculum which centered the history and the culture of African people.

This was the day that the revolution came.

4

BLACK ANTI-SEMITISM

The relationship between African people and Jews is a unique one. According to the Bible, the Hebrews were enslaved in Egypt. It was Moses, the Egyptian raised Hebrew, who eventually led the Hebrews to freedom and in time the Hebrews would develop a nation of their own. The historical accuracy of the Exodus story in the Bible is questionable, but the narrative does demonstrate the centrality of Egypt to the development of the Hebrew religion. The interactions between Africans and the Hebrew people would continue in ways that would profoundly influence both cultures of people. This includes the Nubians saving Jerusalem from an Assyrian invasion and the lineage of the Ethiopian monarchy which is purported to descend from King Solomon.

An aspect of this historical relationship has also included the tensions between African people and Jews. Leo Africanus wrote that the king of Timbuktu was a sworn enemy of the Jews and that he did not allow Jews to enter his city. In general, however, there was not the same level of intolerance towards Jews in pre-colonial Africa as there has been in Europe. Most of the tensions which emerged between Africans and Jews has been due largely to the perception that Jews have participated in and benefited from the exploitation of African people. This is a point that Malcolm X made in one of his speeches. Malcolm spoke about how Jews opened businesses in black communities, taking money out of black communities. Malcolm claimed that Jews were the ones who controlled the economy of Harlem and used the wealth from Harlem for themselves, and for the benefit of Israel. Malcolm also noted that he was on a program in which he made a statement about how Jews controlled 80% of the economy in most black communities in the country. The program was barred from being aired again because of Malcolm's remarks about Jews. Malcolm stated: "Jews believe in censorship more than anybody else [...] They're the most sensitive white people on this earth."

Given the type of injustices which the Jewish people have

endured, this level of sensitivity is understandable and even justified. The problem is, however, that the claim of anti-Semitism is often used to silence legitimate criticisms of Jewish people. This has been at the root of much of the tensions between African leaders and the Jewish community.

One aspect of this clash between Jews and black people has been this question of who the true chosen people are. There have been certain black Hebrew Israelite organizations which have declared that black people are in fact the true Jews and described Jews as frauds. F.S. Cherry founded the earliest of the black Hebrew organizations. The Anti-Defamation League's report on Hebrew Israelite organizations gave the following description of Cherry: "Cherry integrated racism into his teachings, preaching that all biblical prophets and individuals were Black, and that God hates white individuals because they are frauds."

The black Hebrew Israelites who declare that black people are the true Israelites are the product of a quest for a lost identity. During slavery, African people were stripped of a sense of identity. Some of the Hebrew Israelites turned to the Bible to recapture their identity. The connection was a rather natural one given that the story of the Hebrews in the Bible was the story of a people who were enslaved and oppressed in Egypt before being led into freedom. This resonated with enslaved Africans who also longed for freedom. This can be expressed in the spiritual "Go Down Moses." This spiritual was famously performed by Louis Armstrong.

For many Africans, the connection to the Hebrews of the Bible was spiritual or symbolic. The Hebrew Israelites, however, came to view themselves as being the true Israelites. As the ADL report notes, certain Hebrew Israelite groups also claim that Native Americans and Hispanics are among the twelve tribes of Israel. This is a rather curious position, and one which has no basis in the Bible or in history.

One of earlier Hebrew Israelite congregations was the Commandment Keepers, which was founded by Wentworth Arthur Matthew. Matthew preached that Jews are black and that the white Jews were the product of intermarriage between the black Jews and the children of Esau. Matthew did not have any negative views towards white Jews, however. Matthew sought the acceptance from Jewish communities such as the New York Board of Rabbis, but he was not successful.

On some level, this rejection of white Jews by Hebrew Israelites is a reaction to the racism which African people have experienced. Even the ADL report noted that Matthew never found acceptance from white Jews and that he felt like an outcast. The ADL report stated that although "Matthew himself reported feeling outcast by white Jews, he refrained from antisemitic or racist teachings."

The ADL report also noted the criminal conduct of certain Hebrew Israelite groups. This type of activity certainly cannot be excused or defended. The report included some of the murders which were carried out by the Nation of Yahweh in Miami. The founder Yahweh ben Yahweh and fifteen of his followers were indicted on murder charges. Yahweh ben Yahweh was convicted in 1992. Maurice Woodside was a member of the Nation of Yahweh. He later became known as "Michael the Black Man," a supporter of Donald Trump. Maurice claimed that Trump was the greatest president that America has ever had.

It was not only the black Hebrew Israelites who questioned the authenticity of white Jews. John Henrik Clarke explained: "I think this whole thing about anti-Semitic is such a bogus lie. Their word Semitic started off being linguistic. They attach it to a whole people. If it applies to any people at all, it doesn't apply to anybody in Europe. Europeans were belated converts to the Hebrew faith. We must make a clear distinction between a convert to the Hebrew faith and a descendent of the original members of the Hebrew faith. We're dealing with a religion, a faith, not a people." The point that Clarke was making is that white Jews were converts to the Hebrew faith, which is a faith that did not originate in Europe.

The point that Clarke was making was not necessarily to suggest that white Jews are frauds, but that white Jews do not have ownership over the religion of Judaism or the Jewish identity. Clarke also argued that the land of Israel does not belong to white Jews. He stated: "These were Europeans claiming a land that was never the homeland of Europeans." He continued to argue that the only ones who do have a rightful claim to the land are western

Asian Hebrews: "If the western Asian Hebrews claimed it in mythology or folklore, they might have had the shade of a case, if we're to believe what they say about their gods. Since God is not in the real estate business, and God is not the manager of great land surfaces, I would sense to question them. The only people who would have a claim on that land would be people of the Hebrew faith, from western Asia. The people of the Hebrew faith from Europe, has no legitimate claim to Palestine. They were never there. They want to say that God gave them that land. Which God? What time? The European Jew is a European creation."

What is worth noting here is that even the Bible makes it clear that the land did not originally belong to the Hebrews. The Hebrews took Israel from the inhabitants who lived in those lands before the Hebrews. The taking of this land was a very destructive and violent process. In Deuteronomy 20:16-18, God commanded the Hebrews to leave nothing alive in the cities which he offered to the Hebrews. God commands that the Hebrews destroy all of the Hittites, Amorites, Canaanites, Perizzites, Hivites and Jebusites. The reason given for this destruction was that God warned that these groups will teach the Hebrews to worship other gods. This was precisely the reason why the Kingdom of Israel split into two. According to the Bible, King Solomon had 700 wives and 300 concubines. This proved to be his downfall. 1 Kings 11 explained that Solomon's wives led him astray by leading him to worship other gods. As punishment for this, God decided to tear the Kingdom of Israel away from Solomon's son. The Kingdom of Israel was subsequently broken up after 10 of the 11 tribes left to follow Jeroboam. Jeroboam ruled over the Kingdom of Israel in the north and Solomon's son Rehoboam was left to rule over the much smaller Kingdom of Judah to the south.

Based on the Bible's own narrative, the land of Israel which Zionists have claimed and settled on was a land which originally did not belong to the Hebrews. The Hebrews took the land through a violent invasion and eventually the Kingdom of Israel which the Hebrews built fell because the Hebrews strayed away from God, thereby breaking the covenant that they established with God. For this reason, the decline of Israel in the Bible is presented as a form of divine punishment. 2 Kings 24 explains that Zedekiah did great evil in the eyes of God. 2 Kings 25 explains that Zedekiah's fate was that he was defeated by the Nebuchadnezzar of Babylon. Zedekiah was taken captive and forced to watch as his sons were killed before him. Zedekiah then had his eyes put out.

Apart from this question over authenticity, there have been other issues between Jews and African people such as the Jewish role in the slave trade. In *Jews and Negro Slavery in the Old South*, Bertram Wallace Korn noted that although only a relatively small number of Jews participated in the slave trade and were slave owners, there were indeed Jews who did participate in the enslavement of African people. There is also the question of Israel's foreign policy in Africa, which has at times been harmful for African people. For example, Israel has been among the nations which have supported the dictatorship in Togo. Former Israeli Prime Minister Benjamin Netanyahu met Togolese President Faure Gnassingbé, shaking his hand and referring to him as a "great friend." It apparently did not bother the Prime Minister of Israel that his friend was a brutal dictator who came to power through a military coup and retained power through unleashing terror against the Togolese people. Togo's foreign minister Robert Dussey was invited by the American Israel Public Affairs Committee to speak about Togo's relationship with Israel, to the applause of an audience which seemed unconcerned about the human rights abuses committed by the government of Togo. I raise these points to demonstrate that there have been Jews who have been involved in the oppression of African people, whether it was involvement through the slave trade or supporting brutal African dictatorships such as the one in Togo.

African people do have legitimate grievances against certain Jews, although the expression of these grievances has often led to tensions between the two groups. Minister Louis Farrakhan of the Nation of Islam has drawn much condemnation from Jewish organizations for some of the remarks that he has made over the years. In some cases, Farrakhan's anger against Jews has been justifiable, though his reaction only created more controversy.

Farrakhan's problems with Jewish organizations seemed to have begun in 1984, after Jesse Jackson announced that he was going to run for president. The Jewish Defense League launched a negative campaign against Jackson's presidential bid because he held meetings with Arab leaders such as the Syrian President Hafiz al-Assad and Yasser Arafat of the Palestinian Liberation Organization. The campaign against Jackson included threats against his life, which prompted Jackson to request protection from the Secret Service. The Secret Service was reluctant to provide security for Jackson, so Farrakhan provided security for Jackson through the Fruit of Islam. These threats against Jackson angered Farrakhan, who supported Jackson's bid for the presidency. At the 1984 Savior's Day convention, Farrakhan stated: "If you harm this brother, I warn you in the name of Allah, this will be the last one you harm."

Farrakhan would once again come to Jackson's defense after private remarks by Jackson were leaked to the public. Jackson had referred to Jews in New York as "Hymies". Farrakhan responded by threatening to make an example of Milton Coleman, the journalist who leaked Jackson's remarks. Farrakhan stated: "One day soon we will punish with death..."

Throughout the 1990s, Farrakhan made attempts to reconcile with the Jewish community. In 1993, he performed the violin concerto of a well-known Jewish composer named F. Mendelssohn and spoke of reconciliation with America's Jewish population. In a 1994 news conference Farrakhan denounced anti-Semitism in all of its forms and manifestations. He further explained that being anti-Semitic would make him unfit to call himself a servant of God. After the Million Man March in 1995, Farrakhan expressed his willingness to establish a dialogue with Jewish leaders and organizations. In 1996, Edgar Bronfman, the head of the World Jewish Congress, hosted Farrakhan at a dinner in New York, but Bronfman would later cut off contact with Farrakhan. Farrakhan's attempts to improve his relationship with the Jewish community did little to change the media's perception of Farrakhan, however.

Farrakhan has continued to maintain that he has no hatred of the Jewish people. Following being banned from Facebook, Farrakhan delivered a speech in which he stated that he does not hate Jewish people. He also stated that he was seeking to separate the good Jews from the "Satanic" Jews.

Though Farrakhan could be harsh in denouncing certain Jews, there were limits which even he would not cross. This was demonstrated when he dismissed Khalid Muhamad from Khalid's post as a minister in the Nation of Islam following a controversial speech which Khalid delivered at Kean College. Farrakhan described Khalid's remarks as being an improper representation of the teachings of Elijah Muhammad. Farrakhan found the speech to be vile, repugnant, and mean-spirited. He stated that it was against the "spirit of Islam." At the same press conference where Farrakhan announced the suspension of Khalid Muhammad, Farrakhan also criticized a document which the ADL put out about Farrakhan.

Whereas Farrakhan was attempting to reconcile with the Jewish community, Khalid denounced Jews as imposters and even urged rappers not to imitate Italian and Jewish gangsters because black people were the true chosen people of God. After being removed from his position in the Nation of Islam, Khalid Muhammad was free to express himself without worrying about the consequences for Farrakhan. Khalid explained in a speech at Howard University that nothing which he said could be used against Louis Farrakhan since Khalid was no longer the national representative for the Nation of Islam. Khalid proclaimed that he would lock his jaws on the backsides of the "no-good, imposter" Jews. Khalid also expressed love for Colin Ferguson, whom he described as a modern day Nat Turner. Ferguson was a Jamaican born man who killed six people on a train. According to Khalid, Ferguson was sent by God to kill the people that he killed. Khalid felt free to make such a remark because he no longer held an official position in the Nation of Islam.

After being removed from the Nation of Islam, Khalid Muhammad maintained that Farrakhan was his teacher and "spiritual father." He proclaimed that the situation between himself and Farrakhan would play out differently than the split between Malcolm X and Elijah Muhammad. The split between Khalid and Farrakhan did not become as bitter as Malcolm's split with the Nation of Islam became, but differences between Khalid and Farrakhan did emerge. Khalid attempted to avoid a repeat of the situation between Malcolm X and Elijah Muhammad, but this could not prevent a rift from emerging between the two men.

Khalid explained that for years he had called and written to Farrakhan. In five years, Khalid only received one letter from Farrakhan. After Khalid was shot, Farrakhan did not visit Khalid at the hospital nor did he even send a letter. Despite Khalid's repeated attempts to return to the Nation of Islam, Farrakhan continued to ignore him. This bothered Khalid, who claimed that he had supported Farrakhan at a time when even Farrakhan's own children were not supporting him. Not only had Farrakhan removed Khalid from the Nation of Islam because of Khalid's remarks about Jews, but Farrakhan continued to distance himself from Khalid.

Some of Farrakhan's hostility towards Jews stems from Farrakhan's expressed outrage over the Israeli occupation of Palestine. In 1984, he referred to Israel's creation as an "outlaw act" and referred to Judaism as a "gutter religion". Years later, Farrakhan would apologize for these remarks, which he described as a mistake. He explained that his remarks about Judaism being a dirty religion was not a reference to the religion of Jewish people, but to the specific actions of the Israeli government against Palestinian children.

Farrakhan has not been the only prominent African leader to criticize Israel's treatment of Palestinians. Kwame Ture (formerly known as Stokely Carmichael) was a staunch critic of Zionism. Ture decried Zionism as a movement which attached itself to British colonialism to create a Jewish state in Palestine. Ture explained that liberation movements fight against imperialism, not with imperialism. The Balfour Declaration which publicly declared Britain's intention to settle Jews in Palestine stated: "His Majesty's Government view with favour the establishment in Palestine of a national home for the Jewish people and will use their best endeavours to facilitate the establishment of this object." The Balfour Declaration was supported by the United States government, but the Declaration was met with outrage in the Arab world.

Kwame Ture saw Zionism as an obstacle in the way of African unity. This view stemmed from Ture's attempt to build a united front of African organizations in the United States. Ture was sent by the All-African People's Revolutionary Party to meet with Farrakhan for the purpose of organizing a united front. Ture had a prior relationship with the Nation of Islam. As chairman of the Student Non-Violent Coordinating Committee, his first public meeting in America was a meeting with Elijah Muhammad. At that meeting, Elijah Muhammad ordered the Fruit of Islam to provide security for Ture. The Nation of Islam also influenced Ture's views on Zionism. He recalled that as a young man, *Muhammad Speaks* was the only African newspaper in which he could read about the Palestinian struggle against Zionism.

A split was created in the front after John Jacob of the Urban League wrote a letter condemning Farrakhan. Ture explained that it took nine months to get Farrakhan and Jacob to reconcile. Ture blamed this incident on Zionists. He went on to help organize the Worldwide African Anti-Zionist Front. That front included 30 organizations, including the Republic of New Afrika and the Pan African Congress of Azania in South Africa. Ture explained that he was determined to build a united front, even if that front had to be built through fighting Zionism.

Much of what has been labeled as anti-Semitism on the part of African people is merely a response to the Zionist exploitation of Palestine and the Zionist exploitation of African people. This is not to downplay or disregard the injustices which Jews have endured, but one must understand that within the global system of white supremacy, European Jews have been able to participate in and benefit from Western colonialism. I am not suggesting that these criticisms of Jews have always been expressed in an effective or constructive manner. The point I am raising here, however, is that such criticisms should not be merely dismissed without understanding the root of where these criticisms come from. It is true that Jewish people have endured a great deal of suffering and discrimination, but it is also true that there have been Jews who have benefited from the global system of white supremacy and colonization. The creation of Israel is a clear example of this. Zionists not only benefited from the British colonization of Palestine, but Israel's foreign policy in Africa is one which has supported brutal dictatorships such as the one in Togo.

5

THE AWAKENING OF EDDIE WILSON

The clock alarms. It is 6:30 in the morning. A beaten and battered Eddie Wilson reaches out and smashes the alarm clock to turn it off. Eddie then crawls out of bed. His torso is sore and bruised from the beating that he received the night before, but he needs to be at work for 8:00.

Eddie drags himself into the shower, where he tenderly washes himself to avoid aggravating his bruises. He then slowly dresses himself and hobbles out of the door to make his way to Tony's Pizzeria where Eddie works as a part-time pizza delivery driver.

Eddie enters the pizza store. The store is not yet open. Tony is sweeping the floor, as is his usual morning routine before he opens the shop. Tony looks up and notices Eddie opening the door.

Tony, who is surprised to see Eddie, says, "Eddie, what are you doing here today? I thought you got the message I sent you."

"What message?" Eddie replies.

"Business hasn't been doing so well these last few months, so we are cutting costs."

"What do you mean?" Eddie asks.

"That means that we will have to cut your hours. From now on, you will only be delivering on Thursdays."

"But I need the extra money."

"How did the fight go last night?"

"I got knocked out in the third round."

"Well, what can you I tell you," Tony replies, "you'll just have to start winning some more fights. I'm sorry. I really am, but things are getting really tight out here. I am sure you understand."

Eddie nods.

"Alright," Eddie says before leaving, "I will see you on Thursday."

"Take care," Tony tells Eddie as Eddie walks out of the door.

Later that night Eddie decides to go to the gym where he trains. The gym is closed at nights, but Eddie is on such good terms with the owner Manfred that Manfred has given Eddie a key of his own so that Eddie can come back to train at nights after work.

Manfred steps out of his office to see that Eddie is there unleashing his fury on a punching bag. Manfred smiles at Eddie's passion and decides to impart some wisdom on Eddie.

"George Dixon."

Eddie stops hitting the punching bag and turns to Manfred.

"George Dixon. That's the brother who invented that bag that you're hitting there. It's important to know things like this, since the man has tried for so many years to deny us of our historical achievements."

"Manfred. I didn't realize that you were here."

"Yes," Manfred replies, "was just doing some reading in my office and I came out to see what the commotion was out here. I should have known it was you."

"Sorry."

"Don't apologize. I was just about to leave anyway. I've got to get home to my wife."

"I never knew that. What you said about George Dixon. I ain't never even heard of him."

"Most of the brothers who come in here don't," Manfred replies. "That's the way the man wants to keep it. He wants to keep us deaf, dumb, ignorant, and blind to where we have been and the things that we have done. A people who don't know where they have been don't know where they are going."

"How do you mean?"

"What I mean is that you have to know your past to understand where you are going. Have you ever thought about why it is that we have to struggle so hard just to get ahead in this world?"

"I can't say I have. I've always been too busy struggling to get by. It's just the way that it is."

"But it doesn't have to be that way, you know. It wasn't always this way. You know, we black people used to be kings in Africa."

"Look, Manfred, I don't know anything about Africa."

"But you should. You are African ain't ya?"

"I was born here."

"But that's not where our people were stolen from. They stole us from Africa where we lived freely before we was stolen. We had our own civilizations. Great civilizations at that. Ever since we've been in this hellhole the man has been beating us down, trying to make us forget that we ever came from anything great. Why, he got us so good at it that he's even got brothers like you fighting and beating each other up to get ahead in this system. Don't matter how much money you make and how many championships you win, if you ain't got knowledge of self you are a fool. None of the man's accolades will do you any good."

"I don't want to sound ungrateful for your advice, but why are you telling me all of this?"

"Just my way of trying to help. I know that you're disappointed about that last fight but remember that it's just a fight. Don't worry too much about it."

"It's the third fight that I lost in a row."

"Then perhaps this boxing thing isn't for you."

"The problem is that I am sure what it is. I'm a fighter. Not much else makes sense to me, but fighting for survival does because I've been fighting since I can remember."

"You're a smart brother. I'm sure you'll find whatever it is that you are looking for, but just remember that before you find what it is that you want, you have to know who you are and where you come from. That's the power of knowledge of self. That's not something anybody can take from you, no matter how many fights you lose."

After imparting those final words, Manfred walks back to his office to grab his book before making his way outside of the gym to return home, leaving Eddie to continue his training. Eddie returns to striking the punching bag, but this time instead of thinking about the fight that he lost the previous night, Eddie finds himself thinking about Manfred's words. He finds himself wondering about these African civilizations which Manfred mentioned.

6

9/11 AND OSAMA BIN LADEN'S LEGACY OF TERROR

In western Asia, Islam emerged as a very powerful force. The religion was spread by the Prophet Muhammad who began preaching about the one true god, Allah. The Prophet Muhammad claimed that the revelations which he preached were communicated to him by an angel. At this time the people of Arabia practiced a pagan religion. Muhammad's teachings were not well-received, but he was eventually able to establish power over the city of Mecca and established Islam as the most dominant religion in Arabia.

Following the death of Muhammad, Islam spread very rapidly due to Islamic conquests. Syria, Damascus, Palmyra, Antioch, and Jerusalem all fell under Arab domination. In 637, the Arab Muslim forces defeated Persia. These conquests spread into North Africa as well. Arabs conquered Egypt. The conquest continued into Tunisia and Algeria. Queen Kahina is remembered for her valiant defense in the face of the Arab invasion in North Africa, but she was ultimately defeated and killed.

According to the North African historian Ibn Khaldun, Islam served a unifying force for Arabs. He explained: "Arab pride, touchiness and intense jealousy of power render it impossible for them to agree. Only when their nature has been permeated by a religious impulse are they transformed, so that the tendency to anarchy is replaced by a spirit of mutual defense. Consider the moment when religion dominated their policy and led them to observe a religious law designed to promote the moral and material interests of civilization. Under a series of successors to the Prophet [Muhammad], how vast their empire became and how strongly was it established."

The spread of Islam was not merely the spread of a religion. It also spread Arabic culture and the Arabic language throughout the region. Islam helped to produce a distinct regional Arab identity which came to include people who were not ethnically Arab but had adopted Arabic culture and the religion of Islam.

From 1514 to 1638, the Ottoman state of the Turks managed to conquer nearly all the Arab countries. The Ottoman Empire would eventually fall during World War I. The collapse of the Ottoman Empire would have profound consequences for the region. Arab states which had been under Ottoman rule for centuries found themselves under the hegemony of European colonial powers. Vladimir Borisovich Lutsky gave the following description of the situation: "Though free at last from the Turkish yoke, they had been cheated of their long-awaited independence and fallen under the influence of the British and French colonialists. The end of World War I opened a new period in the history of the Arab people, a period of struggle against British and French imperialism for the complete national liberation of the Arab countries."

After Arab countries freed themselves from the domination of British and French imperialism, they were then confronted with the regional influence of the United States, which had frequently intervened in the region to overthrow certain governments or to support regimes which served American interests, even if those regimes were oppressive. I recount this history because the terrorism of Osama bin Laden and other Islamic extremist groups developed in part as a response to Western hegemony over the Islamic world. Bin Laden himself invoked the history of the clash between the Christian Westernized civilization and the Islamic Arabic civilization by referring to Americans as "Crusaders", which is a reference to the Crusade in Europe, which was an attempt to save the Holy Land from Muslim rule.

Osama bin Laden was born in Saudi Arabia. He was the seventeenth of his father's fifty-seven children. In 1979, the Soviet Union intervened in Afghanistan in support of the communist government which was established there in 1978. Muslims from around the world flocked to Afghanistan to join this "holy war" against the Soviet Union. Bin Laden was among those who went to Afghanistan to fight the Soviets. The Afghan forces finally defeated the Soviet Union in 1988. Bin Laden's role in this conflict helped to increase his stature in the Islamic world. This would later help him to organize his campaign of terror against the United

States.

In 1990, Saddam Hussein invaded Kuwait. Bin Laden proposed to the Saudi monarchy that mujahadeen be used to retake Kuwait. Saudi Arabia instead decided to seek the military assistance of the United States. The Saudi royal family also allowed American forces to establish a base in Saudi Arabia. This outraged bin Laden who despised the idea that American soldiers were allowed to be stationed in Saudi Arabia. Bin Laden left the country and in 1994 his citizenship was revoked.

Bin Laden moved to Sudan in 1991. There bin Laden used his construction company to build a new highway in Sudan. Bin Laden had established connections to the government of Sudan in 1989 when Hassan al Turabi requested bin Laden's assistance with fighting the war against African Christians in the south. While in Sudan, bin Laden also supported anti-Saddam Islamists in Iraq. Turabi reportedly got bin Laden to agree to cease supporting anti-Saddam groups in Iraq. Bin Laden's tendency to support radical Islamic organizations in the region would create problems for him in Sudan.

The government of Sudan was receiving pressure from the United States and other nations to cease harboring terrorist organizations. Libya was also one of those nations which pressured Sudan. The Libyans who were members of bin Laden's army were forced to leave Sudan. In secret meetings with Saudi officials, Sudan offered to expel bin Laden to Saudi Arabia. Saudi officials wanted bin Laden out of Sudan, but they were also not willing to allow him to return to Saudi Arabia. Bin Laden no longer felt safe in Sudan, so he decided to leave in 1996. He returned to Afghanistan, which at this point was under Taliban rule. It was in Afghanistan that bin Laden launched his jihad against the United States.

In Afghanistan, bin Laden was given the freedom to publish his appeals for jihad. Unlike in Sudan, the government of Afghanistan allowed Al Qaeda members to freely travel throughout the country. Al Qaeda also used state-owned planes to bring money into the country. Around this time, bin Laden was also apparently working towards cooperation with Saddam Hussein. Hussein was trying to rebuild relations with the Saudis, however. This led him to avoid bin Laden.

Bin Laden was outraged over the presence of American soldiers in Saudi Arabia. He also denounced the American support of Israel and the suffering of the Iraqi people because of the sanctions which were imposed on them after the Gulf War. Bin Laden's solution was to declare a war against "Jews and Crusaders" to liberate the holy places from these intruders. He made it very apparent that in this war against the United States not even American civilians would be safe. When asked if he approved of attacks on civilians, bin Laden stated: "We do not have to differentiate between military or civilian. As far as we are concerned, they are all targets."

Bin Laden's campaign of terror included bombing the American embassies in Tanzania and Kenya in 1998. The attack in Kenya killed 12 Americans and 201 others, most of whom were Kenyans. Another 5,000 were injured. The attack on the embassy in Tanzania killed 11 people, none of which were Americans. Al Qaeda was also responsible for bombing the *USS Cole* in 2000. The attack killed 17 members of the ship's crew and wounded 40 others. Bin Laden's most notorious attack would come in 2001.

Prior to the attack on September 11, 2001, there were reports of a possible terrorist attack involving hijacked planes. The *9/11 Commission Report* noted that in 1998 there were reports of a possible Al Qaeda plan to hijack a plane. There was also mention of a possible plot to fly an explosive-laden aircraft into an American city. In August of that same year, the intelligence community received information that a group of Libyans were hoping to crash a plane into the World Trade Center. None of this information could be corroborated, however. In August 1999, the Federal Aviation Administration's Civil Aviation Security intelligence office concluded that a suicide hijacking operation was unlikely because it would not offer an opportunity for dialogue to achieve the goal of obtaining Omar Abdel Rahman and other captives. It concluded that suicide hijacking was an option of "last resort." At the time Rahman was serving a life sentence for his role in the 1993 plot to blow up sites in New York City.

The *9/11 Commission Report* indicated that officials were aware of the possibility of a terrorist attack involving hijacked planes.

The *9/11 Commission Report* also indicated that this possibility was not treated as a top national security priority. Prior to 9/11, Al Qaeda itself had not been treated as a top national security priority. In 2000 and during the first eight months of 2001, terrorism was not a major public concern. That would change after the events on September 11, 2001.

On the morning of September 11, four planes were hijacked. Most of what is known about the hijacking came from Betty Ong and Madeline "Amy" Sweeney, who were two flight attendants that were onboard one of the hijacked planes. The hijackers had stabbed two unarmed flight attendants and forced their way into the cockpit. How they were able to enter the cockpit is not known, but once inside the cockpit the hijackers sprayed an irritant to force the passengers to the rear of the plane. Contact with Sweeney and Ong was lost minutes before the plane crashed into the first tower.

The North Tower was the first of the two towers to be hit. Hundreds of civilians were killed by the impact of the plane smashing into the building. Hundreds more were trapped. Some of those who were trapped inside the building decided to jump out. The impact from the plane made all three of the building's stairwells impassable from the 92nd floor up. The impact also sent a fireball down the building, which blew out the elevators and burned civilians who were caught in the path of the fireball.

Seventeen minutes after the first tower was hit, the South Tower was struck by another plane. Unlike in the North Tower, the plane which hit the South Tower did leave portions of the building undamaged on the impact floors. One of the stairwells remained passable from the 91st floor down. The destruction caused by the two plane crashes resulted in both towers eventually collapsing. The South Tower was the first to collapse, followed by the North Tower. More than 2,900 Americans were killed because of this attack.

The third plane to crash was American Airlines Flight 77. This one struck the Pentagon, killing all the passengers on board as well as many civilians and military personnel who were in the building. United Airlines Flight 93 was the last of the four planes to leave the airport. The passengers on this flight received calls from family, friends, and colleagues about the two planes which hit the World Trade Center. Two of the callers from the flight reported that the hijackers were aware that the passengers were making calls but, the hijackers did not seem to care. The callers also reported that a passenger had been stabbed and two people were lying on the floor in the cabin, injured or dead. Several callers indicated that the passengers and surviving crew members decided to revolt against the hijackers to retake the plane. The passengers attacked the hijackers. The hijackers, realizing that they were going to be overtaken by the passengers, decided to crash the plane. The plan was to crash the plane into the White House, but the passenger revolt onboard prevented the hijackers from reaching their destination.

Khalid Sheikh Mohammed was the mastermind behind the September 11 attack. He was the one who presented the plans to attack the World Trade Center by flying planes into them. He had previously been involved in the bombing of the World Trade Center in 1993. Sometime in 1991 or 1992, Khalid Sheikh Mohammed learned of Ramzi Yousef's plan to launch an attack inside of the United States. Khalid Sheikh Mohammed discussed the progress of these plans with Yousef through numerous telephone conversations. Khalid Sheikh Mohammed also contributed funds to this plan. The 1993 bombing of the World Trade Center motivated Khalid Sheikh Mohammed to become more involved in planning attacks against the United States. Khalid Sheikh Mohammed explained that his animus towards the United States stemmed from America's support for Israel.

Following the 9/11 attack, the United States demanded that the Taliban turn over bin Laden and other Al Qaeda operatives. In his speech before a joint session of Congress, President George W. Bush declared: "Every nation, in every region, now has a decision to make: Either you are with us, or you are with the terrorists." He also explained that this war went beyond bin Laden, explaining that the war "will not end until every terrorist group of global reach has been found, stopped, and defeated."

The United States launched a military invasion of Afghanistan which forced the Taliban from power, although the Taliban would later regain power again in 2021. Bin Laden escaped being captured during the initial American invasion of Afghanistan. It was not until 2011 that the United States was finally able to locate and assassinate bin Laden.

Bin Laden did not succeed in driving America out of the region, but the ideas which bin Laden preached continued to spread beyond Al Qaeda. Al Qaeda's ideas influenced an Islamic organization in Nigeria known as Boko Haram. Boko Haram translates to Western education is forbidden. This negative attitude towards Western education stems from the fact that Western education is available to a small elite who are typically trained in British universities and then return to rule Nigeria from the capital. Yusuf Muhammad was the founder of Boko Haram. His goal was to end the rule of this elite.

Boko Haram appealed to the frustrations of northern Nigerians who struggle with poverty and lack of opportunity, as well as abuses from the government's security forces. Initially Boko Haram did not target civilian populations. Boko Haram's violent attacks were aimed at the government. The group moved in a more radical direction in 2009 after about 70 Boko Haram members attacked a mosque and police station, killing 55 people. Nigerian security forces retaliated in a crackdown which killed more than 700 people, many of whom were innocent bystanders. Yusuf was captured and paraded before television cameras before he was executed in front of a crowd outside of a police station. This action only further radicalized Boko Haram.

Weeks after the execution of Yusuf, Al Qaeda reached out to Boko Haram to express support for the organization. Boko Haram's remaining members scattered to other countries. Some of them received training in Algerian camps from Al Qaeda. Members of Boko Haram also trained in Somalia with Al Shabab, which is an Islamic organization in Somalia that is also affiliated with Al Qaeda. In 1993, Al Qaeda had sent weapons and trainers to Somalis who were fighting American forces. Bin Laden explained in an interview that he and his followers were preparing for a long struggle in Somalia, but the United States "rushed out of Somalia in shame and disgrace." The withdrawal of the American army in Somalia emboldened bin Laden.

Boko Haram returned to Nigeria as a more sophisticated and

better equipped organization. Under the leadership of Abubakar Shekau, Boko Haram also began staging more lethal attacks. These attacks targeted civilians. This was done to demonstrate the incapacity of the Nigerian state. The brutality of Boko Haram has been such that even fellow jihadists have accused Boko Haram of killing too many noncombatants (*The New York Times* reported on this on May 7, 2014, with a story titled "Abduction of Girls an Act Not Even Al Qaeda Can Condone"). Some jihadists were shocked to hear news that Boko Haram had kidnapped schoolgirls in 2014. Bronwyn Bruton explained that the violence that African rebel groups practice "makes Al Qaeda look like a bunch of schoolgirls."

As stated before, Boko Haram did appeal to legitimate frustrations felt by Nigerians in the north, but since 2009 the organization has become increasingly radicalized to the point that Al Qaeda has found it difficult to support some of Boko Haram's actions. By 2014, when Boko Haram kidnapped over 200 schoolgirls, Al Qaeda was moving towards a more moderate position of avoiding killing civilians for fear of losing potential supporters. Boko Haram, on the other hand, had no such fear. As Al Qaeda was moving in a more moderate direction, Boko Haram was doing the opposite.

I mention Boko Haram not only as an example of how bin Laden's brand of Islamic extremism has expanded to other parts of the world, but also to demonstrate that an insidious aspect of this brand of Islamic extremism is that it appeals to legitimate frustrations on the part of Muslims who are recruited by these organizations to carry out these heinous actions. The *9/11 Commission Report* noted that the image of the United States among Muslim populations around the world was a very negative one. The *9/11 Commission Report* noted that only 15% of Muslims in Indonesia held a favorable view of America, which was a sharp decline from the previous 61%. Among Muslims in Nigeria, America's favorability was 38%. The report noted that many of "these views are at best uninformed about the United States and, at worst, informed by cartoonish stereotypes, the coarse expression of a fashionable 'Occidentalism' among intellectuals who caricature U.S. values and policies." This is true, but I cannot help but feel that the report was also downplaying some of the legitimate criticisms that Muslims have of the United States, such as the continued America intervention in the political affairs of Muslim nations. This would include actions such as the military intervention in Somalia which led to the deaths of several Somalis or organizing a coup in Iran—it was noted before that bin Laden was supporting Somalis in their struggle against the United States. These interventions cannot be so easily explained away as being the result of Muslim intellectuals attempting to caricature the United States.

Bin Laden's terrorism also raised questions about the religion of Islam itself. Following the 9/11 attack, President Bush declared that "the face of terror is not the true face of Islam." Given the rapid expansion of violent Islamic terrorist groups, not everyone has been convinced. The fact is that Islam is a religion which very explicitly allows for violence within certain contexts. Whereas Jesus was an individual who rejected violence and urged his followers to turn the other cheek when struck, Muhammad was a very successful military commander. As was already noted, after Muhammad's death, the religion of Islam expanded throughout the region due to military conquests, so the spread of Islam and Arab culture has been directly connected to Arab imperialism.

I bring Africa up once again in this context because Africans were victims of Arab imperialism. The religion of Islam spread throughout North and East Africa through violent conquests. The Arab expansion also brought with it an expansive slave trade which would predate the European slave trade. During this period, some Arabs also developed some very negative racial attitudes towards Africans.

One historian explained that one of the elements of strength in Islam "lay in the insistence of Islam upon the perfect brotherhood and equality before God of all believers, whatever their colour, origin or status." Malcolm X felt compelled to drop Elijah Muhammad's interpretation of Islam and embrace orthodox Islam following his hajji to Mecca. He explained in his autobiography: "America needs to understand Islam, because this is the one religion that erases from its society the race problem." Malcolm was moved by his experience in Mecca, where he met, talked to, and ate with white people who truly saw him as a brother. This was a display of brotherhood which Malcolm had not experienced among white people in the United States.

One of the appeals of Islam is the idea that Muslims of all races are brothers and sisters who are united together in worship of a common creator. Racial unity has not always been practiced in the Arab world, however. This is demonstrated by an incident in which hundreds of Nigerian women who had made the hajj to Mecca were detained because they did not have a male escort. Some of the women complained that they were being treated like criminals for attempting to make the hajj without being accompanied by a husband or male relative. One of the women who were detained complained that more than 2,000 women were detained in an area where there was only one toilet. The women were made to go several days without bathing as well. Malcolm's experience in Mecca was a very moving one for him, but the reality is that not every African who has made the hajj to Mecca has been fortunate enough to have the experience that Malcolm had.

History demonstrates that the pacifism which Jesus preached has never stopped Christians from engaging in extreme acts of violence, but violence was not something which Jesus had expressly encouraged. The Qur'an, however, does expressly allow for defensive wars. Quran 2:191 states: "Kill them whenever you confront them and drive them out from where they drove you out. (For though killing is sinful) wrongful persecution is even worse than killing." This passage acknowledges that killing is wrong, but that wrongful persecution is even worse and for that reason killing is acceptable if the killing is done to protect oneself from wrongful persecution. Killing is treated as a serious offense in the Qur'an. It is so serious that Qur'an 5:32 declares that to kill one person would be to kill all of mankind and that to save a life would be as if to save all of mankind.

The Qur'an does allow for war, but there are also limitations on what actions can be carried out during war as well. Qur'an 2:190 cautions those who are fighting in the way of righteousness against transgression. Transgression in this verse is not specifically defined, but the intention of this verse clearly suggests that there are certain limitations in war which should be observed by righteous Muslims. A moderate Muslim would likely argue that indiscriminately killing civilians would be an act of transgression, but bin Laden was no moderate. He was a fundamentalist and a violent extremist. The legacy of bin Laden is that he promoted the spread of an Islamic ideology which advocated for extreme displays of violence targeted at civilian populations.

7

MOSHOESHOE

Moshoeshoe (also known as Moshesh) of the Basotho (Basuto) stood out as one of the most notable rulers in southern African history during a time period of great political change and upheaval brought on by the rise of the Zulu kingdom, which was founded by Shaka, as well as European encroachment in the region. Moshoeshoe had to contend with these challenges and others while also working to build a kingdom of his own.

George Theal regarded Moshoeshoe as being the most intelligent and most humane of the chiefs of South Africa. Theal contrasted Moshoeshoe with Shaka by pointing out that Moshoeshoe "built up a great power by his own ability, but he did it without that vast sacrifice of human life which marked the career of the Zulu despot." In praising Moshoeshoe's qualities, Theal also demonstrated views which were typical of European writers at the time. He presented Moshoeshoe as a reasoned chief who favored the introduction of the arts of civilization, but also accused Moshoeshoe of not possessing "the higher virtues of Europeans." Theal claimed that Moshoeshoe was a man who was willing to break his promises to others—as if Europeans were not known to be dishonest in their dealings with Africans. The example of this which Theal provided was Moshoeshoe signing a treaty with Sir George Grey, which Moshoeshoe would later fail to enforce. Hunting parties continued to traverse Orange Free State without asking permission from a landdrost. It is notable here how Theal deemed that Moshoeshoe lacked the higher virtues of Europeans when Moshoeshoe undertook actions which were opposed to the interests of the European settlers. Theal also does not conceal his racism when he explained that no European who lacked honesty and truthfulness should be regarded as a hero, but that Moshoeshoe should be regarded as a hero because Moshoeshoe's vices "were the vices of his race".

The comparison which Theal makes between Moshoeshoe and Shaka was typical of how some of the Europeans viewed

Moshoeshoe. David Coplan explained: "Men like Thomas Arbousset, Eugene Casalis, and F. D. Ellenberger had themselves a powerful interest in promoting the almost Christianized king of the Basotho, who authorized the missionaries' education of his own sons, as an alternative to the anti-Christian (and therefore anti-Christ-like) Zulus, Shaka, Mzilikazi, and Dingana."

Whereas the Zulu kings were depicted as violent savages, Moshoeshoe was generally depicted in a more positive light by European settlers and missionaries. This was not only because Moshoeshoe was more receptive of the missionaries than the Zulu rulers were, but also because Moshoeshoe was not as aggressive as the Zulu rulers were. Unlike Shaka who built an empire through war and conquest, Moshoeshoe was known as a ruler who favored peace and forgiveness.

Moshoeshoe's approach to leadership is credited to Mohlomi. Mohlomi was known as a rainmaker, diviner, and healer. A dying Mohlomi was said to have convinced Moshoeshoe of the value of diplomatic means rather than military subjugation. The story explains that Mohlomi had prophesized the rise of the Zulu empire when he declared that "a cloud of red dust" would come out of the east to devour his tribe. He then instructed Moshoeshoe to abandon the "pursuit of policy by other means," which referred to raiding and warfare. Of course, Moshoeshoe did engage in raids and war for the purpose of subduing rivals and obtaining cattle. Moshoeshoe means "the shaver." He acquired this name from capturing Ramonaheng's cattle, which was referred to among the Basotho people as shaving Ramonaheng's beard.

Moshoeshoe also engaged in political intrigue to eliminate his rivals. This was something which was acknowledged in his praise song. In the final lines of his praises, Moshoeshoe is criticized for failing to rescue his brother Makhabane, who was surrounded and killed during a campaign against the Thembu in 1835. It would appear that Moshoeshoe wanted to get rid of his uncontrollable brother, as well as avoid any challenges to his power which his brother could have posed.

Moshoeshoe was also known for some of the new laws which he implemented. Among the laws which Moshoeshoe implemented included forbidding circumcision, forbidding the sale of liquor, and ending executing people for witchcraft. Of these three new provisions, the ban on executing individuals for witchcraft was the only policy which was successfully changed among his people. Moshoeshoe was also against the idea of killing people as a form of punishment. The Native Laws and Customs Commission acknowledged that among Moshoeshoe's people, murder was settled by fining the offender ten head of cattle. The fine was four or five if the murder was done on accident. Assault, arson, and rape were also punished by fines as well.

Moshoeshoe's decision to ban the sale of liquor was welcomed by the missionaries in South Africa and Europe. According to Theal's account, the Basotho people used fermented liquors made of millet. It was a weak beer which formed a large proportion of their food, but Europeans later introduced strong liquor. Seeing that his people could not resist the temptation to use strong liquor and receiving advice from the missionaries, Moshoeshoe decided to ban liquor. This was a decision which was approved by Moshoeshoe's councilors.

One aspect of Theal's account which is curious is that Theal suggests that Moshoeshoe's decision to ban punishments for witchcraft was done at the advice of the missionaries and that no attempt was ever made to enforce this policy. This claim is curious because it was contradicted by remarks which were made in the Native Laws and Customs Commission. In the commission it was stated that Moshoeshoe banned killing for witchcraft "before he knew Europeans, and there was little killing for witchcraft afterwards in his tribe."

As a peacemaker, Moshoeshoe was known for gifting his rivals with cattle and land. Moshoeshoe did this after his soldiers repelled an attack from the Ndebele people who were led at the time by Mzilikazi. Mzilikazi served as a military leader under Shaka, but he eventually left to form a kingdom of his own. Moshoeshoe did the same for Rakotsoane, the chief of the cannibals who had eaten Moshoeshoe's grandfather, Peete. Rakotsoane and his cannibals were captured by Moshoeshoe's forces. Instead of executing Rakotsoane, Moshoeshoe had the cannibals ritually purified as the living tombs of his ancestor. He then gave Rakotsoane a gift of cattle. In order to abolish cannibalism in the region, Moshoeshoe provided cannibals with cattle and encouraged them to till the soil.

In "The *mfecane* as Alibi: Thoughts on Dithakong and Mbolompo," and "Grasping the Nettle: The Slave Trade and the Early Zulu," Julian Cobbing argued that Shaka's conquests never occurred and that Shaka's legend was inflated by Europeans who were attempting conceal European slave raiding in the area. It is possible that Europeans exaggerated certain aspects of Shaka's conquests. Europeans certainly had no problems with exaggerating the brutality of the Zulus to justify their colonization of the Zulu people. It would be a stretch to suggest that the conquests did not occur at all, however, considering that Shaka's conquests are attested not only in the history of the Zulu people, but also by groups who were impacted by Shaka's conquests, such as the Basotho people. The Basotho view is that cannibalism in the region was an aberration which was produced by the impact of the Zulu expansion.

Moshoeshoe himself recognized that cannibalism was a product of the political upheaval which was taking place in the region at the time. Moshoeshoe's own people faced a food shortage. Moshoeshoe explained that forgiving the cannibals made the cannibals more willing to share grain which they had stored in underground baskets in their caves at a time when the crops of the Basotho were burned during Shaka's wars. Moshoeshoe considered the real cannibals to be those who "had brought war and devastation to the country," such as his rivals Mzilikazi and Mantatisi.

Moshoeshoe's kingdom became a protectorate in 1868. He sought protection from the British against Orange Free State, which Moshoeshoe had previously fought against. The British colonial government did not offer much protection, however. Two-thirds of Lesotho's arable land was lost to the Free State. British colonial policy also subsidized Free State farmers at the expense of the Basotho people by restricting Basotho exports into South Africa.

Some of the Basotho reverted to cannibalism during the wars against Orange Free State. This is hardly surprising considering that one of the tactics which Orange Free State engaged in was destroying the crops of the Basotho people. As Theal explained: "The Free State forces, on their part, were doing what they could to weaken their enemy by destroying the crops and picking up a few cattle here and there."

A Baphuthi chief named Morosi distinguished himself in the war against Orange Free State. For his service, Morosi was awarded land by Moshoeshoe. Morosi would later clash with the British colonial administration after Morosi's son Dodo was arrested for refusing to pay a hut tax. Despite putting up fierce resistance, Morosi was killed in battle and his head was removed to be displayed on a staff. Morosi's four wives were taken as prisoners after his defeat. Morosi's conflict against the British took place after Moshoeshoe's death, but the conflict is worth recounting here because of his relationship to Moshoeshoe and his role in the war against Orange Free State.

Moshoeshoe died in 1870 at the age of 77. Theal explained that to "the Basuto his decease transformed him from a help less old man, for whom even his nearest relatives had no regard, to the highest object of their worship." The reverence for Moshoeshoe was due to his capacity as a leader and the peaceful manner in which he ruled. These qualities earned him the respect of Europeans who contrasted Moshoeshoe's relatively peaceful nature with Shaka's warlike ways. In the end, however, Moshoeshoe came into conflict with the European colonizers just as the Zulu rulers did. Moshoeshoe was forced to seek the protection of Britain to preserve his lands, which meant that he had to accept becoming a subject of the British crown. Moshoeshoe stands out as one of the many remarkable African leaders who came into direct conflict with the European colonizers. European colonizers sought to undermine Africa's sovereignty and disrupted the nation building efforts which were taking place throughout Africa.

Further References:

David B. Coplan, "History is Eaten Whole: Consuming Tropes in Sesotho Auriture," *History and Theory*, Vol. 32, No. 4, Beiheft 32: History Making in Africa (Dec. 1993), pp. 80-104

James Grant, *Recent British Battles on Land and Sea*

George Theal, *History of South Africa: From 1795 to 1872*, April 1916.

Report and Proceedings with Appendices of the Government Commission on Native Laws and Customs, 1883.

8

MASSA DAY DONE: THE ANTI-COLONIALISM OF GABBY

The Mighty Gabby composed a song titled "Massa Day Done." The title of the song comes from Eric Williams' famous "Massa Day Done" speech in which he decried colonialism. In Gabby's song, Gabby chastises America's imperialism. He notes how Europeans settled North America by stealing land away from Native Americans, spreading diseases, disaster, and woe in the process. Gabby continues to recount America's acts of imperialism such as placing an embargo on Cuba, bombing Grenada, and locking up Manuel Antonio Noriega. Gabby also notes America's mistreatment of prominent black men such as Marcus Garvey, Martin Luther King, and Muhammad Ali. Gabby also includes O.J. Simpson as well, suggesting that O.J. Simpson was being unfairly treated by the United States.

Gabby developed his anti-colonial views from an experience that he had as a child in Barbados. One day the British Prime Minister, Harold Macmillan came to Barbados to deliver a speech. The children who attended this speech were fainting due to hunger. Gabby did not live too far from the location, so he decided to leave. It was discovered that Gabby walked out on the British prime minister's speech. For this, Gabby was reprimanded for disgracing and dishonoring the Queen's representative. Gabby was made to write twenty-five lines stating that he will respect the British crown and the crown's representative. Gabby wrote one-hundred lines in the book. This was the first time that Gabby had ever heard the term "insubordination" because he failed to do as he was instructed. Gabby was then made to write five hundred lines as a punishment. Gabby was also given lashes from his mother. Gabby's mother explained to him that the Queen was "the Lord's anointed." Gabby explained that after this incident, he swore that he would always be against colonialism, though at that time he did know the word colonialism. He simply saw that white people were ruling over black people in Barbados and he was against this. At the age of ten, Gabby developed the view that black people in

Barbados must have their own country.

Gabby's anti-colonialism was accompanied by an embrace of African culture and roots. This is displayed in another song by Gabby titled "Wuk Up." This song is an angry response to priests in Barbados who were condemning the crop over celebration in Barbados for being too sexual. Gabby defends "wukking up" on crop over by pointing out that it is an African tradition. Gabby declares: "They want to take the African out of the picture, but Africa is buried in me."

Gabby was also named a chief in Nigeria and given the name Omowale. Gabby was sent to Nigeria as an official representative of the government. One day Gabby received a phone call. Gabby picked up the phone. At first, Gabby thought it was a friend of his named Owen. He eventually realized the Owen who was calling him was Owen Arthur, the prime minister. Gabby came to the prime minister's office. There he met with Owen Arthur who made Gabby a cultural ambassador and gave him an official passport. Owen Arthur also explained to Gabby that some of the chiefs in Nigeria requested that representatives from Barbados be sent to Nigeria to participate in a ceremony which was designed to make amends for the involvement of Nigerian chiefs in the slave trade.

Gabby was sent to Nigeria along with Ikael Tafari. The immigration officials in Nigeria were not very friendly when Gabby arrived. Gabby was interrogated by an immigration official. The official was attempting to take a bribe from Gabby. Gabby not only refused to pay the bribe, but he also explained that if the king knew that this official was trying to make Gabby pay a bribe, the official would lose his job. When the officials realized that the kings and high officials were waiting for Gabby, the man doing the interrogation apologized and allowed Gabby to leave. Gabby was then picked up by the chiefs at the airport. Afterwards, he participated in a ceremony which was attended by several high chiefs in Nigeria. It was at this ceremony that Gabby became chief Omowale and received his chiefly beads to symbolize his status as a chief.

9

THE CULTURAL ROOTS OF THE YORUBA SINGERS OF GUYANA

The African Society for Cultural Relations with Independent Africa (ASCRIA) emerged as a very important cultural organization for African people in Guyana. This organization was co-founded by Eusi Kwayana, who had also been a member of the People's Progressive Party. After Eusi Kwayana left the PPP, he helped to form ASCRIA as a cultural organization for Africans in Guyana.

One of the lasting cultural legacies of ASCRIA is the fact that it was out of ASCRIA that the Yoruba Singers emerged. The lead singer of the band was Eze. Eze was named after a Nigerian prince named Eze Ogueri. Eze had studied at Harvard and taught at Bethune-Cookman College in the United States. Eze's visit to British Guiana was a very significant occasion. It was so important that December 27, 1951, was declared to be Eze Day and an Eze Day Ball was held at the African Welfare Convention Hall.

Eze joined ASCRIA as a teenager. He wanted to join an organization which resonated with him. He also wanted to learn more about his culture. Eze's membership with ASCRIA was also simultaneous with his membership in the Young Socialist Movement. Eze was also influenced by Kwame Nkrumah because his father would always speak about Kwame Nkrumah.

One of the songs that Eze wrote was a song called "African People." The song was a message to African people around the world. The lyrics stated in part:

African people everywhere
African people do not despair
African people wherever you go
African people we love you so
African people the struggle is on
Let's organize, mobilize, educate, and learn
This principle is ours

Let's practice it too
Don't let the enemy take what belong to you

In the song Eze also called the names of nations such as Brazil and Zimbabwe to include African people from everywhere. Eusi Kwayana encouraged Eze to perform this song and the song became somewhat of a theme for ASCRIA. The Yoruba Singers traveled all around Guyana performing for ASCRIA. In fact, the band was originally known as the Young Ascrians. The Yoruba Singers were among many of the cultural groups which emerged out of ASCRIA. Two other groups were the Black Showcase and Tutashinda. David Hinds of the Working People's Alliance was a member of Tutashinda as well.

The Yoruba Singers are part of the tradition of musical bands in the African Diaspora who have used their music as a means of expressing a cultural connection to Africa. This tradition would include Earth, Wind, and Fire, which is a band that has utilized Egyptian symbols on their album covers. Maurice White of the group visited Egypt and studied Egyptology. He wanted to use his music as a means to share what he was learning about Egypt with the public. This tradition also includes La Compagnie Créole, whose song "Africa Music" invokes an ancestral connection to Africa. This song includes the line "And always deep in my memory, the kora player." This is a reference to a West African instrument, which La Compagnie Créole proclaimed was still held deeply in their memory. Likewise, the very name of the Yoruba Singers invokes an ancestral connection to the Yoruba people of West Africa from which many Africans in Guyana descend.

10

REFLECTIONS ON MALCOLM X AND MARTIN LUTHER KING

In "Malcolm X: The Man and His Contribution to the Pan-African Struggle," I mentioned how following the assassination of Malcolm X, Martin Luther King's approach to the struggle of black Americans noticeably shifted in a direction which was much more aligned with Malcolm's views. In this essay, I will explore this topic in a bit more detail. I explained in "Malcolm X: The Man and His Contribution to the Pan-African Struggle," that Malcolm and King had their differences. Of the two, Malcolm seemed much more willing to condemn King in public. These condemnations were often very harsh and even insulting at times. For instance, Malcolm called King a religious Uncle Tom in an interview with Kenneth Clark. In his "Message to the Grassroots" speech Malcolm pointed out King's failure to desegregate Albany, Georgia and criticized King's role in the March on Washington. In a 1963 interview with *Playboy*, Malcolm was asked by Alex Haley if he respected any other black American leaders, such as King. Malcolm responded that as a Muslim he saw Elijah Muhammad as the only leader who was qualified to unite black Americans. In Malcolm's view, Elijah Muhammad was the leader who had the true solution for black people and King was a misguided preacher who was teaching black people to love their oppressors. In another interview in which Malcolm was asked about King, he responded by stating that any black man who teaches black people to turn the other cheek is doing black people an injustice, and he's a traitor to his own people. After leaving the Nation of Islam, Malcolm's criticisms of King were not so harsh, but he did refer to King as "Uncle Martin" rather than referring to King as an Uncle Tom.

In my essay, I noted that a great display of King's self-control and humility is that he never responded by verbally lashing out at Malcolm in return. This is not to suggest that King hesitated to voice his disagreements with Malcolm X. King made his differences with Malcolm very clear in an interview with *Playboy* in 1965:

> I met Malcolm X once in Washington, but circumstances didn't enable me to talk with him for more than a minute. He is very articulate, as you say, but I totally disagree with many of his political and philosophical views—at least insofar as I understand where he now stands. I don't want to seem to sound self-righteous, or absolutist, or that I think I have the only truth, the only way. Maybe he *does* have some of the answer. I don't know how he feels now, but I know that I have often wished that he would talk less of violence, because violence is not going to solve our problem. And in his litany of articulating the despair of the Negro without offering any positive, creative alternative, I feel that Malcolm has done himself and our people a great disservice. Fiery, demagogic oratory in the black ghettos, urging Negroes to arm themselves and prepare to engage in violence, as he has done, can reap nothing but grief.

King's comments on Malcolm were measured and respectful in comparison to some of the remarks which Malcolm made about King. The *Playboy* interview is an example of this. Another example was King's interview with Kenneth Clark. In the interview, King defended himself against Malcolm's criticisms while avoiding any personal attacks against Malcolm. I wrote that the closest King may have come to putting down Malcolm was when he was asked about Malcolm following Malcolm's assassination. In the interview, King stated that Malcolm had catchy slogans, but did not have a solution. I thought that the remark was very dismissive of Malcolm's work. It gave the impression that Malcolm was little more than an orator who had no real solution or plan, which was untrue.

King also never confronted Malcolm in a debate. Malcolm had debated other prominent leaders of the civil rights movement such as Bayard Rustin, James Farmer, and Wyatt Tee Walker. King, however, seemed to have little interest in challenging Malcolm in a public debate.

As I pointed out in my essay, I think the differences between the two men often gets overstated, but differences did exist. The most striking difference was their views on nonviolence. King was profoundly influenced by Gandhi's use of nonviolence and passive resistance in India's liberation struggle. King heard a speech by Mordecai Johnson, who was the president of Howard University at the time. Johnson gave this speech after he returned from India. King was so deeply moved by what Johnson said about Gandhi that King bought several books on Gandhi.

Malcolm's position on nonviolence was different. Malcolm believed that black people had a right to defend themselves when attacked. For this, Malcolm was often branded as being a man who advocated violence, but this was not the case. Malcolm did not advocate for indiscriminate acts of violence, nor did he see violence as the ultimate solution for black people. He merely believed that black people should use any means necessary to protect themselves from violent attacks.

There were other differences as well, but the point of this piece is not so much the differences between the two men, but how King's public statements were beginning to resemble some of the remarks which Malcolm had been making. After Malcolm's assassination, the circumstances in the struggle were changing in ways that were very challenging for King. In *The Black African Crisis in the Age of a Black President*, there is a chapter titled "King's Dream." In that chapter I pointed out that although King remained committed to nonviolence, the masses were growing impatient with nonviolence. In that chapter I noted that King was in a very difficult situation. He could not bring himself to support violence, but he understood the frustrations of the masses. King also expressed disillusionment with integration. He complained privately to Harry Belafonte that he feared that he had integrated his people into a burning house. He could not give up the dream of integration, however. He suggested to Belafonte that they should become "firemen" to put out the fire.

The greatest challenge for King came when he finally denounced the war in Vietnam. In 2010, Tavis Smiley was interviewed on National Public Radio about King's position on Vietnam. At the time, Smiley was promoting a program about King and Vietnam. In the interview, Smiley pointed out that 168 major newspapers denounced King after he gave his speech. King was also disinvited from the White House and polling showed that nearly three quarters of the American people were against King, including over fifty percent of black people. Opposing the Vietnam War was not a popular position. King and his advisors knew this, which is why King had been consistently advised against speaking out about the war.

Smiley suggested that if King was alive during Barack Obama's presidency that there would be tensions between King and Obama on the issue of nonviolence and American militarism. Obama himself acknowledged the different philosophies of the two men during his speech to the Nobel Committee after winning the Nobel Prize. Obama pointed out that as the leader of the United States, he was confronted with threats such as al Qaeda, and therefore could not embrace King's doctrine of nonviolence. Obama stated:

> I make this statement mindful of what Martin Luther King, Jr. said in this same ceremony years ago: "Violence never brings permanent peace. It solves no social problem: it merely creates new and more complicated ones." As someone who stands here as a direct consequence of Dr. King's life work, I am living testimony to the moral force of nonviolence. I know there's nothing weak—nothing passive—nothing naïve—in the creed and lives of Gandhi and King.
>
> But as a head of state sworn to protect and defend my nation, I cannot be guided by their examples alone. I face the world as it is, and cannot stand idle in the face of threats to the American people. For make no mistake: Evil does exist in the world. A nonviolent movement could not have halted Hitler's armies. Negotiations cannot convince al Qaeda's leaders to lay down their arms. To say that force may sometimes be necessary is not a call to cynicism—it is a recognition of history; the imperfections of man and the limits of reason.

Obama continued on to explain: "The world rallied around America after the 9/11 attacks, and continues to support our efforts in Afghanistan, because of the horror of those senseless attacks and the recognized principle of self-defense. Likewise, the world recognized the need to confront Saddam Hussein when he invaded Kuwait—a consensus that sent a clear message to all about the cost of aggression." Obama felt that the use of violence was necessary, which was why during his presidency the United States dropped a total of 26,171 bombs in 2016. This was an average of about 72 bombs dropped a day. The majority of these bombs landed in Iraq and Syria.

Smiley responded to these remarks from Obama by stating: "Had the president stopped by giving Martin King his just respect—as he did, to his credit—it would have been okay. But when he turns the corner and then says, essentially, that Martin's philosophy wouldn't work in today's world, he goes on to say that Dr. King didn't know al Qaeda's, as if to suggest that Martin didn't understand evil, that Martin didn't understand violence, that he himself had not been subjected to it. He was stabbed at one time. His house was bombed."

King was certainly not naïve about the usage of violence, but he felt that violence was not necessary for the struggle he was waging. He explained: "I'd be the first to say that some historical victories have been won by violence; the U.S. Revolution is certainly one of the foremost. But the Negro revolution is seeking integration, not independence." Malcolm X had ridiculed the idea of a nonviolent revolution. He explained: "There's no such thing as a nonviolent revolution. The only kind of revolution that's nonviolent is the Negro revolution. The only revolution based on loving your enemy is the Negro revolution." Malcolm continued to explain: "The Cuban Revolution—that's a revolution. They overturned the system. Revolution is in Asia. Revolution is in Africa. And the white man is screaming because he sees revolution in Latin America. How do you think he'll react to you when you learn what a real revolution is? You don't know what a revolution is. If you did, you wouldn't use that word."

Speaking out against the war placed King in an interesting position. It alienated him from some of the people that once supported him, but it also placed King on the same side of the Vietnam War issue as figures such as Elijah Muhammad, Muhammad Ali, and Kwame Ture (then known as Stokely Carmichael)—figures with whom King had significant ideological differences. In fact, it was Ture, who was the chairman of the

Student Non-Violent Coordinating Committee (SNCC), and others in SNCC who worked to get King to take a position against the Vietnam War. The Nation of Islam was clear about rejecting the idea that black people should be made to fight in America's wars. Though King was very critical of the teachings of the Nation of Islam, he and the Nation of Islam both opposed the Vietnam War. King had a private meeting with Elijah Muhammad. If Elijah Muhammad's account of the meeting in *The Fall of America* is to be believed, King privately expressed agreement with Elijah Muhammad's teachings that white people are devils but did not want to state these things in public.

I want draw attention to two speeches which were delivered by King after Malcolm's assassination which demonstrate the ways in which King's public positions were becoming more aligned with Malcolm. The first are remarks from a speech in which King explained: "No document can do this for us. No Lincolnian emancipation proclamation can do this for us. No Kennedisonian or Johnsonian civil rights bill can do this for us. If the Negro is to be free, he must move down into the inner resources of his own soul and sign with a pen and ink of self-assertive manhood his own emancipation proclamation." King went further by also calling for racial pride. He called on the audience to be proud of their heritage, and to be proud to be black. The message which King delivered here is not unlike the message of racial pride and self-determination which was preached by the Nation of Islam and Malcolm X.

King's call for the audience to be proud to be black is interesting when one considers that Malcolm X had denounced the word Negro. Malcolm had explained in an interview that if white people regard themselves as white, then black people should regard themselves as black. In the 1960s, there was a gradual shift away from the usage of the word Negro and towards the usage of the word black. King's speech here represents this shift.

The second speech I want to draw attention to is the last speech which King delivered before he was assassinated. I specifically want to examine two sections of that speech. In one part of this speech, King spoke about the struggles being waged in Africa and in the United States: "Something is happening in our world. The masses of people are rising up. And wherever they are assembled today, whether they are in Johannesburg, South Africa; Nairobi, Kenya; Accra, Ghana; New York City; Atlanta, Georgia; Jackson, Mississippi; or Memphis, Tennessee—the cry is always the same: 'We want to be free.'"

His statement certainly demonstrated a concern about the global nature of the black struggle for liberation. Indeed, King did recognize that there was a global connection among the oppressed non-white people of the world. In the previously mentioned interview with *Playboy*, King stated: "Consciously or unconsciously, the American Negro has been caught up by the black Zeitgeist. He feels a deepening sense of identification with his black African brothers, and with his brown and yellow brothers of Asia, South America and the Caribbean. With them he is moving with a sense of increasing urgency toward the promised land of racial justice."

It is also worth noting that, like Malcolm, King felt that African governments should support the struggles of black people in America. King stated: "I think that in every possible instance Africans should use the influence of their governments to make it clear that the struggle of their brothers in the U.S. is part of a world-wide struggle. In short, injustice anywhere is a threat to justice everywhere, for we are tied together in a garment of mutuality. What happens in Johannesburg affects Birmingham, however indirectly. We are descendants of the Africans. Our heritage is Africa. We should never seek to break the ties, nor should the Africans." King did not become as committed to Pan-Africanism as Malcolm was, but King did recognize that there was a connection between Africans around the world.

The second passage of King's final speech that I want to bring attention to is the part of his speech in which King stated, "we've got to strengthen black institutions. I call upon you to take your money out of the banks downtown and deposit your money in Tri-State Bank. We want a 'bank-in' movement in Memphis. Go by the savings and loan association. I'm not asking you something that we don't do ourselves at SCLC. Judge Hooks and others will tell you that we have an account here in the savings and loan association from the Southern Christian Leadership Conference.

We are telling you to follow what we are doing. Put your money there. You have six or seven black insurance companies here in the city of Memphis. Take out your insurance there." I think it would be going too far to suggest that King became a Black Nationalist in his thinking, but he certainly understood the need for black people to build and control their own institutions. Again, the need to strengthen black institutions is a call that the Nation of Islam was making.

I make these points to show that although King and Malcolm disagreed very strongly, some of the positions which King took after Malcolm's assassination were closely aligned with the position of Malcolm and the other Black Nationalist leaders of the 1960s. King never rejected nonviolence or integration, but he did begin to advocate for racial pride and for the building of strong black institutions.

I must confess that I do have a bias towards Malcolm X. I think that between the two men, Malcolm had a more realistic understanding of the struggle which black people were facing, particularly as it relates to nonviolence. A point that I have raised in my writings is that the gains which were made by the civil rights movement could not have been made if not for the willingness of the masses to engage in violence when necessary to make their frustrations known. Malcolm X had pointed out on numerous occasions that it took violent rioting in Birmingham for John F. Kennedy to finally take action on civil rights.

I observed the same situation regarding the protests in Ferguson and Baltimore during Obama's presidency. Following the killing of Michael Brown in Ferguson, there were protests which became very destructive. Obama denounced the destructive protests in Ferguson, yet his government also launched an investigation into the police force in Ferguson. The investigation uncovered that the police in Ferguson regularly violated the civil rights of the black population there. The same scenario happened in Baltimore where Freddie Gray was killed by police officers. This resulted in destructive rioting which Obama denounced. The Department of Justice then investigated the police force in Baltimore. The investigation uncovered racial discrimination and the use of excessive force.

In both scenarios Obama condemned the destructive protests, yet it was the same destructive protests which prompted his government to act by investigating these police forces which were engaging in racism. This, in my view, was yet another example of the correctness of Malcolm's approach. One cannot be nonviolent with a violent oppressor. This is not a call for wanton acts of violence. It is simply a recognition that the violent nature of the United States has been such that the only time the humanity of black people is respected has been when black people fight back. It took a violent civil war for slavery in America to finally be abolished. It took violent rioting to get the federal government to take serious action on civil rights. It also took destructive rioting to get Obama's government to investigate police racism. Nonviolence has never prompted the same type of urgency from the government that violent reaction has prompted.

A great irony of King's life is that his advocacy of nonviolence helped to prepare others to engage in violent struggle. I mention Kwame Ture again in this context. As the chairman of SNCC, Ture marched alongside with King. During the march, Ture agreed to nonviolence, but he also told King that if anyone touched King then nonviolence was over. Ture was true to his word. Ture explained that when King was assassinated, he called everyone that he had contacts with throughout the country to tell them to start burning. According to Kwame Ture, King's commitment to nonviolence was a mistake which was corrected by the masses who buried King the way that a guerilla should be buried, with fires burning in the camps of the enemy. Ture argued that King made the same mistake which Nelson Mandela made by not understanding the level of human quality of the enemy which they were fighting. Of course, unlike King, Mandela did not reject violent resistance in South Africa.

Ture explained that King's greatest contribution was that he taught black people to confront their enemy without fear. King mobilized people—including the children and the elderly—to use nonviolence to confront a violent enemy. According to Ture, he learned how to confront his enemy without guns from King, so it was very easy for Ture to pick up guns to confront white people. He said, "Dr. King in fact helped prepare me for picking up the gun." King had stated: "I don't agree with everything that Stokely Carmichael says. I don't feel that we can win the struggle through violent means. I don't believe in guerilla warfare. I think it would be both impractical, ineffective, and immoral, so I can't believe in this at all." In the end, King's assassination only strengthened Ture's belief that King's nonviolent strategy was a mistake and that a violent enemy can only be confronted through violence. This was the same point which Malcolm X had articulated when he called for black people to defend themselves against violent attacks from white racists.

In conclusion, both men made very important contributions to the liberation struggle. Though they had their disagreements, the two men did not see each other as enemies or rivals in the struggle. I will close with the words of King's daughter Yolanda: "And with my father, everyone wants to stop with 1963 and 'I have a dream.' They don't deal with my father's last years, when he leveled very harsh but accurate criticisms of our country. He talked about how violent we are, how materialistic, how we must stop counting profits before people. Right before he died, he was talking to poor whites in Appalachia, he was talking about mass civil disobedience of the have-nots. Nonviolent, of course. That's what killed him."

11

ON THE FALL OF ROME

I noticed that one of the reviews of *The Devastation and Economics of the African Holocaust* seemed to have taken issue with my remark that the fall of the Western Roman Empire led to a period of decline and stagnation. One of the justifications for the colonization of Africa was this idea that African people were uncivilized. In that passage of *The Devastation and Economics of the African Holocaust*, I merely made the point that following the fall of the Western Roman Empire, Africa continued to produce thriving civilizations as Europe struggled with the aftermath of the fall of the Roman Empire. It should be made clear that the fall of Rome was an event which brought about very profound societal changes in Europe.

I point to a discussion which took place on "Context with Brad Harris" with Bryan Ward-Perkins, the author of *The Fall of Rome, and the End of Civilization.* Ward-Perkins pointed out that the fall of Rome resulted in a real decline in the material conditions of people in Western Europe. Ward-Perkins found himself frustrated with historical interpretations of the fall of Rome which downplayed the consequences of the fall of Rome. This interpretation came about as a response to the popular conception of the fall of Rome resulting in the "Dark Ages" in Europe. Ward-Perkins argued that historians became too obsessed with some of the positive changes which happened during this period, while forgetting that even though intellectual and religious developments were taking place, there was a significant change in the quality of life in Europe following the fall of Rome.

Ward-Perkins gave some examples to demonstrate the profound societal changes caused by the fall of Rome. One example was that the use of the potter's wheel to make pots disappeared in Britain following the fall of Rome. During the Roman period, there was an industry producing quality pots in Britain. There was also a decline in the production of bricks and tiles. These examples indicate that following the fall of Rome, living standards declined and economies became less sophisticated than during the Roman period.

The other point that I will raise is that the fall of Rome also signaled the global weakening of Western power. The Roman Empire was a mass international empire which was established through the military dominance of Rome. Rome not only controlled most of Europe, but the Roman Empire established control over territories in Asia and North Africa. It would be several centuries before a Western power could once again establish a powerful empire built on international conquest in the way that Rome did. Spain was the first of the European nations to begin the exploration of the Americas, which ultimately resulted in the establishment of a global Spanish empire. Spain was only able to accomplish this after freeing itself from centuries of Moorish domination. I mark the rise of the Spanish Empire as a revival of European imperialism.

12

TAKE DOWN NELSON

The removal of the statue of Horatio Nelson in Barbados was a welcomed development. For many decades there had been calls to remove Nelson's statue. Among those voices who called for the removal of Nelson was the Mighty Gabby who recorded a song calling for Nelson's statue to be removed. David Commisong, who had advocated for the removal of the Nelson statue two decades prior to the removal, stated that he was inspired to see that the younger generation had built upon the work of the previous generation.

The removal of Nelson's statue has been part of a global effort on the part of African people to remove symbols and monuments of racism and colonialism. In Cameroon, Andre Blaise Essama became well known for toppling and destroying colonial monuments. One particular statue that Essama targeted was the statue of Philippe Leclerc. Leclerc was a French general who was sent to Africa to conscript the locals to fight for France during World War II. On several occasions Essama removed the head of the statue. Each time the government replaced the head and even built a fence around the statue. For his activities Essama has been arrested, jailed, and fined. Despite these punishments, Essama has continued his work. He argued that national statues are important because they bring national pride. Essama has done more than just tear down statues. He also formed an association which included sculptors who sculpt works to honor Cameroonian heroes.

This effort to take down monuments which honor the colonizers of African people is a necessary aspect of our struggle for liberation, but one must remember that tearing down the symbols of colonialism is not enough. I am reminded of Kid Site's song on the situation. In "Take Down Nelson," Kid Sire notes the calls in Barbados to remove the statue of Nelson and questions why people are calling for the removal of Nelson's statue rather than removing others who seem to do more harm to Barbadians than Nelson's statue. Kid Site sings: "I didn't know he bring so much pain to the people. Standing up in town so peaceful, man it got me real puzzle, how you could remove he and not other people."

Kid Site suggests that drug dealers and other criminals should be removed. Kid Site also questions why no one is moving black people in Barbados who harm other black people. He sings: "Some black men neglect their children, physically abuse their woman, and you don't move them." Kid Site concluded that if the government of Barbados could do nothing else to address the other, more serious issues in the country, then at the very least the government of Barbados could move Nelson's statue.

I think the point which Kid Site raised in his song is an important one. The removal of symbols of colonialism is important, but decolonization means more than the mere removal of colonial symbols and monuments. Decolonization also means a real material transformation in the lives of colonized people.

13

OBAMA AND SOCIALISM

Sarah Palin claimed that President Barack Obama is a socialist who believes in taking money from small business owners. The view with Palin expressed was a rather curious one and she certainly was not the only Republican to attempt to assign socialism to Obama. Representative Paul Broun also accused Obama of being a socialist. The reality is a bit different. Obama supported providing a bailout to Wall Street. He then expressed anger that Wall Street bankers were giving themselves bonuses at a time when they were also asking for taxpayers to help to sustain them. Obama acknowledged that the bailout for the banks was not easy. It was something that he hated, but he also felt that it was necessary to stabilize the market. As president, Obama was very critical of the conduct of Wall Street bankers. After leaving office, Obama received $400,000 from Wall Street for a speaking engagement. Bernie Sanders described this payment as being "unfortunate."

Obama was not the only one in his administration who benefited from Wall Street. Eric Holder, who served as the Attorney General under Obama's administration, worked at a law firm known as Covington & Burling prior to working in Obama's administration. After his tenure as Attorney General ended, Holder returned to Covington & Burling. Covington & Burling's clients include some of the very banks which escaped prosecution during Obama's administration. Obama's administration is one which served the interests of Wall Street and was rewarded for so doing. Obama may have been critical of the conduct of Wall Street bankers as president, but the conduct of his administration demonstrated that Obama was no socialist.

One could go even further and look at some of Obama's policies. Take for example the Affordable Care Act or Obamacare. Obamacare most certainly cannot be described as a socialist policy, although Paul Broun argued that Obama wanted a government takeover of healthcare in America. When Mitt Romney ran against Obama in 2012, one of the things that Romney claimed he would do was repeal Obamacare. The problem was that in 2006, Romney passed a healthcare act which was not much different from Obama's plan. Jonathan Gruber helped to design Romney's healthcare act and then served as an advisor for Obama's healthcare act. Gruber described them as the same plan. In other words, Obama's healthcare plan was the same one that his Republican opponent had implemented. Obama himself acknowledged that in the 1980s, he would be considered a "moderate Republican" for his policies. Moderate is a good word to describe Obama. Far from ushering in radical, socialist policies which dramatically changed America, Obama's approach was a very moderate one. One could argue that Obama's approach was too moderate and that not enough was changed during the eight years that he was in office. This is an argument that I made in *From Colin Kaepernick to Donald Trump: A New Age of Crisis* in which I argue—through the voice of the fictional persona of Eddie Wilson—that Donald Trump's victory in 2016 was a product of the fact that not enough had changed and Americans were not eager to show up to vote for another Democrat.

Paul Broun declared that Obama did not believe in the Constitution. This is a rather curious claim given some of the remarks which were made by some of the Republicans who attempted to run against Obama for the presidency. There was Romney, who ran for the nomination of the Republican Party in 2008 and then again in 2012 when he won the party's nomination. In one of the Republican primary debates, Romney was asked if he would need to get authorization before attacking Iran's nuclear facilities. Romney responded by stating that as president he would have to sit down with his attorneys to find out what to do. Romney's position was that it was lawyers who needed to figure out whether the president needs authorization to engage in military action. When Ron Paul was asked about the same issue, he stated that he was baffled by the suggestion that the president needed to sit down with attorneys. He pointed out that it was written in the Constitution that the president could not go to war without a declaration of war from Congress.

There were others. Herman Cain stated that he would not

appoint a Muslim to his cabinet if he was elected president. The Constitution explicitly states that "no religious test shall ever be required as a qualification to any office or public trust under the United States."

Michele Bachman declared that the Founding Fathers worked tirelessly to end slavery. Not only was this false, but anyone who read the Constitution would be familiar with the clause stipulating the return of runaway slaves. If the Founding Fathers were working so tirelessly to end slavery, why was this clause included in the Constitution? Why was the Thirteenth Amendment required to abolish slavery—and, in fact, the Thirteenth Amendment did not truly abolish slavery. Bachman displayed not only ignorance of the Constitution, but ignorance of basic American history. In a short paper from 2006 titled "Slaveholding Presidents," Gleaves Whitney pointed out that twelve American presidents owned slaves. Whitney further explained that during 50 of the first 60 years of America's existence as a republic, the president was a slave owner. This is not to suggest that all of the Founding Fathers supported the institution of slavery. President John Adams was not a slave owner. In fact, Adams provided support for Toussaint L'Ouverture's struggle against slavery in Haiti. Benjamin Franklin served as the president of Pennsylvania Society for promoting the Abolition of Slavery. It is true that some of the Founding Fathers opposed slavery, but to say that the Founding Fathers worked tirelessly to end slavery is simply false. Bachman also managed to confuse John Adams with his son, John Quincy Adams.

Newt Gingrich was another Republican who ran for the nomination of his party in 2012. Gingrich denounced Obama as a "food stamp president" who put more people on food stamps than any president in American history. Eusi Kwayana described Gingrich as being a representative of the character of Mr. Jones in Bob Dylan's song "Ballad of a Thin Man." Kwayana described Mr. Jones as being the representative of some "self-important wizard that has all the answers" but cannot solve any problems. This was an apt description of Gingrich.

For whatever remarks can be made about Obama being too moderate, what is clear is that the Republican Party which opposed him was a very anti-intellectual party. It was a party led by individuals who professed to be upholding the Constitution, which was a document that they apparently did not spend much time reading. Worst of all was Donald Trump, who was Obama's successor.

Not only was Obama moderate in his political approach, but he was a bit of an idealist as well. He once declared that there was not a black America or a white America. In his view, there was only a United States of America. It was a nice sentiment, but it did not match the reality of American politics. Obama also expressed the belief that Trump would not become president because of the faith that he had in the American people. That faith was clearly misguided on Obama's part. Obama declared that tolerance, democracy, and justice were on the ballot in 2016. Tolerance, democracy, and justice lost. The American people elected Trump. In the eight years that Obama was president, the shift to socialism never occurred.

The struggles that the American people—particularly African Americans—endured under Obama was something that Trump himself campaigned on in 2016. At the Republican National Convention, Trump noted that four in ten African American children live in poverty. He stated: "Household incomes are down more than $4,000 since the year 2000. Our manufacturing trade deficit has reached an all-time high—nearly $800 billion in a single year. The budget is no better." He also stated: "Every action I take, I will ask myself: does this make life better for young Americans in Baltimore, Chicago, Detroit, Ferguson who have as much of a right to live out their dreams as any other child America?"

One interesting display of Trump's populism during this speech was when Trump criticized Hillary Clinton's popular campaign slogan, "I'm with her." To this Trump said, "I'm with you—the American people." Trump declared that he was the voice of the American people. None of this was true, but it is noteworthy that Trump campaigned as the populist candidate who represented the voice of struggling Americans. He declared that he would bring back the jobs and prevent companies from being able to move to other countries without consequences. Implementing government policies to punish American companies for outsourcing jobs to other countries seems like a socialist policy which is aimed at restricting the freedom of companies for the benefit of working people.

The election of Obama was certainly a very emotional moment for African Americans who experienced a strong sense of pride in finally seeing a black man being elected as the president of the United States. The conditions for African Americans did not improve significantly, however. Upon hearing that Obama won the election in 2008, Sandy Booker stood in tears as she declared that America was more united than ever. She shouted, "We did it!" Years later, she was much less optimistic. She explained that there were still a lot of people who were suffering. In Booker's view, Obama had more of an impact in other communities than in his own. Booker herself remained frustrated by the fact that even after earning a graduate degree, she still lived in fear for her life. Tears of happiness at seeing Obama's election in 2008 were replaced with tears of sorrow for the difficulties that she and others continued to experience.

Booker was right to be concerned for her safety. In the eight years that Obama was president, the nation witnessed several publicized incidents of black people being violently killed. One particular story was that of Shirley Chambers, an African American woman who lost four of her children to gun violence. Obama was not unaware of the reality of gun violence in America and how gun violence impacted African Americans. In his eulogy to Clementa Pinckney, who was a victim of gun violence, Obama stated: "For too long, we've been blind to the unique mayhem that gun violence inflicts upon this nation." In his remarks on Trayvon Martin's death, Obama also acknowledged that African Americans are the victims of violence in America. Yet what Chambers' story represented to me was the continued struggles and grief of African Americans under Obama's presidency. This was a mother who lost four of her children to violence. What did the election of a black president mean to her?

Of course, there were many other victims in addition to Chambers' children. Trayvon Martin was mentioned. There were the killings of Eric Garner and Freddie Gray which led to riots in Ferguson and Baltimore. Clementa Pinckney was one of nine African Americans who were killed as the result of a mass shooting in 2015. There was also Oscar Grant, who was killed by police officers shortly after Obama's victory. There were other incidents of black people being tragically killed, such as Walter Scott, who was shot in the back as he attempted to run away from a police officer. Jordan Davis was shot and killed for playing loud music. Hadiya Pendleton was shot and killed not long after attending Obama's second inauguration. There was also Sandra Bland, who died in police custody after she was arrested during a traffic stop in which the officer who arrested her threatened to "light" her up.

In response to Donald Trump's claim that there has never been a worse time to be a black person in America, Obama joked that Trump missed the civics lesson on slavery and Jim Crow. This line received cheers and applause from his audience, but the problem was that the fact that things had been worse for black people in America was of little comfort to those who were burying their children and their grandchildren. That Jim Crow no longer existed was of little solace for the grandmother of Aiyana Jones, who cried as she recounted how her granddaughter was shot in the head. It was little solace to the mother of Ramarley Graham who felt that it was a slap in her face to learn that the officer who killed her son was allowed to resign. The mother of Tamir Rice, a child who was shot and killed by police, expressed her disappointment with Obama. Black people were really suffering during Obama's presidency and Obama had little to offer these individuals but to remind them that things had been worse for black people in the past.

In the view of Glen Ford of the Black Agenda Report, Obama's presidency helped to make black people in America less skeptical of those in power and more supportive of America's military aggression. He also agreed with Cornel West's remark that Obama was a black mascot of Wall Street. This is certainly not the description one would expect of a socialist. Ford also stated that having Obama as president helped remove the illusions of what it means to have a black person at the head of a national party.

Unlike Obama, Bernie Sanders actually is a socialist, a democratic socialist to be more precise. In his campaign, Sanders spoke directly to the material conditions of African Americans. After visiting Baltimore, Sanders described the conditions of the community as looking like a Third World country. At a rally, Sanders compared the conditions in Baltimore to nations such as North Korea, Palestine, India, and Nigeria. This was the condition that African Americans were living in under Obama's presidency.

The differences between Sanders and Obama were very apparent on the topic of the Trans-Pacific Partnership (TPP). Obama supported the TPP. Obama argued that the TPP was a necessary response to the global economy of which America was a part of. Sanders, on the other hand, opposed the TPP. This was consistent with his long-time opposition of America's trade policies. Sanders pointed out that these trade agreements were written by corporate America for the purpose of benefitting corporations at the expense of the American workers. The issue of the TPP placed Clinton in a tough situation. She had initially supported the TPP, claiming that the TPP set the "gold standard" of trade deals. Clinton expressed support for the TPP in numerous speeches. Clinton later stated that she was not in favor of the TPP. This is something that both Sanders and Trump used against Clinton in their campaigns against her. Sanders highlighted the fact that he was opposed to the TPP before Clinton was. In a debate between the two, Trump pointed out that Clinton had changed her position on the TPP after she heard what he said about the TPP. Terry McAuliffe only made matters worse when he expressed his view that Clinton would support the TPP if she became president. McAuliffe would later claim that he misunderstood the question that was asked of him and affirmed that Clinton would not support the TPP, but the damage had already been done. Trump seized on McAuliffe's remarks to further criticize Clinton's position on the TPP. Opposition to the TPP was something which Trump campaigned on. He stated: "The TPP will not only destroy our manufacturing, but it will make America subject to the rulings of foreign governments. I pledge to never sign any trade agreement that hurts our workers, or that diminishes our freedom and independence."

Clinton found herself in a very difficult position regarding the TPP because she initially supported the TPP, but the TPP was a very unpopular trade deal, which seemed to force Clinton to oppose the same TPP which she had supported. Her views on the TPP were not quite clear, however. She had stated the TPP was the "gold standard," yet she later stated that she was against the TPP because she did not have all the details about the TPP. If she did not have the details, then why was she so supportive of the TPP to begin with? How could she have known that the TPP set the gold standard?

Obama himself had been aware of Clinton's flaws as a candidate. In fact, he pointed out these very flaws when the two ran against each other for the nomination of the Democratic Party. Despite claiming that Clinton was more qualified than anyone who had ever run for the presidency, when Obama and Clinton ran against each other, Obama noted that Clinton took more money from lobbyists than any other candidate. Obama also noted that Clinton once campaigned for NAFTA, only to now claim that she was opposed to NAFTA. Obama's views on Clinton had apparently changed, but Clinton's tendency to switch on important issues was the reason why Clinton was not viewed as a trustworthy candidate. This lack of trustworthiness was demonstrated when Clinton falsely claimed that she encountered sniper fire when she visited Bosnia in 1996. She claimed that she had to run to her car when she arrived. This was not true. The video footage of Clinton's arrival in Bosnia showed that she was in no immediate danger. Clinton had time to shake hands, greet a child at the tarmac, and take photos. Clinton later clarified that she made a mistake when she described her trip to Bosnia. It was a rather odd mistake to make, but one may generously grant that lapses in memory do happen. The problem is that Clinton had told the story of this Bosnia trip on numerous occasions before.

In the end, Sanders failed to secure the nomination for the Democratic Party. The Democratic Party would not nominate a socialist to run for president. This was apparent even to Trump, who declared that the system was rigged against Sanders. What is interesting is that Trump claimed that those who supported Sanders would join his movement. Trump recognized that there were splits within the Democratic Party and he hoped that those who supported Sanders would support him as well. Trump did offer a similar populist appeal, but Trump obviously was not a socialist. He referred to Sanders as "crazy Bernie."

Obama's Republican critics attempted to portray him as a socialist, but Obama was not a socialist who sought to radically alter the United States. In the view of Obama's Republican critics, he was too radical and he was doing too much to change the United States. The reality is that not enough had changed during Obama's presidency. This was especially true for African Americans, who continued to suffer even under the administration of the nation's first black president.

14

CULTURE AND REVOLUTION: THE IDEOLOGY OF KWAME TURE

After relocating to Guinea, Stokely Carmichael adopted the name Kwame Ture and became a member of the All-African People's Revolutionary Party. As an activist in the United States, Ture called for Black Power. The concept of Black Power was articulated in a book which Ture co-wrote with Charles Hamilton. After moving to Guinea, Ture adopted the ideology of Nkrumahism-Toureism which was based on the political ideologies of Kwame Nkrumah of Ghana and Sekou Toure of Guinea. One of the most important aspects of Nkrumahism-Toureism as espoused by Kwame Ture is the importance of placing the culture of African people at the center of the Pan-African liberation struggle. Nkrumahism-Toureism is a socialist ideology rooted in the historical and cultural experiences of African people. In this regard, Nkrumahism-Toureism distinguishes itself from other anti-capitalist ideologies such as Marxism, Marxism-Leninism, and Maoism.

Ture saw the tendency towards unification as being an innate evolutionary process which was interrupted by colonialism and slavery. As such, Ture argued that the unification of Africa could now only be obtained through a revolutionary process rather than an evolutionary one. Indeed, throughout Africa there was a process of nation building which produced large multiethnic kingdoms. In West Africa, several large multi-ethnic empires had emerged, such as the empires of Mali and Songhai. In South Africa, Dingizwayo was working towards uniting the disunited and warring tribes. Dingizwayo served as a mentor for Shaka who would later develop the Zulu Empire. These are just some examples to illustrate the point which Ture made. Walter Rodney explained: "All of the large states of nineteenth-century Africa were multiethnic, and their expansion was continually making anything like 'tribal' loyalty a thing of the past, by substituting in its place national and class ties."

Not only did colonialism disrupt Africa's development, but it also forced the creation of new nations in Africa. These new nations conformed to the borders which were established during colonialism. One area of conflict that Kwame Ture had with Marxist-Leninists was on the question of nationalism. Marxist-Leninists denounced nationalism, but in Ture's view nationalism was positive in situations where people went from being a state to a nation.

Former African colonies had to become nations as part of their struggle for liberation. This was noted by Julius Nyerere who complained that he was often seen as being an African rather than a Tanzanian. He illustrated this in a speech in which he mentioned that people asked him about the problems in Rwanda. Nyerere pointed out that it would have never occurred to him to ask Tony Blair about the war in Bosnia or to ask Helmut Kohl about the war in Chechnya, but Nyerere was asked about Rwanda because Westerners failed to distinguish between Rwanda and Tanzania. Nyerere continued to explain that the Europeans and North Americans were correct for viewing him as an African because Tanzania was a nation which he created. Tanzania was formed as a union between Tanganyika and Zanzibar following the revolution in Zanzibar. Nyerere wanted East Africa to be unified at independence rather than becoming independent as separate states. Nyerere even argued that Tanganyika should delay its independence to unite with other East African states at independence. This did not happen, which merely made the process of establishing political unity in East Africa more challenging.

I mention Nyerere in this context because he was a Pan-Africanist who recognized that because of colonialism he was forced to engage in the process of creating a nation. This demonstrated Ture's point about the fact that anti-colonial leaders in Africa had to develop nationalist ideologies to not only confront colonialism, but to create independent societies.

Another area where Ture and Marxist-Leninists had differences was on the question of religion. Ture recognized that not only are African people deeply religious, but Africans often used religion as a tool in their struggle for liberation. He mentioned Martin Luther

King and Malcolm X as two examples. For this reason, he did not preach atheism as being a necessary aspect of the revolutionary struggle as certain Marxist-Leninists did. Ture noted the irony of the fact that the Communist Party USA advocated that atheism was a fundamental aspect of the struggle for freedom, but the only place in the south the Communist Party USA could organize was in the church. Ture himself organized in the church when he was working with the Student Non-Violent Coordinating Committee.

Ture argued that a people's ideology must come from their culture and their history. This too created some disagreements with those who practiced a different ideology. Ture recalled meeting a Maoist who was very dismissive of Nkrumahism because of the perception that Nkrumah had not accomplished as much as Mao Zedong (alternatively spelt as Mao Tse-tung in English) accomplished in China. Ture explained that Mao simply had to fight Japanese imperialism and Chinese feudalism. Nkrumah, being a Pan-Africanist, sought to liberate Africa from all of the Western powers which had colonized and subjugated Africa. As such, Nkrumah faced greater odds than the odds which confronted Mao in China. In defending Nkrumah, Ture was also demonstrating the need for Africans to develop their own ideologies to confront the challenges which face Africans around the world.

Ture described Mao as a great man for whom he had the greatest admiration and respect for. Mao was indeed an influential revolutionary leader. Under Mao's leadership China provided support for revolutionary struggles in Africa. Amilcar Cabral received military training in China before he returned to wage an armed struggle against Portuguese imperialism in Africa. China also provided military and political support for Sam Nujoma's South West Africa People's Organisation as it struggled against imperialism as well. Mao's policies in Africa are not without their contradictions, however. Mao's support of the imperialist backed dictator Joseph Mobutu is one example of this. China's support for Mobutu was such that when Zaire (as the country was known under Mobutu's leadership) clashed with Angolan troops over the border which the two nations shared, China provided military support to Zaire.

Mao's revolutionary movement in China is relevant to the analysis of culture and revolution because Mao sought to challenge certain entrenched aspects of China's culture through the Cultural Revolution. Whereas Kwame Ture advocated that embracing African culture was a necessary aspect of the revolutionary struggle for African people, Mao saw China's traditional culture as a challenge to the objectives of his revolution. In 1966, Mao launched the Cultural Revolution.

The Cultural Revolution was aimed at transforming the thinking of the masses. Mao stated: "Once the correct ideas characteristic of the advanced class are grasped by the masses, these ideas turn into a material force which changes society and changes the world." Implementing correct ideas meant doing away with what was called the "Four Olds". The "Four Olds" were customs, culture, habits, and ideas.

Confucius became one of the prominent targets of the Cultural Revolution. Confucius was not only one of the most important philosophers in China's history, but his ideas have also impacted other parts of Asia as well, including Japan. In the view of Maoists, the doctrines of Confucius and Mencius (another prominent Chinese philosopher) represented a remnant of the exploiting class which shackled the minds of the people. For this reason, Maoists in China argued that these doctrines needed to be challenged to advance the revolutionary struggle of the working class in China. The targeting of Confucius was part of the process of targeting and eliminating old cultural ideas which were entrenched in the minds of the Chinese people. The doctrine of Confucius was not the only aspect of ancient Chinese culture that was targeted by the Cultural Revolution. During the Cultural Revolution many cultural artifacts were destroyed. This included smashing and burning statues. Books, temples, and works of art were destroyed as well. Many of these historical sites were later recreated after Mao's death.

The Cultural Revolution was a period of civil unrest in the country. In addition to transforming the thinking of the masses, Mao also called for purges within the Communist Party of China. Mao called on Chinese citizens to assist with this effort. What followed was an event in which a large number were killed. Those who were targeted by the Cultural Revolution were publicly humiliated and executed by the Red Guards. The Red Guards were made up of students who were ordered to carry out attacks on behalf of the Cultural Revolution. Estimates of the total number killed during the Cultural Revolution range from hundreds of thousands to millions. Among those who were killed in the purge was the individual who wrote the lyrics for China's national anthem.

The Cultural Revolution also turned family members against each other. Zhang Hong Bing was an example of this. Bing denounced his mother because she criticized Mao. She was subsequently arrested and killed for her actions. This was an action that Bing later looked back on with regret. He argued that the Cultural Revolution was not a revolution at all and that it actually moved China backwards.

The Communist Party of China was engaged in the process of transforming the culture of China to ensure that a new bourgeoisie would not be able to emerge in the country. The reasoning for this was explained in an editorial from the December 12, 1975, edition of the *Peking Review*. The editorial explained: "Socialist society is a society which has just emerged from capitalist society and is thus in every respect, economically, morally and intellectually, still stamped with the birth marks of the old society. In this society there are still classes, class contradictions and class struggle, the remnants of private ownership and the spontaneous capitalist tendencies of the small producers, the influence of the bourgeoisie and the force of habit of the old society, bourgeois right with respect to distribution and exchange, and so forth." For this reason, the aim of the Cultural Revolution was to create conditions in which it would be impossible for the bourgeoisie to exist or for a new bourgeoise to arise.

There was also a political motive behind the Cultural Revolution as well. Mao's public image was damaged following the failure of the Great Leap Forward campaign. That campaign resulted in a massive famine which killed millions. The Cultural Revolution provided Mao with an opportunity to strengthen his position by ridding the country of ideas and individuals who were perceived as threats to Mao's vision for a communist China.

The Cultural Revolution came to an end following Mao's death in 1976. Mao's successor, Hua Guofeng, had the "Gang of Four"—which included Mao's wife—arrested. Their arrest signaled the end of the Cultural Revolution. Deng Xiaoping, who had been stripped of his leadership positions by Mao in 1976, returned to politics after Mao died. Deng managed to take power away from Hua Guofeng. Deng had been purged during the Cultural Revolution, but he managed to emerge as the leader of China.

In the decades that followed Mao's death, Mao continued to be honored as a hero in China and the father of the country, but the Cultural Revolution became an uncomfortable topic for which some Chinese avoid speaking about because they prefer to remember the good things which Mao did. The Chinese government itself did nothing to mark the 50th anniversary of the Cultural Revolution in 2016. The Chinese government's position on Mao is that he was 70% right and 30% wrong. One would have to assume that the Cultural Revolution was among the 30% of the time that Mao was wrong. One certainly understands the logic in trying to rid China of a culture which had sustained thousands of years of feudalism, but the Cultural Revolution was carried out in a manner which was very destructive and traumatic for Chinese society.

I mention the Cultural Revolution here to present two contrasting approaches to culture and revolutionary struggle. Whereas Mao felt that it was necessary to do away with the old aspects of Chinese culture to implement a revolutionary transformation of China, Ture embraced African culture as an aspect of Africa's revolutionary struggle. Ture argued that the values of socialism came from communalism. He further argued that communalism rested in Africa for a long period of time and that feudalism in Africa did not reach "the terroristic aspects" that it reached in other areas of the world. Ture argued that Pan-Africanism is an objective. That objective is to achieve a unified socialist Africa. In the pursuit of achieving this objective, Ture did not view Africa's traditional culture as an obstacle which needed to be removed to establish socialism in Africa. He instead viewed Africa's culture as a tool to be utilized in the service of the revolutionary struggle.

The extent to which communalism remained a dominant feature in Africa's social organization is debatable. In *African Voices of the Atlantic Trade*, Anne Bailey argued that communalism in Africa was not as dominant as Walter Rodney had claimed and that the veneer of communalism in some African societies did not take away from the underlying presence of different social relationships. Rodney himself had pointed to the existence of these different social relationships and wrote about the role that these different social relationships played in the slave trade, just as Anne Bailey did. What is clear, however, is that for many revolutionary Pan-African leaders, the communal elements of pre-colonial African culture presented a basis for developing a revolutionary ideology. This is certainly the case with the ideology of Nkrumahism-Toureism as espoused by Kwame Ture.

Ideology also played a role in Ture's split with the Black Panther Party. The ideology which was adopted by the Black Panther Party was Marxism-Leninism. In a document titled "On the Ideology of the Black Panther Party," Eldridge Cleaver elaborated on the ideology of the Black Panther Party. He explained that the Black Panther Party viewed the struggle of black people in America through the prism of Marxism-Leninism. The Panther's embrace of Marxism-Leninism was inspired largely by Frantz Fanon. In Cleaver's view, Fanon was the first major Marxist-Leninist theoretician "who was primarily concerned about Black people, wherever they may be found." Cleaver added that Fanon was primarily focused on Africa and that it "is only indirectly that his works are beneficial to Afro-Americans." Cleaver also noted that "Fanon delivered a devastating attack upon Marxism-Leninism for its narrow preoccupation with Europe and the affairs and salvation of White folks, while lumping all third world peoples into the category of the Lumpenproletariat and then forgetting them there; Fanon unearthed the category of the Lumpenproletariat and began to deal with it, recognizing that vast majorities of the colonized people fall into that category."

Cleaver acknowledged that Marxism has not dealt with the United States of America, though some attempts were made.

Cleaver also noted that on "the subject of racism, Marxism-Leninism offers us very little assistance." He points out that evidence suggests that Marx himself was a racist, but he also expressed the view that the founding of the Democratic People's Republic of Korea and the People's Republic of China injected something new into Marxism-Leninism. Kim Il Sung and Mao applied the principles of Marxism-Leninism to their conditions and made the ideology of Marxism-Leninism useful to their people. The struggles in Korea and China demonstrated to the Black Panther Party that the ideology of Marxism-Leninism could be applied to the struggles of non-white people.

The challenge which the Black Panther Party confronted was how to take an ideology which developed in Europe and apply it to the struggle of black people in the United States. The revolutionary struggle led by Mao in China and Kim Il Sung in Korea demonstrated to the Black Panther Party that Marxism-Leninism as an ideology could be applied to the revolutionary struggles of non-European people. Fanon also demonstrated to the Black Panther Party that Marxism-Leninism could be applied to the struggles of black people.

The Black Panther Party adopted Marxism-Leninism, but also applied the Marxist-Leninist ideology to their situation as an oppressed people—Cleaver argued that black people in America are a colonized people—in America. This also meant understanding that American capitalism was something different than the capitalist system which Marx had written about. Cleaver explained: "The Working Class that we must deal with today shows little resemblance to the Working Class of Marx's day. In the days of its infancy, insecurity, and instability, the Working Class was very revolutionary and carried forward the struggle against the bourgeoisie. But through long and bitter struggles, the Working Class has made some inroads into the Capitalist system, carving out a comfortable niche for itself." Cleaver noted that labor unions, collective bargaining, the Union Shop, and social security all played a role in transforming the working class into a "bought-off" labor movement that is only interested in higher wages and more job security. He denounced A. Phillip Randolph as a traitor to the proletariat, but he acknowledged that Randolph represented the aspirations of the working class in America because the

American working class looked to the Democratic Party for its salvation.

Yet another area where the Panthers differed with Marx is on the role of the lumpenproletariat. Cleaver challenged the view that the lumpenproletariat was a parasite upon the working class. He argued that it was actually the American working class which was a parasite to the lumpenproletariat.

Whereas the Black Panthers attempted to apply Marxism-Leninism to the struggles of black people in America, Ture ultimately embraced an ideology which emerged out of Africa's revolutionary struggle. This was not necessarily a rejection of Marxism-Leninism by Ture, however. Though he was not a Marxist-Leninist, Ture did not disagree with Marxism-Leninism in theory. He studied Marxism-Leninism. Ture also described Karl Marx and Vladimir Lenin as great men. In Ture's view, one's ideology must come from one's culture.

15

C.L.R. JAMES AND CLASS

C.L.R. James was a Marxist who expressed the following view: "The race question is subsidiary to the class question in politics, and to think of imperialism in terms of race is disastrous. But to neglect the racial factor as merely incidental is an error only less grave than to make it fundamental." James obviously recognized that the racial factor was an important factor in the struggle, but in his view the race question was secondary to the class question. James' position on class and race was one of the reasons why he was so critical of Marcus Garvey.

James saw Garvey as a reactionary who was comparable to Adolf Hitler. In some ways Garvey's views were comparable to the white supremacists of his day. Garvey opposed interracial relationships and promoted the concept of racial purity. Garvey's views often led him to form associations with white supremacists such as Earnest Cox. Tony Martin explained that Garvey's "fierce love for his own race placed him in the unlikely position of sharing, with America's most notorious white racists, a hostility to integrationists and an advocacy of emigration."

James, on the other hand, had married and had a child with a white woman named Constance Webb. He clearly differed with Garvey on the question of preserving racial purity. The marriage between James and Webb would end in a divorce, which is hardly surprising given that Webb was having an extramarital affair and James was engaging in many different extramarital affairs of his own. The marriage between the two was James' second and Webb's third. After divorcing Webb, James married another white woman named Selma. For James, the question of race versus class was not merely a political question, but a personal one as well.

James was influenced by Leon Trotsky, whom he described as "one of the most gifted men who ever lived." Trotsky was a revolutionary leader who assisted Vladimir Lenin with overthrowing the Tsarist regime in Russia and establishing the Soviet Union. After Lenin died, Joseph Stalin came to power in

Russia. Trotsky would oppose Stalin, which forced him into exile. Trotsky was eventually murdered in Mexico. Following Trotsky's murder, James would write: "With the death of Trotsky, the movement is for the first time without an authoritative spokesman—and such a spokesman is needed now as never before."

In James' view, Trotsky represented the type of leadership which black people needed. He compared Trotsky to the celebrated boxer Joe Louis. James pointed out that Louis allied himself with Franklin Roosevelt because Louis "has something to defend." The thing that Louis had to defend was the fame and money that Louis achieved through his success as a boxer. James noted that Louis was given "the job of encouraging the exploited, oppressed, humiliated, starving Negroes, to die for a democracy that they have never had, and will never have under capitalism." Whereas Trotsky remained committed to revolution, Louis was willing to serve the capitalist class.

James, who wrote under the pen name J.R. Johnson, would eventually break with the Trotskyite movement over the Soviet Union. Trotsky was critical of the Soviet Union under Stalin, but James came to realize that Trotsky's analysis of the Soviet Union was wrong because Trotsky was unwilling to admit that the bureaucracy which developed in the Soviet Union constituted a capitalist class. James wrote in 1941 that Trotsky's "initial and overwhelming mistake was to identify state property indivisibly with the proletariat as ruling class." James explained: "Thus Trotsky and we who followed him failed to distinguish between first, means of production in the hands of the state where the state is merely an economic form like a trust, a bank, or a cartel; second, state ownership as a purely juridical relation, which tells us no more than that it is the duty of the state to organize production and distribute the product; and third, a workers' state, i.e., a state transitional to socialism; this last is not a juridical question at all but a question of the economic conditions and social relations of production, which can be summed up in one phrase: is the working class master or not?"

James argued that the bureaucracy in Russia became what Marx always insisted the capitalist class is because the bureaucracy maintained the means of production. James also argued that under Stalin the conditions of laborers became worse even as production increased. He explained: "The relationship of capital and wage-labor has certain consequences. It constantly increases the misery, oppression and degradation of the workers. I can show, not only from the testimony of Victor Serge and Yvon, but from independent investigation of Stalinist sources, that the average income of the Russian workers which in 1936 was already less than it was in 1913, is today somewhere between 50 and 75 percent of the 1913 level, despite the manifold increase in production. The workers' oppressions, slavery and degradation are the worse in the world. Never before has there been a regime in which the gap has been so wide between what is preached and what is practised. The degradation of human personality has reached unbelievable depths. Socialism will be built by free men, not by driven slaves. Stalinist society can build only capitalist barbarism."

James noted that in 1936, Trotsky admitted that 15% of the population in Russia received as much income as the remaining 85%. James saw this as a typical example of Marx's theory of capitalist distribution. James continued: "Stalin remains where he is because he knows better than to attempt any fundamental change in distribution without a fundamental change in class relations. Only when production is ruled by the producers themselves and, without too much delay, on an international scale, can the permanent crisis be resolved. When the crisis is suppressed economically it breaks out politically. It is suppressed politically by a gigantic apparatus of repression and wholesale massacre. Planned terror cements the planned economy."

James pointed out that to his dying day Trotsky insisted on referring to the bureaucracy in Russia as a caste. He refused to view the labor bureaucrats as a class since they performed "an organizational, administrative social function which is only remotely if at all connected with the actual productive and distributive process."

In James' view, Trotsky was wrong. James argued that the distinction between caste and class which Trotsky maintained was meaningless and harmful. James wrote that "the final proof of the weakness, the impossibility, of maintaining Trotsky's theory is this. To remove that bureaucracy today would require a revolution greater in scope than the October Revolution. Now what kind of caste is this that is more powerfully established as a government than the old combination of landlords, bureaucrats and capitalists who ruled Russia up to 1914?"

James also argued that Stalinism was a menace to labor movements around the world. James pointed out that class conscious revolutionaries opposed Stalin for different reasons than the United States did. He wrote: "A class-conscious revolutionary opposes Stalinism because it betrays revolutionary struggle and, as far as it can, manipulates the working-class movement for its imperialist ends. Thus while American capital and American labor are both threatened by Stalinism, that makes for no solidarity between American capital and American labor on this issue. The class line is as sharp here as elsewhere."

In 1946, James expressed the position of the Workers Party of which he was a member. He wrote: "The Workers Party denounces above all the conception that Russia is any kind of a workers' state." He continued to explain: "For the Workers Party, a workers' state must be a state in which the workers rule. The governmental form of workers' rule is the workers' council or soviet. That is its distinctive mark, the guarantee of workers' democracy, and it is worth description."

James gave the following description of democracy in the Soviet Union: "The genuine soviet form of government is entirely different. Elections take place on the basis of the individual's type of labor. Workers in individual factories elect workers' representatives. Farmers elect farmers' representatives. White collar workers elect representatives on the basis of their particular organization of work. In theory, therefore, with all of heavy industry in the hands of the state, there is a genuine equality of individuals in so far as election rights are concerned. A large factory, for example, will have the largest number of representatives. In such elections, therefore, the weight of labor is overwhelming. And it is just that which Lenin and Trotsky and the early Bolsheviks looked upon as decisive and new in the Russian constitution."

James noted that this form of government was not invented by a single individual. He explained that this system of organization emerged among the workers themselves who could not prepare electoral lists or organize any elaborate procedures. James explained that the 1917 constitution merely legalized and formalized a system which the workers had spontaneously discovered by themselves. This was undone by Stalin who abolished the constitution. James argued that the "reactionary step of abolishing the soviet constitution in Russia was merely the preliminary to the most open abandonment of revolutionary principles by the Communist International abroad."

James' analysis of Stalinism in the Soviet Union and his willingness to break with Trotsky's analysis of the situation demonstrated his commitment to a Marxist analysis which was centered on the conditions of the working class. For this reason, he rejected the notion that Stalinist Russia was anything but a capitalist state where workers were brutally oppressed.

James, Raya Dunayevskaya, and Grace Chin Lee developed what became known as the Johnson-Forest Tendency. The Johnson-Forest Tendency took its name from James' pen name J.R. Johnson and Raya Dunayevskaya's pen name, Freddie Forest. Of the Johnson-Forest Tendency, Selma James stated: "I was committed to Johnson-Forest. It was a different way of looking at the world from the rest of the left. Working-class people were central—not backward and to be led, but the source of the revolution." Selma James also explained that the Johnson-Forest Tendency challenged the concept of a vanguard party: "The vanguard party, we were told, made the revolution in 1917 and we all had to form a vanguard party to make the revolution elsewhere. The fact that the party was out of V. I. Lenin's control and resulted in Stalinism was not considered. Even Trotskyism, the prime enemy of Stalinism, formed a vanguard party in which the intelligentsia were in charge. Johnson-Forest was based on the rejection of a vanguard and experimented with new ways of organizing within the working-class movement, twenty years before the mass movements of the 1960s undermined the whole hierarchical concept of a vanguard."

Selma James explained that James' greatest contribution was

"creating a new kind of working-class organization in which the autonomy of black people, of women, and of young people was integral to our political focus, the way the organization was structured, and our relationships." Yet another significant aspect of James as a Marxist was his unwavering commitment to the struggles of working people. This commitment was summed up by Walter Rodney who explained: "James has become a model of the possibilities of retaining one's intellectual and ideological integrity over a protracted period of time…I've always said to myself that I hoped at his age, if I'm still around, I still have some credibility as a progressive, that people wouldn't look at me and say, 'This used to be a revolutionary.'" David Austin wrote that the Guyanese historian and writer Jan Carew was another individual who could fit this description as well. In the history of the Pan-African struggle—particularly in Caribbean politics—such reversals are unfortunately not uncommon. James could have easily joined the neo-colonial ruling class in the Caribbean, but he did not.

James had worked closely with Eric Williams leading up to the independence of Trinidad and Tobago. At the time the two men shared the common goal of liberating Trinidad from colonial domination. Eventually political differences between the two men became apparent. James would eventually join the Workers and Farmers Party (WFP) which contested the general election in Trinidad in 1966. The party sought to challenge the incumbent People's National Movement party which was led by Eric Williams and the Democratic Labour Party which was the main opposition party in Trinidad at the time. Hamid Ghany gave the following description of the WFP: "In 1966, the first manifestation of the ideological desire for the formation of a labour party was realised with the creation of the Workers and Farmers Party (WFP). The dominance of the political landscape by the PNM and the DLP at the time was such that the electorate was largely divided between them. The other political party that was formed that year (the Liberal Party) also failed miserably. The idea of a true labour party has never captured the imagination of voters in Trinidad and Tobago. In the 1966 general election, CLR James could only muster 274 votes in the Tunapuna constituency for the

WFP. In the same election, Basdeo Panday, contesting the Naparima South constituency, could only garner 326 votes as a WFP candidate." Following the defeat, James got out of politics in Trinidad. Panday would go on to form the United Labour Party (ULF) to challenge the PNM. The ULF would fail to win a seat as well and the ULF was subsequently split up.

George Weekes was a member of the ULF. He would later join with the National Alliance for Reconstruction which was led by A.N.R. Robinson. The Mighty Chalkdust (Hollis Liverpool) would comment on this in his song "Qualifications of a Politician." In that song, Chalkdust played the role of a father advising his son on the necessary qualifications to be a politician. He explained in his song: "You must sell your soul like George Weekes cheaply, for position in the NAR Party." In the same song, Chalkdust also declared: "You must know NJAC is the best, but to the public you must not confess." This is a reference to the National Joint Action Committee which was led by Makandal Daaga. NJAC at the time still maintained its credibility as a leading anti-imperial political party. This is a point which Chalkdust made in his song "Chauffeur Wanted", in which he portrays Prime Minister Robinson as an ineffective driver. At one point in the song Chalkdust notes that NJAC warned Robinson against going to the International Monetary Fund (IMF), but Robinson did not listen and the IMF ended up robbing Robinson. NJAC would later join with the People's Partnership government, which is a move that Chalkdust would criticize. Daaga and Weekes were leading figures in the Black Power movement of the 1970s in Trinidad, yet both men ended up making political decisions which were viewed as betrayals of the values which they previously held. James engaged in no such betrayal. He remained firmly committed to the struggles of the working class.

Notes:

Caryl Phillips, "Constance Webb: Writer wife of CLR James," *The Guardian*, April 14, 2005.

C.L.R. James, "A Tribute to Our Fallen Leader, Leon Trotsky,"

Labor Action, vol. 4 No. 21, 2 September 1940.

___ "Marcus Garvey," *Labor Action*, Vol. 4, No. 11, 24 June 1940, pp. 3

___ "Russia–A Fascist State," *New International*, Vol. VII No. 3, April 1941.

___ "Russia No Workers' State," Labor Action, Vol. X No. 14, 8 April 1946.

___ "The Stalinist Menace to World Labor," Labor Action, Vol. X No. 13, 1 April 1946.

___ "Which Type of Leader Should Negroes Follow?," *Labor Action*, Vol. 4 No. 21, 2 September 1940

Dr. Hamid Ghany, "The labour party concept," *Trinidad Guardian*, August 13, 2011.

David Austin, "The gentle revolutionary: Jan Carew at 90," *Stabroek News*, September 27, 2010.

Selma James and Ron Augustin, "Beyond Boundaries," *Monthly Review*, September 1, 2019.

The Mighty Chalkdust, "Chauffeur Wanted," (1989).

___ "The Qualifications of a Politician," (1992).

Tony Martin, *Race First: The Ideological and Organizational Struggles*, (The Majority Press, 1986).

Walter Rodney, *How Europe Underdeveloped Africa*, (Bogle-L'Ouverture Publications, 1972).

16

JOSEPH ROBERT LOVE: PROFILE OF A PAN-AFRICANIST

Joseph Robert Love, who was originally born in the Bahamas, arrived in Jamaica in 1889. He started a newspaper known as *Jamaica Advocate*. The *Jamaica Advocate* concerned itself with African affairs. This included publishing writings by Pan-Africanists such as Edward Wilmot Blyden and Joseph Casely Hayford. The *Jamaica Advocate*'s views on Africa were demonstrated by a comment which was published, which stated: "'Africa for the Africans' is the new shape of an old cry ... This cry will waken the so-called civilised world to a consciousness of the fact that others, who are not accounted as civilised, think with regard to natural rights, just as civilised peoples think..." The paper also reported on African American affairs, including reporting on the work that Booker T. Washington was doing in the United States. Love had described Washington as the "Negro Apostle of Industrial Education for the African Race", though Love was also critical of Washington's acquiescence to racism. Love also quoted a pamphlet on racism which was published by an African American journalist named John E. Bruce. Love and Bruce maintained a correspondence with each other. Bruce would later work for Garvey's *New World*.

Love also involved himself in the politics of Jamaica. Love was met with resistance from whites and mulattoes. At the time most of the black population in Jamaica was disenfranchised. In 1906, Love campaigned for a seat of St. Andrew in the general elections and won. He was also the Justice of the Peace for Kingston. Love's political career was short-lived, however. He became ill in 1906 and was forced to resign from politics in 1910.

Despite his success in politics, Love was not able to establish a mass movement in Jamaica. This was in part due to the fact that his movement did not appeal to the masses. Rupert Lewis explained that "Love reflected the middle-peasantry—the better-off blacks—whose advance in all areas (professional, mercantile, social, cultural and political) faced the stonewall of colonial racism."

Lewis contrasted this with Bedwardism, an anti-colonial religious movement in Jamaica which was named after its founder, Alexander Bedward. Bedwardism attracted the poor peasantry. Bedward became a target of the colonial authorities because of his preaching. He was arrested and charged with sedition in 1891. He was deemed to be insane. In 1921, Bedward was placed in a mental asylum after an attempted protest march. Garvey would later declare in 1927 that the colonial authorities in Jamaica would have a hard time putting him in the asylum as they had done with "poor Bedward."

Love died in 1914. He left a lasting impact on the development of the Pan-African movement in Jamaica. Barry Chevannes identified "the Pan-African years, from the launching of [Trinidadian H. Sylvester Williams's and Jamaican] Robert Love's Pan-African Association in 1901 and Marcus Garvey's Universal Negro Improvement Association (UNIA) in 1914 to 1930" as being one of the four major periods of idealization of Africa in Jamaican history. The other three periods include the pre-Christian period, the period of Christian evangelization from 1784 to 1900, and the Rastafari years.

References:

BAAM magazine article on Robert Love from the 2015 issue.

Nathaniel Murrell, William Spencer, and Adrian McFarlane (editors), *Chanting Down Babylon: The Rastafari Reader*, (Temple University Press, 1998).

Rupert Lewis, "Garvey's Forerunners: Love and Bedward," *Race Class*, January, 1987. vol. 28 no. 3, pp. 29-40

17

THE MAROONS OF JAMAICA

Throughout the Americas, enslaved Africans ran away from their slave masters and formed independent societies. These runaway slaves would come to be known as maroons. There were maroon societies established throughout the Americas. One of the most notable examples of maroon societies in the Americas were the Maroons of Jamaica. Since the British captured Jamaica from the Spanish in 1655, the British administration struggled to deal with runaway slaves who would form independent communities in the forests on the interior of the island. These maroon communities grew and developed different settlements.

The Maroons came from various West African tribes, although the Akan cultural influence was very noticeable among the Maroons, as demonstrated by the number of Maroons who had Akan names. The white planters in Jamaica referred to the Akan people as Coromantees. Michael Sivapragasam argued that the Maroons likely started as a mix of different African tribes and over time began to acquire more Akan culture in the eighteenth century when more slaves from the Gold Coast were imported into Jamaica. The Maroons also practiced the African tradition of polygamy. Bryan Edwards argued that the practice of polygamy would make it difficult to teach Christianity to the Maroons. Edward also added that "if a clergyman was to be sent to them, instead of listening to his doctrines, they would eat him up." This remark by Edwards demonstrated the common European stereotype about Africans being cannibals. There is no evidence that the Maroons cannibalized missionaries, but they did practice polygamy.

The Maroons grew their own crops such as cocoa, sugar cane, plantains, and yams. The Maroon villages also traded with each other. The Maroons also traded food products with slaves on the plantation and with free blacks in the urban market. Trade allowed the Maroons to acquire supplies for war. During the First Maroon War, the Maroons purchased ammunition from the marketplace.

The Maroons of Jamaica established their own social hierarchy.

Jonathan Brooks pointed out that Maroon society was structured more like a federation than a monarchy, and that the leadership was communal. Hierarchy was based on age, with elders ranking at the top. "Obeahs" had the second highest position in society. They served as advisors to the elders. Cudjoe, who was one of the most prominent Maroon leaders, claimed legitimacy based on his lineage on the basis of being the brother of Nanny. He consolidated his power among the villages by taking power away from the obeah women. Nanny was known to be one of the obeahs. She developed a reputation as a fierce warrior who carried a large knife belt with 12 knives. Apart from Cudjoe and Nanny, Quao and Accompong were also prominent Maroon leaders who fought against the British.

After several years of war against the Maroons, it was apparent that the British could not defeat the Maroons. The British decided to offer peace instead. Sivapragasam explained: "The admission that they could not defeat the Leeward Maroons embarrassed the colonial elite. Many white Jamaicans were not pleased that the authorities chose to agree peace terms with a community supposedly more primitive than their own." The 1739 treaty which was signed with Cudjoe allowed him to keep all of the runaways who joined his town before he signed the document, but the Windward Maroons were required to return all runaways who joined them in the three years prior to Quao signing the 1740 treaty.

Nanny, who was named a national hero of Jamaica in 1975, is a unique figure among the Maroons. Not only was Nanny the only woman leader among the Maroons, but she is also a very mysterious figure as well. Not much is known about Nanny, since very little information about her appears in the colonial records. In a 1969 book, Carey Robinson questioned whether Nanny even existed at all given the scant information about her. Even the circumstances around Nanny's death are uncertain. During the Maroon War, the colonial authorities rewarded a slave named Cuffee for killing Nanny, who was described as the "old obeah woman" of the rebels." Sivapragasam suggested that the Nanny in question was probably another woman named Nanny, since there were multiple women among the Maroons named Nanny.

Nanny's view on the peace treaty which was signed by the Maroons is also in question. Some have argued that whereas Cudjoe agreed to sign the peace treaty with the British, Nanny opposed the treaty. This view seems to come from a report by Philip Thicknesse. Thicknesse reported that Quao had confided in him that Nanny opposed peace with the British. Nanny also ordered that the white officer who arrived to inform the Maroons that Cudjoe had accepted peace with the British be beheaded. Sivapragasam explained that this incident occurred while the Windward Maroons were still at war and that Nanny seemed to moderate her position after the war. Maroon oral history mentions that Nanny reluctantly accepted peace with the British. This is demonstrated by the fact that although Nanny did not sign the 1740 treaty, she also ceased her war with the British. Nanny also accepted a patent of land. The terms of the land patent explained that Nanny was required to be ready to serve the British in the event of any insurrection, mutiny, rebellion, or invasion.

After agreeing to peace with the British, the Maroons would regularly assist the British with suppressing slave rebellions in Jamaica. Maria Alessandra Bollettino explained: "Free Blacks formed a small but important component of local militias. On Jamaica, when they were not themselves at war with them, Whites relied upon the martial prowess of the Maroons, free descendants of escaped slaves who lived in independent communities in the highlands. Planters hired their slaves out to the government to build the fortifications that lined the coasts and to serve as pioneers for the militia and for the regiments of British regulars stationed on the islands."

The terms of the treaty meant that the Maroons would have to intervene to assist the British whenever there was unrest, even if that unrest was a rebellion by enslaved Africans. An example of this was the rebellion which was led by Tacky in 1760. This rebellion was put down with support from the Maroons. Tacky was killed by one of the Maroons.

The decision by the Maroon leaders to agree to these terms with the British is a decision that has been criticized. Such criticism is not misguided because the Maroons were willing to collaborate with the British to put down rebellions and fight against runaway slaves who desired the same freedom which the Maroons enjoyed, yet one must also understand the circumstances which the Maroons were faced with. Continuous warfare with the British posed the risk that the Maroon societies could be completely defeated at some point. Sivapragasam explained that the Maroon leaders "did not see themselves as liberators of slaves throughout Jamaica, but rather as leaders who wanted to protect the freedoms of the members of their respective towns." A peace treaty with the British ensured that the Maroons would retain their freedom while protecting their communities from the suffering caused by continuing war. It is also worth noting that Cudjoe only signed the 1739 peace treaty after demanding that the provisions be changed in order to protect the freedom of recent runaways who joined his forces. Sivapragasam explained: "All Maroon leaders accepted peace treaties with the colonial authorities in order to preserve the existence of their communities."

The decision to collaborate with the British also demonstrated the nature of Jamaica's slave society in which white people retained power. Not only did the Maroons help to put down Tacky's rebellion, but other enslaved Africans participated as well because they were promised freedom in return. The British paid the blacks and mulattoes who fought for the British during the Second Maroon War. Being able to determine who remained free and who remained enslaved allowed the British to turn Africans against each other when necessary. In the case of the Maroons, the Maroons would be left alone to live in freedom so long as they aided the British in putting down rebellions. It was an arrangement that was favorable for the Maroons, but not so much for the rebellious slaves who were often forced to fight both the colonial authorities and the Maroon collaborators. It must also be noted that the freedom for the Maroons meant freedom from being enslaved, but the British would continue to erode the political authority of the Maroons. The Maroons were not enslaved, but they had been reduced to being subjects of the British colonial administration. This was a gradual process.

With the passing of strong leaders such as Cudjoe and Nanny, Maroon communities came under the control of white superintendents. The British were unable to defeat the Maroons in combat, but they were able to establish authority over the Maroons. Claude 15 of the 1739 treaty listed Cudjoe as the leader of Trelawny Town and also listed his successors. One of those successors was Accompong. Accompong succeeded Cudjoe after Cudjoe died. Accompong remained in charge of his town, but the British appointed a new Maroon commander in Trelawny Town. When Accompong died, a superintendent named Alexander Forbes appointed his successor. The British broke the terms of the treaty which they signed with the Maroons by ignoring the succession clause. In the past the Maroons had independent control over their economic, political, and social systems. After the 1739 treaty, the British began to exercise control over the Maroon towns. Brooks explained that "it was through external and internal coercion that Maroon autonomy was stifled."

The clash between the Maroons and the colonial government can be demonstrated by the Second Maroon War in 1795. This was a conflict between the Maroons of Trelawny Town and the colonial government. The Maroons of Trelawny Town were dealing with the problem of land encroachment by the planters and the disappearance of their hunting grounds. They also made a petition for more land which had been rejected. The war was sparked when two Maroons of Trelawny Town were flogged for shooting hogs which belonged to a planter. This outraged the Maroons, who once again requested more land. Alexander Lindsay, the Earl of Balcarres, who was the governor of Jamaica from 1795 until 1801, decided to resort to force to deal with the Trelawny Town Maroons. Some of the Maroons wished to avoid a conflict. Six Maroon captains went to Spanish Town to seek a resolution. Balcarres ordered these six to be arrested. Thirty-seven more Maroons were arrested after going to Montego Bay to seek peace. The arrest of these Maroon representatives who sought peace ensured that there could be no peaceful resolution to the conflict.

The Trelawny Town Maroons proved to be difficult to defeat in battle because they employed guerrilla tactics. Balcarres was completely unprepared for the Maroon resistance and underestimated their fighting ability. The colonial authorities actually suffered more casualties than the Maroons did during the Second Maroon War, although the Maroons were ultimately defeated. The colonial forces employed a scorched-earth policy which made it impossible for the Maroons to sustain their guerilla tactics. The Maroons were also unable to get a regular supply of ammunition to continue the fighting and the colonial forces deprived the Maroons of their water supply. The Maroons finally surrendered after the colonial authorities imported hunting dogs from Cuba. As punishment for the war, some of the Maroons were deported to Nova Scotia in 1796 and then to Sierra Leone in 1800.

Balcarres believed that the slave uprising in Haiti (then known as St. Domingue) inspired the Trelawny Town Maroons to rebel. The uprising in Haiti was such a serious concern in Jamaica that the Assembly attempted to prevent free blacks and coloureds from St. Domingue from going to Jamaica due to their fear that these free blacks would spread rebellion in Jamaica. This did not prevent the influx of blacks and coloureds, however. Balcarres blamed the rebellion of the Trelawny Town Maroons on France. He frequently complained about the impact of revolutionary France and deported a large number of French people back to Saint Domingue.

The runaway slaves who fought on the side of the Trelawny Town Maroons did not surrender at the end of the war. They continued to attack and kill white men in Jamaica. The runaway slaves were also armed with weapons which were left behind by the Trelawny Town Maroons. Balcarres complained that the Maroons surrendered only weapons of poor quality and left the other weapons in the woods. These weapons were apparently left with the runaways who fought alongside the Maroons of Trelawny Town.

Runaways became a serious problem for planters in Jamaica. Two years after the war ended, Balcarres and the planters were complaining about a community of runaways who were terrorizing Jamaica. In 1798, a slave named Cuffee escaped from an estate and led a group of runaways into the forests of territory which was formerly controlled by the Trelawny Town Maroons. Balcarres believed that a number of the runaways with Cuffee had fought with the Trelawny Town Maroons or secured their freedom during the Second Maroon War. Cuffee's forces raided plantations for supplies and waged war against the slave owners. Cuffee's followers also destroyed plantations throughout Jamaica. Cuffee's community expanded as more runaway slaves joined him.

The Accompong Maroons joined the colonial forces in trying to subdue Cuffee, but they were unsuccessful. Balcarres became so desperate to capture Cuffee that he offered a reward, but Cuffee was never captured or killed. Balcarres himself admitted that "the Parties in search of the Negroe Cuffee have not been able to lay hold of him." Other rebels had been captured and killed by the Maroons, however. The failure to capture Cuffee caused anxiety among the planters. Most refused to return to their lands. A planter named Peter Scarlett did return to his plantation only to be shot and killed by an individual who was never caught.

The Maroons not only assisted in putting down rebellions because it was the part of the terms which they had agreed to, but they were also financially rewarded for their service in suppressing rebellions, though this pay was not always timely. Some of the Maroons complained about not being paid promptly by the British for their services rendered during the suppression of Tacky's rebellion. The debts owed to those who assisted in putting down Tacky's rebellion would not be paid off until 1780.

The Maroons would continue to help suppress rebellion in Jamaica. Jack Mansong—also known as Three-Fingered Jack— was a runaway slave who led a band of runaways. This group was so troublesome for the colonial authorities that the colonial authorities offered a reward for Jack and the members of his community. Jack and his gang committed robberies and carried away other slaves. Jack was killed in 1781 by a party which consisted of six Maroons. The Maroons who were responsible for killing Jack would not receive their reward until two years later. The Maroons also contributed to suppressing Sam Sharpe's rebellion in 1831. The Maroons were late in joining the effort to suppress this rebellion, however. The Maroons of Accompong Town killed one of Sharpe's deputies and captured 27 runaway rebels.

The missionaries in Jamaica highlighted how the British had supported the brutality of the Maroons. A Baptist missionary named John Clarke wrote that the colonial authorities rewarded the Maroons for the numbers of ears that they cut off of the rebel slaves that they had killed. A Methodist missionary named Henry

Bleby alleged that "scores of slaves innocent of all participation in the revolt were shot by Maroons, for no other purpose than to obtain their ears for sale."

Employing Maroons to suppress rebellion would continue after the end of slavery in Jamaica. The Maroons were called to assist with suppressing the Morant Bay Rebellion in 1865. The Maroons were praised by the governor for assisting in suppressing the rebellion, but they were also criticized for their brutality in suppressing the revolt. This would be the last time that the Maroons were called to put down a rebellion in Jamaica.

The Jamaican Maroons paradoxically represent both freedom and resistance against slavery, as well as collaboration with the slave masters. The Maroons were runaway slaves who engaged in fierce resistance to maintain their own freedom. They were successful in maintaining their freedom from slavery, but the peace terms which they agreed to meant that the Maroons would have to collaborate with the British to suppress rebellions in Jamaica. Tacky, Cuffee, Sam Sharpe, and Paul Bogle were all mentioned as examples of men in Jamaica whose acts of rebellion were put down with the help of the Maroons. What's more is that the terms of the peace treaty allowed the British to gradually erode the authority of the Maroon settlements.

References:

Jonathan Brooks, "From Freedom to Bondage: The Jamaican Maroons, 1655–1770," University of North Carolina Wilmington.

Maria Alessandra Bollettino, "Slavery, War, and Britain's Atlantic Empire: Black Soldiers, Sailors, and Rebels in the Seven Years' War," doctoral dissertation, 2009.

Sivapragasam, Michael (2018) After the treaties: a social, economic and demographic history of Maroon society in Jamaica, 1739-1842. University of Southampton, Doctoral Thesis

18

DID BURNHAM KILL RODNEY?

The death of Walter Rodney is a very contentious issue in the political history of Guyana. Rodney died on June 13, 1980, after a bomb exploded in the car in which he was sitting. Rodney had picked up a walkie-talkie, which turned out to be an explosive. This aspect of his death is not contested. What is contested is why did this happen and who was responsible. There were those who blamed the prime minister, Forbes Burnham, for the assassination of Walter Rodney because he saw Rodney as a potential threat to his government. That Burnham was concerned about being ousted by a popular uprising was no secret. In *The Grenada Revolution in the Caribbean Present*, Shalini Puri wrote: "Cognizant of the threat that the Grenada Revolution posed to unpopular authoritarian governments in the region, Forbes Burnham declared it a military offence for Guyanese soldiers to discuss events in Grenada." Did Burnham's concern about being overthrown drive him to kill Rodney? The Commission of Inquiry which investigated Rodney's death concluded that Burnham was involved, but there are also those who disagree.

Gerald A. Perreira of the Organization for the Victory of the People (OVP) wrote a letter in which he criticized the COI. He described the COI as a farce, which was aimed at demonizing Burnham, discrediting the PNC prior to the May 15 general elections, and fracturing the unity of A Partnership of National Unity (APNU). I do not think that these are unreasonable conclusions. The PPP was in a very vulnerable position leading up to the 2015 elections. Creating disunity within the APNU coalition was one way that the PPP could strengthen its position going into the election. Even so, I do not think that this is enough to dismiss the findings of the COI.

For those who are supporters of Burnham, the problem posed by the COI was its conclusion. That conclusion was that Burnham was responsible for the murder of Walter Rodney. This is not a new revelation. There had long since been suspicions of this, but no investigation was ever carried out so there was never any conclusive evidence that Rodney's murder was part of a conspiracy which was carried out by the PNC government to silence him.

In his letter, Perreira attempted to discredit the COI. Perreira wrote: "A long list of people appeared before the commission, each of them offering mere opinions and hearsay, because they had nothing more to offer, while important witnesses, such as Assistant Commissioner of Police under Burnham, Cecil 'Skip' Roberts, who now resides in the US and travelled to Guyana to give evidence, was accommodated at a hotel in Georgetown for 10 days, all expenses paid by the Commission, but was not called upon to give evidence. At the time of the events supposedly being examined by the COI, Mr. Roberts was the chief investigator into the circumstances surrounding Dr Walter Rodney's death—so surely an important witness."

Two things stood out to me about this remark from Perreira. The first is his dismissal of the long list of people who appeared before the commission. Among those who testified at the commission were members of the WPA; Donald Rodney, who was in the car with his brother Walter when the bomb exploded; and Joseph Hamilton, who was a member of the House of Israel. The COI also made use of the reports from three experts who conducted a forensic analysis of Rodney's body after he was killed. These were individuals who were directly involved in the circumstances surrounding the activism and assassination of Rodney. It is not clear why Perreira believed that Roberts was a more important witness than the others who spoke before the commission. Perhaps Perreira hoped that Roberts would provide information which would have cleared Burnham of any accusations of wrongdoing.

The other thing that stood out to me is that Perreira mentioned the fact that Roberts did not testify. He did so to discredit the COI, but he did not explain why Roberts did not testify at the COI. Hamilton Green provided a similar criticism of the COI over the failure to take evidence from Roberts. In response to Green, Tacuma Ogunseye (a member of the WPA who worked with Walter Rodney) wrote: "If truth be known I attended every session of the Commission's hearings and I can testify that from the very first occasion and on every subsequent occasion that the Attorney for the PNCR, Mr. Basil Williams raised this matter, the Commission's Chairman always gave an explanation of what took place." Ogunseye also wrote: "For the benefit of those who do not know the Chairman was always at pains to point out that Mr. Roberts was brought to Guyana based on the assurance he gave to them that when he arrived in Guyana he would produce his statement. The Chairman had also on numerous occasions reminded consuls present of the Commission's rule that a witness must submit a written statement before he/she can take the stand and give evidence. It was said that Mr. Roberts refused to comply with the Commission request in spite of the several attempts made by the officials of the Commission to get his cooperation."

Glen Hanoman, the Commission's senior lawyer who dealt with Roberts, wrote, "I think he came because he got a free trip, because he had nothing material to say". It is not clear from Perreira's letter what it was that he felt Roberts would have contributed to the COI, but based on Ogunseye's account, Roberts was not seriously interested in participating in the COI, nor did he have anything of importance to add.

Perreira continued his criticism of the COI by providing some context for the circumstances surrounding Rodney's death. He wrote: "Walter Rodney who was then, and remains an esteemed intellectual warrior, decided to oppose Burnham at a time when the CIA was waging a very real and threatening campaign to destabilize Burnham's government and roll back the revolution." Perreira viewed this "attempt to destabilize and overthrow the revolutionary and anti-imperialist regime of Forbes Burnham" as an erroneous one. The problem here is that Perreira himself ignored some important context.

Rodney did not view Burnham's regime as a revolutionary and anti-imperialist regime. Rodney recognized that Burnham's regime had been helped into power by the CIA in an attempt to suppress the spread of communism in Guyana—this is an important detail which Perreira left out. After Burnham came to power, his turn towards socialism created some tensions with the United States. In the 1970s American aid to Guyana had stopped, but Rodney did not view Burnham as an anti-imperialist leader. Not only because of the Western support that Burnham had received in the 1960s, but also because of the fact that under Burnham's government Guyana found itself accepting loans from the International Monetary Fund (IMF). To meet the demands of the IMF, Burnham's government implemented hardships upon the Guyanese people.

It should also be noted that Rodney's opposition to Burnham's government was also influenced by the fact that when Rodney decided to return to Guyana to teach at the University of Guyana (UG), his appointment was revoked by Burnham's government. Why would the revolutionary and anti-imperialist government of Burnham seek to bar Rodney from teaching at UG? Rodney at the time had acquired an international reputation as an intellectual who spoke out on behalf of the oppressed working class. It was for this reason that Rodney was barred from returning to Jamaica. One would think that Burnham would have gladly welcomed Rodney back to Guyana, but this was not the case at all.

Perreira's exclusion of this incident is critical because Burnham's decision to ban Rodney from teaching in Guyana would shape the political relationship between Rodney and Burnham moving forward. The decision to ban Rodney from teaching at UG ensured that from the beginning of Rodney's return to Guyana, his relationship with the PNC and Burnham would be a hostile one. Ogunseye speculated that Hamilton Green was the one responsible for this. He wrote: "It is Green who I believe poisoned Burnham's mind against Rodney with his lies when he returned from Tanzania and it was he who instigated Rodney's banning from UG." Ogunseye argued that were it not for Green's deception the history of Guyana could have been different as it relates to the relationship between Rodney and Burnham, as well as the PNC and the WPA.

Perreira posed two questions: "At the time, who would have benefitted most from disunity and warfare between two anti-imperialist formations in Guyana, namely the PNC and the WPA? Who would have tried to ratchet up the disunity rather than facilitating unity?" By leaving out the fact that Rodney was banned from teaching at UG, Perreira leaves out the fact that the PNC's own actions indicated that the leadership was not interested in unity. Perreira blamed the CIA for instigating conflict between the WPA and the PNC. I certainly cannot deny the possibility that the CIA was working to create disunity in Guyana, especially since the CIA had done so in the past, but I also think one cannot ignore the fact that real contradictions existed between Rodney and Burnham. Burnham's conduct ensured that the only resolution to these contradictions would have been a direct confrontation between the WPA and the PNC.

Perreira stated that "the WPA was amassing weapons in an attempt to overthrow Forbes Burnham's government, which was also facing a very real threat of destabilization and overthrow from the CIA." In his defense of Burnham, Minette Bacchus also mentioned the fact that the WPA was amassing arms. One important piece of information which came from the COI was Ogunseye's testimony, which stated that it was only certain cells within the WPA which were amassing weapons. The WPA as a collective party did not adopt a policy of amassing weapons. Secondly, the context around why the WPA was amassing weapons should be understood. Perreira presented this as an attempt to overthrow Burnham's government, but Ogunseye stated that the weapons were acquired for self-defense. At the COI, Ogunseye spoke about the extrajudicial killings which took place under Burnham's government. Prior to Rodney's murder, two members of the WPA named Ohene Koama and Edward Dublin were killed. Bernard Darke had been stabbed to death. Critics of Burnham's government also faced physical attacks from the House of Israel. Members of the WPA were seriously concerned for their safety and well-being. Perreira does not acknowledge any of this in his defense of Burnham and neither does Minette Bacchus, but all of this is important for understanding the context of the WPA's struggle against Burnham's government. Burnham stated that members of the WPA should make their wills. It is difficult for supporters of Burnham to justify this apparent threat and the very real violence which members of the WPA experienced, so Perreira and Bacchus simply refuse to acknowledge that Burnham made such a threat. Doing so hurts their attempts to defend Burnham, however.

Minette Bacchus suggested that Rodney supported armed

revolution based on "extracts from Rodney's mentor, the world-renowned CLR James; and WPA co-leader Rupert Roopnarine". At the COI, Eusi Kwayana dismissed some of James' remarks about the situation in Guyana. Kwayana disagreed with the notion that Rodney was preparing for an armed rebellion to take power. Kwayana also pointed out that James was not in Guyana at the time that Rodney was killed, so some of James' views on the situation were misinformed. Roopnarine did admit that the WPA was getting weapons and that some of these weapons were coming from the military, but these remarks should be understood within the context of the previously mentioned information regarding the WPA's attempt to defend itself from state violence.

Perreira wrote: "A seasoned and astute leader, Burnham knew that the homegrown opposition was being fuelled by the imperialists. He knew that the WPA, whose leadership comprised mainly of middle-class academics, would be an easy target for CIA operatives." Perreira's admiration for Burnham is apparent. He also wrote that Burnham was "nothing short of a brilliant strategist," but this praise of Burnham as being brilliant, seasoned, and astute does little to address the allegation that Burnham was involved in Rodney's death.

Perreira continued on to write that "the very worst thing he could have done, akin to shooting himself in the foot, would have been to order the assassination of a world renowned academic such as Dr Walter Rodney. It is clear that this would have been political suicide." Could this perhaps be why there was no serious investigation into Rodney's death on the part of Burnham's government? There was even some suggestion that the government attempted to cover up the murder of Rodney. David Hinds and Ogunseye held the view that the bomb which killed Rodney was meant to disfigure his face so that he would be unrecognizable and then that way the government could claim that Rodney was not really dead, but the bomb did not blow up Rodney's face. It was reported in the news that Rodney was not recognizable, but this was not the case at all.

Perreira also stated: "As a political analyst, having studied Amilcar Cabral, Frantz Fanon, and CLR James, Burnham understood the middle-class character and contradictions of the WPA and what he described as their hollow, revolutionary rhetoric, borne out of their immersion in theoretical analysis and the culture of critique without any revolutionary praxis." Here Perreira listed three Pan-African thinkers that Burnham studied in an attempt to somehow connect these men to Burnham. None of this information is relevant for dispelling the notion that Burnham was behind the killing of Rodney or that the COI was a farce. Rodney studied Cabral, Fanon, and James as well, so one is not clear on why studying these three men gave Burnham some type of special insight into the character of the WPA. This information is included merely to bolster Burnham's image as a great revolutionary thinker, but it does little to address the topic of whether or not Burnham killed Rodney.

I will close by noting an irony in Perreira's attempt to defend Burnham. At no point in his letter does Perreira acknowledge the suppression of free speech or the rigging of elections which took place during Burnham's government. These issues were critical to the WPA's opposition to Burnham. In 2020, Perreira's political party, the OVP, withdrew its support for the APNU+AFC over electoral irregularities. The results table showed 155 votes for the OVP in Region 1, which was a region which the OVP did not even contest. The OVP also received 250 votes in the General Election, despite contesting only at the regional level. Perreira wrote: "Despite serious political and ideological differences with the ruling Coalition, we offered them critical support to prevent the return of a Jagdeo-led PPP/C regime. Following the events of Thursday, our National Directorate has now taken a decision to withdraw forthwith all support for APNU+AFC." The OVP withdrew support from the APNU+AFC because the APNU+AFC was engaged in the very thing which the WPA had denounced Burnham for doing, which was interfering with elections.

Cited Articles from *Kaieteur News*

Minette Bacchus, "The facts do not support Burnham killing Rodney," May 26, 2013.

Tacuma Ogunseye, "Ogunseye accuses Hamilton Green of terrible past violations," March 16, 2016.

Gerald A. Perreira, "Forbes Burnham had nothing to do with Walter Rodney's death," March 16, 2016.

___ "We have decided to withdraw all support for APNU+AFC," March 7, 2020.

19

DIANE RWIGARA

The story of Diane Rwigara's bid for the presidency in Rwanda was one which I found to be very fascinating for what it exposed about Paul Kagame's government in Rwanda. Kagame is a leader who has managed to gain support from Western countries for the perception that he has created of himself. This perception is that Kagame is a leader who has managed to develop Rwanda. This perception has been maintained through the suppression of dissenting voices. This suppression has targeted political opposition leaders and journalists.

Rwigara attempted to run against Kagame in 2017. Rwanda's Constitution previously limited a president to two terms, but this provision was scrapped so that Kagame could run for a third term. In 2017, Kagame won 99% of the votes, which certainly raises some questions about how fair and free the 2017 election was. What also raises questions about the electoral process in 2017 was the fact that Rwigara did not even get her name on the ballot.

Rwigara was harassed throughout the whole process. The government first began circulating nude pictures of her, which she claimed were fake. Even if the photos were real, one wonders why the government decided to stoop to such levels to try to discredit Rwigara. Some of the people who worked with her were also beaten and jailed. These actions suggest that the government of Rwanda was trying to intimidate her to get her to drop out of the race, but she refused.

In Rwanda, candidates need at least 600 signatures to get their name on the ballot. Rwigara surpassed this number, but the government refused to validate the signatures and suggested that the signatures were invalid. After the election, Rwigara was arrested for forging signatures. Her mother and sister were arrested as well.

The charges against Rwigara kept piling up. She was accused of forgery and tax evasion. The government later arrested her again and accused her of planning an insurrection against the government. This is not the first time that Rwanda has done this to a woman who attempted to run against Kagame. Victorie Ingabire attempted to run against Kagame in 2010. She was the presidential candidate of a union of opposition parties, but she was barred from contesting the election. She was later arrested and sentenced for terrorism. Other critics of Kagame's government have been killed under mysterious circumstances, such as Patrick Karegeya and Charles Ingabire.

After a year of being detained, Rwigara was acquitted of the charges against her. After being released, Rwigara suggested that Kagame was afraid that the people of Rwanda would raise up against him, which is why he utilized very repressive measures to silence any criticisms of his government. Rwigara explained that Rwanda looks very beautiful for tourists, but the Rwandan people themselves continue to struggle. She suggested that Kagame's focus has been on trying to impress foreigners and that he forgot the citizens of Rwanda. Kagame has certainly been successful in attracting the admiration of the West, though this has not been enough to benefit the people of Rwanda. David Himbara, who worked for Kagame, left Rwanda after he realized that the "economic miracle" in Rwanda was based on statistics which were not credible. Himbara explained that the clean streets of Kigali were not a measurement of development because a large number of Rwandans still lived in poverty.

20

AN AFRICAN-CENTERED ASSESSMENT OF SELF-ACTUALIZATION

Abraham Maslow's concept of self-actualization is one which I have mentioned in my prior writings because I find his concept to be very useful for understanding human development. Maslow's concept is rooted in the search for self, particularly the search for one's highest self. This conception is not a new one. Egyptian temples inscribed the phrase "know thyself." This phrase was later used by Greek thinkers such as Socrates. Maslow's conception of self-actualization is not new, but it is a concept that I have been fascinated with since I first encountered his ideas when I was a student in high school. Maslow's concept also has certain limitations which I will elaborate on in this essay.

Maslow wrote about the concept of self-actualization in an essay titled "A Theory of Human Motivation." In his essay, Maslow organized human needs into a hierarchy. The starting point in the hierarchy are physiological needs. This is a logical starting point since humans need things such as food, water, and sleep to survive. As Maslow explained, "a good way to obscure the 'higher' motivations, and to get a lopsided view of human capacities and human nature, is to make the organism extremely and chronically hungry or thirsty." Next are safety needs. Safety needs refers to the need to feel safe from things such as wild animals, extremes of temperature, criminals, and tyranny. Maslow viewed religion as being part of the attempt to satisfy one's safety needs. He wrote: "The tendency to have some religion or world-philosophy that organizes the universe and the men in it into some sort of satisfactorily coherent, meaningful whole is also in part motivated by safety-seeking."

Once the physiological and safety needs are "fairly well gratified," next are the love needs. This refers to the desire for companionship in the form of friends, a spouse, or children. Next are the esteem needs. Maslow explained: "All people in our society (with a few pathological exceptions) have a need or desire for a stable, firmly based, (usually) high evaluation of themselves, for self-respect, or self-esteem, and for the esteem of others. By firmly based self-esteem, we mean that which is soundly based upon real capacity, achievement and respect from others." Maslow classified the esteem needs into two subsidiary sets. The first set is the desire for strength, achievement, adequacy, confidence, and independence. The second set refer to the desire for reputation, recognition, attention, and appreciation. The satisfaction of the esteem needs leads to feelings of self-confidence, worth, and strength. The thwarting of these needs produce feelings of inferiority, weakness, and helplessness.

Once all of these needs are satisfied, the individual then seeks to be self-actualized. Maslow explained: "Even if all these needs are satisfied, we may still often (if not always) expect that a new discontent and restlessness will soon develop, unless the individual is doing what he is fitted for. A musician must make music, an artist must paint, a poet must write, if he is to be ultimately happy. What a man *can* be, he *must* be. This need we may call self-actualization."

Maslow pointed out that each need does not need to be completely satisfied before the next need emerges. He explained: "In actual fact, most members of our society who are normal, are partially satisfied in all their basic needs and partially unsatisfied in all their basic needs at the same time. A more realistic description of the hierarchy would be in terms of decreasing percentages of satisfaction as we go up the hierarchy of prepotency, For instance, if I may assign arbitrary figures for the sake of illustration, it is as if the average citizen is satisfied perhaps 85 per cent in his physiological needs, 70 per cent in his safety needs, 50 per cent in his love needs, 40 per cent in his self-esteem needs, and 10 per cent in his self-actualization needs."

Maslow argued that the search for self was partly a search for one's life work. Therefore, the self-actualized individual is one who has discovered his or her vocation. This vocation then becomes a defining characteristic of the self. Maslow explained that the self-actualized individual must do that which the self-actualized individual loves to do, otherwise that individual would not be himself or herself. The fascination with this work is such that the self-actualized person forgets about the ego and about pride. The work becomes worthwhile in itself.

Another trait of self-actualized individuals is that they are autonomous. They are not like weathervanes, which move in whichever direction the wind blows. Rather, self-actualized individuals are firm in their convictions. Maslow described such individuals as being their own bosses. One example which Maslow gave was Abraham Lincoln. Maslow explained that Lincoln could not be diddled around once he made up his mind. The self-actualized individual is an individual who does what he or she thinks is best, even if it means taking a very unpopular position.

Maslow seemed to suggest that the self-actualized individual is one who is not motivated by a desire to be loved or by a desire to receive adulation. Rather, self-actualized individuals are motivated by a desire to do that which they are passionate about doing or that which they feel compelled to do.

One significant shortcoming of Maslow's concept of self-actualization is that it is very Eurocentric. This is understandable. After all, Maslow was a white man who analyzed human behavior from his own cultural view of the world. The historical frame of reference which Maslow drew from were primarily other white Americans such as Abraham Lincoln, Thomas Jefferson, and Eleanor Roosevelt. These were his models for what a self-actualized individual looks like. The limitation here is that Maslow's conception of self-actualization was confined to a particular cultural outlook.

Maslow himself recognized that motivations differ across cultures and societies. He wrote: "This classification of basic needs makes some attempt to take account of the relative unity behind the superficial differences in specific desires from one culture to another. Certainly in any particular culture an individual's conscious motivational content will usually be extremely different from the conscious motivational content of an individual in another society. However, it is the common experience of anthropologists that people, even in different societies, are much more alike than we would think from our first contact with them, and that as we know them better we seem to find more and more of this commonness. We then recognize the most startling differences to be superficial rather than basic, *e. g.*, differences in style of hair-dress, clothes, tastes in food, etc. Our classification of basic needs is in part an attempt to account for this unity behind the apparent diversity from culture to culture. No claim is made that it is ultimate or universal for all cultures."

Though Maslow recognized cultural differences, he also viewed the self-actualized individual as an individual who exists independent of culture. He explained that such individuals "all seem to be like each other, and I would guess, independent of the century, independent of the culture even." In Maslow's conception, the self-actualized individual seems to be an individual who stands apart from others and even stands apart from the culture which they come from. It is not that I disagree with this necessarily, but I would raise the possibility that a culture itself can produce self-actualized individuals. In such a scenario an individual who is self-actualized cannot be viewed as being independent of the culture but is a product of the culture. Maslow seems to be operating from the view that a self-actualized individual is so independent and so autonomous in their thoughts and their actions that they are even independent of the cultures that produce them. I do not think Maslow explored the possibility that the culture itself has a significant role in human development. This is because Maslow's approach is a more individualistic approach which is very much aligned with his own cultural background.

Maslow certainly recognized the role that society played in creating self-actualized individuals. Concerning safety needs, Maslow wrote: "The healthy, normal, fortunate adult in our culture is largely satisfied in his safety needs. The peaceful, smoothly running, 'good' society ordinarily makes its members feel safe enough from wild animals, extremes of temperature, criminals, assault and murder, tyranny, etc." What of those who do not live in societies which satisfy safety needs? An example of this would be individuals who live under an oppressive military dictatorship. Such a regime often denies its citizens the ability to satisfy physiological and safety needs. One can go further to assess Maslow's own culture because when he writes that the healthy, normal, fortunate adult is largely satisfied in their safety needs in

American culture, he obviously was not referring to African people in American culture at the time.

Maslow's conception of self-actualization was not particularly concerned with a race of people who are struggling against an oppressive system. His concept was not addressed to the question of how an individual becomes self-actualized in a society which is actively ensuring that individuals of a particular race do not have any of their needs satisfied. In such a situation, I would argue that resistance and rebellion then become hallmarks of a self-actualized individual who strives to break the chains of oppression for himself and for others. This is not Maslow's conception, however. As stated previously, Maslow's conception is largely rooted in his own experience and worldview as a white American.

Maslow's conception of self-actualization centers around the needs of the individual. This is most apparent to me when Maslow discussed the love needs. Maslow acknowledged that love must be both given and received, which seems to give the impression that love is a transaction. Relationships in Maslow's hierarchy are one of the needs which must be satisfied before an individual can move to the next set of needs on the hierarchy. Maslow's whole concept centers around how self-actualized individuals stand apart from those who are not self-actualized. He seems to have little to say about the relationships of self-actualized individuals in terms of how they interact with their loved ones or with people within their community. The self-actualized individual needs family and friends to satisfy the need for love, but this seemed to be the extent to which Maslow was concerned with love and relationships regarding the self-actualized individual.

In Maslow's conception, the self-actualized individual is an individual who does identify with humanity and seeks to serve humanity. Maslow does describe the self-actualized individual as being sympathetic, compassionate, and unselfish. These are individuals who feel a sense of love towards others. He mentioned Eugene Debs as an example of a loving person who tried to help humanity. Maslow presented Walt Whitman as another example of this. Maslow also described the self-actualized individual as one who can identify with individuals beyond social boundaries such as class or caste. Such individuals have a feeling of commonness with mankind. Maslow referred to this as *gemeinschaftsgefühl*, a

German word which refers to social interest or a feeling of commonness. It is apparent that Maslow does not conceive of the self-actualized individual as an individual who is disconnected from humanity, but his conception of self-actualization is centered on the thoughts and the actions of the individual in a manner that views the self-actualized individual as acting independently from the wider community.

The individualistic nature of Maslow's concept is something which Na'im Akbar pointed out when he explained: "European American Psychology takes as its arena of study the individual ego, behavior and consciousness. The commonality in the European American approach to personality is its emphasis on individuality. From Adler's 'creative self' through Maslow's 'actualized self' and Mead's 'looking glass self,' the conception is consistent that self is an individual phenomenon. All of these approaches give the highest credibility to the individual and his unique experiences." Akbar adopted an African-centered approach which saw the individual as belonging to a collective. Akbar described the African conception as follows: "Whatever happened to the individual impacted on the corporate body, the tribe and whatever happened to the tribe reverberated into the individual."

Akbar pointed out that individualism was one of the characteristics of the traditional Western model. He explained: "The model is also primarily individualistic. It assumes that the person is best understood as separate from others and characteristics suggestive of interdependence are viewed as deviant. In the psychological literature, dependence has been identified as endemic in a broad array of mental abnormalities from depression to schizophrenia. As a result, the general motif of the culture is one of individualism and a defiant independence." Akbar points out that for this reason African Americans are consistently shown to be pathological or abnormal because African Americans "show higher tendencies of interdependence, dependence and internal fate control."

Akbar also pointed out that the Western model is one which views competition and conflict as being signs of mental health. He referenced David McClelland who wrote that the "need for achievement is an essential ingredient for entrepreneurial success." In McClelland's view, black Americans lack the achievement drive. Akbar pointed out that McClelland failed to see the correlation between the need for achievement and the authoritarian personality.

In Akbar's view, Maslow's hierarchy is also part of the Western tradition of viewing human motivation as being directed towards gratification: "The European American approach sees the person as essentially directed towards pleasurable gratification based on material achievements. The Behaviorists assume that, all behavior hinges on rewards and punishments. Freud assumes the primal need of immediate gratification of either sexual or aggressive drives and Maslow assumes a hierarchy of needs for gratification at various levels." The needs that Maslow wrote of are universal across all cultures, but it is also true that in certain cultures the denial of such needs can be an important practice. The example which I give here is how Muslims fast during Ramadan. This is the deliberate denial of the physiological needs which Maslow wrote about. This is done for spiritual reasons as opposed to a desire for physical gratification.

The entire premise of self-actualization is subjective as well. An individual who may be viewed as being self-actualized by one group may be viewed differently by another group. Thomas Jefferson was among the historical personalities whom Maslow presented as being examples of self-actualization. This is understandable since Jefferson achieved great things in his lifetime. Jefferson was one of the leading figures in America's revolutionary struggle for freedom against Britain. Jefferson would later become the president of the United States. These accomplishments are undeniable. Jefferson was also a slave owner and a racist who believed that African people were inferior. In Jefferson's view, Native Americans were savages who deserved to be exterminated. Given these facts should Africans and Native Americans view Jefferson as being a self-actualized individual?

I want to make clear that none of this is intended to be a complete rejection of Maslow's concept of self-actualization. Maslow himself was aware of some of these limitations of his concept. For instance, he did acknowledge that cross-cultural studies needed to be done because his research was done among

Americans. Most of Maslow's examples of self-actualized humans are white, but he did also include individuals from outside of his culture. This included a chief of the Blackfoot people, whom Maslow came to refer to as his "father." Maslow's work is limited by cultural bias, yet his work does speak to certain universal desires such as the desire to satisfy one's needs and the desire for understanding one's truest purpose in life.

21

RACE IN AMERICAN POLITICS

W.E.B. Du Bois stated: "The problem of the twentieth century is the problem of the color-line,—the relation of the darker to the lighter races of men in Asia and Africa, in America and the islands of the sea." Du Bois understood that racial discrimination had become the most serious problem of the twentieth century. It became so because of the position of power and dominance which white people maintained in the world. European nations set out to conquer and colonize the entire world. This gave birth to a philosophy which saw the white man as being racially superior to those whom he subjugated. The United States of America was one of the nations which was a product of this global racial imperialism.

America was created out of an act of rebellion against the colonial order which European nations created, yet America's birth was not a rejection of the racism which had justified the colonial ambitions of European nations. America rejected Britain's rule over a foreign colony, yet America had not rejected the idea that the white race was a superior race. David Brion David stated: "Even most history books fail to convey the extent that the American government was dominated by slaveholders and proslavery interests between the inaugurations of Presidents Washington and Lincoln. Partly because of the clause in the Constitution that gave the South added political representation for three-fifths of its slave population, Southern slaveholding presidents governed the nation for roughly 50 of those 72 years. And four of the six Northern presidents in that span catered to Southern proslavery policies. For example, Martin Van Buren, who came from a New York slaveholding family, sought to undermine the nation's judicial process and send the captives from the slave ship Amistad back to Cuba—and certain death. Millard Fillmore, also from New York, signed the Fugitive Slave Law of 1850, which enforced return of escaped slaves even from free states." This statement by David should give one some idea of how racist attitudes profoundly shaped the early decades of America's political history.

The problem of racism in American politics is a problem in which the basic human rights of African Americans have been denied by political leaders who have not viewed African Americans as equal human beings. There is an apparent inability to truly confront the extent to which racism has shaped American politics or how this racism has impacted the lives of African people. Joe Biden displayed this when he stated that Donald Trump was the first racist to be elected president in America. This is not true. Biden's remarks demonstrated the unwillingness to be honest about race in American politics and this unwillingness to confront racism has resulted in an analysis of America's political history which looks at presidents as individuals who are removed from the consequences of their policies. The racism of these presidents is often treated as a minor issue or often not even addressed at all. This can be demonstrated by remarks which Barack Obama made in an interview with AllAfrica. Obama stated: "I'd say I'm probably as knowledgeable about African history as anybody who's occupied my office. And I can give you chapter and verse on the—why the colonial maps that were drawn helped to spur on conflict, and the terms of trade that were uneven emerging out of colonialism."

Obama's response seems to ignore how racist some of the previous presidents were and how that racism impacted America's policy towards Africa. Some examples which come to mind are America's role in overthrowing Kwame Nkrumah, America's role in assassinating Patrice Lumumba, and America's support for apartheid in South Africa. The overthrow of Nkrumah is especially significant here because the interview with Obama was conducted ahead of his visit to Ghana. In the interview Obama also stated, "I'm a big believer that Africans are responsible for Africa." If he truly believed this, then why not allow Africa to handle the responsibility of the unrest in Libya, instead of intervening there? Obama was correct to point out that Africa is ultimately responsible for its own leadership, but it is disingenuous to speak of the issue of governance in Africa without acknowledging

America's history of intervening in Africa's affairs.

The admiration which Franklin Roosevelt enjoys within the Democratic Party is yet another example of this point. When asked to name a political leader that they admire, both Hillary Clinton and Bernie Sanders named Roosevelt. Roosevelt is admired in American history for his New Deal policy which implemented government programs to assist impoverished Americans during the Great Depression. The problem with the New Deal is that it did not address the racial inequality in America. In the 1930s, the unemployment rate among African Americans was much higher than it was among white people. The policies of the New Deal not only failed to address racial inequality, but the manner in which the deal was implemented reflected these inequalities. For example, Social Security excluded African American men in certain occupations from its benefits. In response to the Social Security program, the *Crisis* stated: "Just as Mr. Roosevelt threw the Negro textile workers to the wolves in order to get the Cotton Textile code adopted in July of 1933 by exempting them from its provisions, so he and his advisors are preparing to dump overboard the majority of Negro workers in his security legislation program by exempting from pensions and job insurance all farmers, domestic, and casual labor." This is not to suggest that African Americans did not benefit from any of the provisions of the New Deal. The availability of low rent housing certainly did benefit African Americans, but the benefits were greatly hindered by the racial discrimination which African Americans faced. African Americans were the group that suffered the most during the Great Depression, but also received the least amount of help from the New Deal.

The African American community expressed other issues with Roosevelt as well. Roosevelt appointed Hugo Black to the Supreme Court, despite protests from the black community. Black was a former member of the Ku Klux Klan. Black initially refused to answer a question about his membership in the Klan, although Black later admitted that he was a member of the Klan and that he never rejoined the Klan after he resigned from the organization. Black wrote the majority opinion for *Korematsu v. United States*, which was a Supreme Court case that upheld Roosevelt's executive order in which citizens of Japanese ancestry were detained in "relocation centers." Black wrote: "Korematsu was not excluded from the Military Area because of hostility to him or his race. He was excluded because we are at war with the Japanese Empire, because the properly constituted military authorities feared an invasion of our West Coast and felt constrained to take proper security measures, because they decided that the military urgency of the situation demanded that all citizens of Japanese ancestry be segregated from the West Coast temporarily, and, finally, because Congress, reposing its confidence in this time of war in our military leaders—as inevitably it must—determined that they should have the power to do just this." Black stated that Korematsu was not excluded because of his race, but then specifically mentions the segregation of citizens of Japanese ancestry. Justice Roberts accurately noted that it was "the case of convicting a citizen as a punishment for not submitting to imprisonment in a concentration camp, based on his ancestry, and solely because of his ancestry, without evidence or inquiry concerning his loyalty and good disposition towards the United States."

There was also the problem of anti-lynching legislation. Roosevelt refused to commit to supporting anti-lynching legislation. The reason for this was political. The Democratic Party included senators who outright opposed laws banning lynching, such as Huey Long. Long argued that such a law would actually harm black people. Senators Pat Harrison and Ellison Smith saw the anti-lynching legislation as a threat to white civilization, southern women, and the Democratic Party. Roosevelt admitted: "If I come out for the anti-lynching bill now, they will block every bill I ask Congress to pass to keep America from collapsing. I just can't take that risk." *The Crisis* reported that Roosevelt was willing to "spend billions to keep people from relief rolls, but is unwilling to say one word to prevent his fellowmen from being murdered by mobs."

There was a decrease in lynching activity in 1935 when the anti-lynching bill was being debated, but after the bill was defeated in Congress there was an increase in lynching. Roosevelt was content to remain silent on the matter. He was content to allow black people to be lynched, so long as he did not risk losing the support of Congressmen in the south. This silence on the matter resulted in a group of black women picketing the National Democratic Headquarters in New York City to condemn Roosevelt's silence. Rexford Tugwell stated that "Franklin had watched the fight, but had not intervened. He had been urged again and again to exert his leadership, but he had turned his back."

Roosevelt would not risk alienating a portion of the Democratic Party by offering public support for anti-lynching laws. The unwillingness of Democratic presidents to forcefully challenge racism in America would continue in the years that followed. Take for example Lyndon B. Johnson. As Obama pointed out, for the first twenty years that Johnson was a senator, he had opposed civil rights legislation. Johnson did support civil rights legislation once he became president, yet Johnson was also the same man who sided with segregationists in Mississippi against the Mississippi Freedom Democratic Party. Much like Roosevelt, Johnson would not risk alienating southern segregationists within the Democratic Party. Of course, Obama did not mention this aspect of Johnson's politics. Obama merely stated that Johnson was "not a perfect man." The issue is not whether Johnson was perfect or imperfect. The issue is how Johnson's policies impacted African Americans. One cannot deny that Johnson did sign important civil rights legislation into law, but his unwillingness to challenge racism within his own party had the effect of ultimately undermining civil rights in America.

The Republican Party provides more examples of racism on the part of an American president. Richard Nixon was infamously forced to resign following the Watergate scandal in which burglars broke into the office of the Democratic National Committee. Nixon lied about not being involved in the attempt to cover up the break-in. Following Nixon's resignation, Gerald Ford was sworn in as president and Ford pardoned Nixon. Nixon was also a racist. Nixon's views on black people were summed up by H.R. Haldeman, who noted that Nixon expressed the view "that there has never in history been an adequate black nation—and they are the only race of which this is true. Says Africa is hopeless—and the worst there is Liberia, which we built." In a recorded exchange between Nixon and Ronald Reagan, Nixon was heard laughing after Reagan referred to African leaders as monkeys.

Reagan's administration was marked by several scandals such as "Debategate" in which documents from the campaign of Jimmy Carter were illegally transmitted to Reagan's team. A much larger scandal was the Contra scandal. This scandal involved a deal made between Iran and the American government in which the American government sold missiles to Iran, which was a violation of the arms embargo which was in place. The deal secured the release of American hostages who were being held hostage. The funds which were acquired through the sale were used to finance the Contras who were fighting against the government in Nicaragua. Reagan also provided CIA assistance in supporting the UNITA rebels in Angola. Nixon and Reagan were two racists who oversaw scandal ridden presidencies. Nixon felt that Africans never had an adequate country and Reagan saw Africans as monkeys. Obama's claim to have the same level of knowledge about Africa's history as men such as Nixon and Reagan was hardly reassuring.

The racism of American political leaders has often posed a challenge for African Americans, who have struggled to engage in the political system in a manner which can truly advance their interests. W.E.B. Du Bois provides an example of this. Du Bois stated that he "espoused the cause of Woodrow Wilson" and even went so far as to resign from the Socialist Party which he joined to avoid being disciplined for not voting for the Socialist ticket. He explained: "I could not let Negroes throw away votes." He wrote: "We sincerely believe that even in the face of promises disconcertingly vague, and in the face of the solid caste-ridden South, it is better to elect Woodrow Wilson President of the United States and prove once for all if the Democratic Party dares to be democratic when it comes to black men. It has proven that it can be in many Northern states and cities. Can it be in the nation? We hope so, and we are willing to risk a trial."

Du Bois noted that after Wilson was elected, he proceeded "to segregate nearly all of the colored Federal employees, of whom there were a considerable number, herding them so far as possible in separate rooms with separate eating and toilet facilities." William Monroe Trotter was dismissed by President Wilson when Trotter attempted to lead a delegation to protest the president's segregationist policies.

Du Bois explained that black people found themselves politically helpless in 1916 and there was little choice but to vote for Wilson. In 1912, Du Bois had supported Theodore Roosevelt and the Progressive Party, otherwise known as the "Bull Moose" movement. He saw this as an opportunity to develop a third party. Du Bois wrote a proposed plank for the Progressive Party. The plank stated: "The party, therefore, demands for the Americans of Negro descent the repeal of unfair discriminatory laws and the right to vote on the same terms on which other citizens vote." Roosevelt wanted nothing to do with Du Bois, whom he described as a "dangerous" person. The Progressive Party would not even seat most of the black delegates at its convention.

Smaller parties have offered a platform for political figures who would otherwise be unable to find a platform within the Democratic or Republican parties. An example of this is the fact that Clifton DeBerry was able to secure the nomination of the Socialist Workers Party in 1964. DeBerry was nominated again in 1980. In the 1964 campaign, DeBerry identified unemployment and civil rights as the chief domestic issues in America. He also described the Republican and Democratic parties as "the two cold-war, big business parties". Third parties have not been innocent of racism, however. The struggles which Claudia Jones experienced within the Communist Party demonstrated this.

Jones was born in Trinidad in 1915. Her family migrated to New York in 1922. Jones eventually became active in the National Urban League. The event which exposed Jones to the Communist Party was the Scottsboro Nine case in 1931. Nine black boys were accused of raping two white prostitutes. They were tried without an attorney. The Communist Party intervened to support the nine boys through the International Labor Defense group. After several years, the nine were found not guilty and were released.

Jones joined the Young Communist League in 1936. By 1941, she became the National Director of the Youth Communist League. Jones' position in the party did little to attract support from the black community. Connie Johnson explained: "Despite her position as one of the few African-American women in a leadership position within the CP, Jones did not have tremendous success in converting large numbers of black men or women to

Communism. This, in part, may have had more to do with fear of Jim Crow brutality and retaliation if caught engaged with the CP than an unwillingness to consider the merits of social change or equality." The racism of white socialists was also a significant factor in why black people avoided engaging with the CP.

Jones' work within the Communist Party also made her a target of the American government. She was deported to Britain in 1955. In Britain, Jones encountered the racism of the British Communist Party. Jones believed that white communist workers had "a special responsibility" to support black women's autonomous struggles because "they inevitably resisted race, class, and gender exploitation and thereby took aim against the whole capitalist system." The problem that Jones experienced was that some of her white communist comrades did not believe that they held such a responsibility towards black women. Jones died in Britain at the age of 49. Johnson summed up Jones' struggle within the Communist Party as follows: "Jones obviously felt that African-Americans were members of an oppressed group whose salvation was firmly rooted in Marx's Communism. That Jones would be forced to fight for support and approval within the Communist Party itself is certainly painful and ironic. Although Jones' efforts and commitment to the Party would prove to be a bittersweet victory during her lifetime, one can only hope that she found some consolation in the final pay-off at death: a gravesite next to that of Karl Marx."

Where matters of race are concerned, third parties have often not been much different than Democrats or Republicans. This was a point made by Marcus Garvey when he stated that "socialism is only another form of white control that the white man is going to fasten around the neck of the Negro peoples of the world." Garvey further declared: "Before you can accept socialism as a cure, you have to change the white man's soul; and that, the Negro socialists have not done yet." Garvey also stated that the socialist "is the same Republican, the same Democrat as other white men." By this, Garvey meant that socialists were just as racist as Republicans and Democrats were. This merely demonstrates just how pervasive the problem of racism in American politics has been. Even political parties that have presented themselves as alternatives to the two major parties have also displayed racism towards African Americans.

Selected References:

Connie Johnson, "Reclaiming Claudia Jones: When a Black Feminist Marxist Defies McCarthysim" *Michigan Feminist Studies*

Earlene Kelly Parr, "Franklin D. Roosevelt and the Negro in the 1930's," 1965.

Fred Halstead, "Socialist Workers Party Nominates DeBerry as Candidate for President," *The Militant*, January 13, 1964.

Federal Election Commission October 22, 1980.

Marcus Garvey, *Selected Speeches and Writings of Marcus Garvey*, (Dover Publications, 2005).

Peter Scott Dale, "Contragate: Reagan, Foreign Money, and the Contra Deal," *Crime and Social Justice*, 1987.

Remarks by the President at LBJ Presidential Library Civil Rights Summit, April 10, 2014.

Stephen E. Ambrose, "Why Didn't Nixon Burn the Tapes and Other Questions About Watergate," *Nova Law Review*, Volume 18, Issue 3, 1994.

22

A STORY OF HOPE FROM THE CONGO

The Democratic Republic of Congo is a nation which has suffered greatly over the centuries. It was one of the countries in Africa which was targeted during the slave trade. The Congo also endured the brutalities of Belgian colonial rule, which resulted in millions being killed. Since independence, the Congo has struggled with dictatorship, poverty, corruption, and armed conflict. Among the problems which continue to plague the Congo is that of rape. This is particularly a problem because rape in the Congo has been used as a weapon of war used by armed groups. Punishment for rape in the Congo is also rare.

Denis Mukwege has received international attention for the work that he has done to address the problem of rape in the Congo. Mukwege is a doctor who opened the Panzi Hospital in 1999 to treat women who have been raped. Panzi Hospital does not only treat the physical wounds. Panzi Hospital offers a place of refuge for the women as they recover from the psychological effects of the rape. There they are treated by psychologists and social workers. Claudine M'Mirambo was among those who were treated by Mukwege. She was at home with her husband when five men broke into their house. Her husband escaped and left her to be raped by a group of men in front of her children. The rapists nearly killed her. She developed a fear of men not only because she was raped by men, but she was abandoned by the man that she loved.

The hospital also includes as a center for the children who are born from rape—these children are known as "snake children." At this center, women who have been raped are assisting with forming an emotional bond to their children. Some of the children at the Panzi Hospital are also victims of rape themselves.

Mukwege's work has earned him the title, "The Man who Mends Women." It has also made him a target as well. Mukwege was attacked and nearly killed by five armed men. He was at home with his children at the time. Mukwege believed that this was an attempt to silence him. Mukwege left the country for his own safety, but Mukwege eventually returned where he was greeted by hundreds of cheering admirers.

Mukwege's work stands out as a story which inspires hope and optimism in a nation that has endured great hardships and suffering over the years. Mukwege is a deeply religious man who spends his Sundays preaching a message of peace as the pastor of a church. He explained that his faith allowed him to face the difficulties that he encountered on a regular basis. He was also encouraged by the women that he has treated. Mukwege stated that he felt very small compared to the women whom he has treated. Despite the suffering and humiliation that these women have experienced, many of them remain optimistic and hopeful. Their story is one of triumph in the face of great hardship and suffering.

23

NOTES ON THE REPUBLIC OF NEW AFRIKA

The Republic of New Afrika was formed around the idea that African Americans represent an independent nation within the United States. This concept was not a new one. Martin Delany had argued that African Americans were a nation within a nation in his book, *The Condition, Elevation, Emigration, and Destiny of the Colored People of the United States*. The Nation of Islam also expressed a similar view. It demanded that the United States secede territory to the Nation of Islam so that Muslims could create a nation of their own. The Republic of New Afrika took the concept of being a nation within a nation even further. The Republic of New Afrika claimed that New Afrika was sovereign over Mississippi, Louisiana, Alabama, Georgia, and South Carolina. Whereas the Nation of Islam was a religious organization which framed its arguments for separation in religious terms, the Republic of New Afrika saw itself as a political organization.

Prior to becoming a citizen of the Republic of New Afrika, Assata Shakur heard about the organization and was interested in checking the organization out. She described the first Republic of New Afrika event that she attended as being "gay and carnival-like." She explained that a group of brothers were pounding out Watusi, Zulu, and Yoruba messages on drums, while people danced. There were also speeches in-between songs and poems. At the event, Shakur became a citizen after signing her name in the citizen's book. The citizen's book was the official roster to keep track of everyone who was a citizen of the Republic of New Afrika, although Robert Williams noted that some people claimed to be citizens of the Republic of New Afrika, although they did not belong to the roster.

The event which Shakur described was a cultural event, but the Republic of New Afrika was more than just a cultural organization. The aim of the Republic of New Afrika was to establish an independent nation for African Americans. The Republic of New

Afrika was not focused on class struggle, although its members did not dismiss the significance of class struggle. Herman Ferguson stated: "Once we have established our national liberation, our national independence, at that time when we feel that we perhaps can become involved in a class struggle. But before then, it would be, to say the least, premature for us to talk in terms of a class struggle, especially when on the other side, among whites, there's still so much chaos and confusion, and we're clear as to what's happening." In the same interview, Ferguson also explained that "it seems to be extremely difficult" for white leftist groups to "completely free themselves of their white nationalism and accept our right to self-determination."

In the view of the Republic of New Afrika, African Americans are a colonized people. As such, the struggle of "New Afrikans" is akin to the anti-colonial struggles in Africa which were aimed at forming independent nations in Africa. The Republic of New Afrika desired to create an independent African nation in America. Herman Ferguson explained: "As long as we are a colonized people the colonizer can do anything with us and to us that he wants."

Robert Williams was elected as the president of the Republic of New Afrika while he was living in exile. Williams was a member of the NAACP who had been organized the black community in self-defense against white racism. Unlike Martin Luther King and other civil rights leaders, Williams openly supported violent self-defense in reaction to white violence. Williams' position resulted in the NAACP denouncing him for provoking racist violence. Williams was later forced to take refuge in Cuba after he had been charged with kidnapping a white couple. In reality, Williams had taken the couple to his house to protect them from an angry mob of black people who mistook the couple for being Ku Klux Klan supporters. In Cuba, Williams operated a radio program known as Radio Free Dixie. In Cuba, Williams came to know some of the members of the Communist Party, including Fidel Castro and Che Guevara.

Williams began to experience problems in Cuba. The *Workers Vanguard* reported that "Cuban officials began to obstruct his activities and demanded that they be allowed to censor his newsletter and radio program." There were ideology issues as well.

Williams was a professed nationalist, but he found that the Cubans were opposed to nationalism. Williams explained, "they had a black population in Cuba and they did not want these ideas to catch on among their people." Alberto Benvenuti explained: "Despite the fact that Williams maintained good relations with Castro and Guevara, many Cuban communists ostracized his work. The communists—who were gaining influence within the Cuban government as a consequence of the alliance between Cuba and the Soviet Union—feared that Williams, who was a non-communist black revolutionary, would inspire separatist sentiments among Afro-Cubans, in particular in the Oriente province, which had a numerous black population."

Williams explained that the view of the leaders in Cuba was that "the race issue in America is due to class oppression, that this class struggle, rather than racial struggle, and the Cubans maintained that—in fact, they insisted that the white workers are being exploited in the United States and the white workers, the working class, is a natural ally of the black people and that eventually the white workers will—the working class will unite with the black people and that they will bring about the necessary changes to improve conditions for all people including the black people." Williams was not convinced, however. Williams expressed the view that as long as white workers "have jobs and can buy automobiles and homes, they've no real reason to rise up against the capitalists. Only those like, like us Blacks, who are victims of severe economic discrimination and racism, have the motivation to want to overthrow the system." Williams also could not help but notice the racism in Cuba. When he went to Radio Havana, he noticed that all of the faces there were white. He found the same thing in the foreign ministry. Williams noted that some black Cubans were eventually brought into the foreign ministry, but the people they got were not qualified.

Williams left Cuba and went to China where he was supported by the Chinese government. At the time that Williams arrived in China, the Cultural Revolution was taking place. Williams later left China and spent some time in Tanzania before returning to the United States where he faced the kidnapping charge from which he fled eight years earlier. During his return to the United States, Williams was held up in Britain. The British government detained him and planned to fly him to Cairo. Williams refused and pressure from civil liberty groups forced the British government to abandon this plan. After returning to the United States, Williams left the Republic of New Afrika and severed all connections with the organization. The differences between Williams and the Republic of New Afrika were apparent after he returned to America. The *New York Times* reported during a speech which Williams delivered in front of members of the Republic of New Afrika that "Mr. Williams appeared, in some instances, to contradict the often strident militancy of some spokesmen for the republic."

The liberation movement in the United States came under attack from the American government. This attack was carried out by the Federal Bureau of Investigation (FBI), which aimed to neutralize black leaders across the country. It was within this environment that the Black Liberation Army emerged. The Black Liberation Army included individuals who were members of the Black Panther Party and the Republic of New Afrika. Assata Shakur, who was a member of this movement, explained: "The idea of a Black Liberation Army emerged from conditions in Black communities: conditions of poverty, indecent housing, massive unemployment, poor medical care, and inferior education. The idea came about because Black people are not free or equal in this country." She also explained that the Black Liberation Army was not an organization. She described it as "a concept, a people's movement, an idea."

Shakur was among the many activists of the 1960s who were targeted by the FBI. She faced numerous charges, including charges of kidnapping and bank robbery. Shakur was acquitted of those charges, though she was tried and convicted for killing a police officer. Shakur later escaped from prison and fled to Cuba where she has lived in exile. Shakur eventually made history by becoming the first woman to be listed on the FBI's most wanted list.

Mutulu Shakur was among the members of the Black Liberation Army who was arrested and tried for his activities. In his defense, Shakur attempted to argue that he was a prisoner of war and was immune from prosecution for the acts for which he was charged.

Shakur's counsel stated an intention to move to dismiss the indictment under international law. Marilyn Buck joined this motion as well. Buck was facing a conspiracy charge for her role in breaking Assata Shakur out of prison. The defendants also argued that they were immune from prosecution because the acts which were charged in the indictment were political in nature. On July 6, 1988, the United States District Court in New York ruled on the motion to dismiss the charges. The arguments which were put forward by Shakur were rejected by the court. Even so, the arguments do present an interesting insight into the Republic of New Afrika's ideology.

The defense expressed the view that Africans in the United States are a colonized people who have a right to self-determination. The defense stated: "As is the case with every colonial experience, the New Afrikan Nation as a colony has no independent economic structure. The vast majority of the population of New Afrika, however, has at all points in history been contained within the same imperialist economic structure, and has shared the misfortune of suffering discriminatory treatment within it. Indeed it is appropriate to say in the case of New Afrika, as in the case of most colonies, that New Afrikans as a National population are an underclass frozen at the bottom of the American economy."

The defense further asserted that as a colonized people who are engaged in a struggle for self-determination, New Afrikans are entitled to judicial recognition of the war-like nature of their struggle. The defendants here argued that a prisoner of war status exempted them from prosecution. This argument relied on the Geneva Convention Relative to the Protection of Prisoners of War and the first two protocols to the Geneva Conventions of 1949. As noted, the court rejected this argument. Nevertheless, these arguments display the Republic of New Afrika's view that New Afrikans are a colonized people engaged in a struggle for self-determination. As such, in the view of the Republic of New Afrika, any acts of violence committed by New Afrikans should be viewed as acts of war aimed at politically liberating New Afrikans from a colonial power.

Further Reading:

Alberto Benvenuti, "African American Radicals and Revolutionary Cuba from 1959 until the Black Power Years"

Assata: An Autobiography, 1988.

Testimony of Robert F. Williams, 1970.

United States v. Buck, 690 F. Supp. 1291 (S.D.N.Y. 1988).

Workers Vanguard, November 8. 1996 issue

24

THE SWAZI MONARCHY

The history of eSwatini (formerly Swaziland) is unique. In 1968, Swaziland succeeded in gaining independence from colonial rule as a sovereign monarchy. The constitution which was crafted was one which established a parliamentary government based on the Westminster model. Swaziland is a nation which has struggled to balance this mix of traditional monarchy with the Western parliamentary model. At times the monarchy clashed with the parliamentary model. This was demonstrated in 1973 when the constitution was suspended and opposition parties were banned.

The people of Swaziland live in abject poverty, as well as terror because the Swazi monarchy has utilized repressive methods to silence any form of criticism. The situation is such that wearing a t-shirt which displays the name of an opposition party is treated as an act of treason. Opposition parties have been banned and those who have dared to organize opposition parties have put themselves at risk. The People's United Democratic Movement (PUDEMO) is an example of this. PUDEMO became the largest opposition party in Swaziland. Members of this organization have been targeted by the government. Bheki Dlamini was among those who were targeted. On one occasion, his homestead was ransacked by the police. His mother was there during the raid. Dlamini was also arrested and beaten before being taken to prison. He spent almost four years in prison. During this time, he was tortured and nearly killed. The repression forced Dlamini into exile.

Even members of the royal family have been silenced for expressing views which displeased the king. In 2006, *Mail and Guardian* reported on a situation in which Princess Sikhanyiso was silenced for remarks which she made regarding polygamy. She reportedly told the media that polygamy was evil because it brought all of the advantages in a relationship to men. It was reported that King Mswati was not happy after listening to a recording of the interview. King Mswati himself has several wives and is known for engaging in the practice of taking a virgin to be his new wife on an annual basis. Princess Sikhanyiso is his oldest child by his first wife. Sikhanyiso reportedly directed her remarks about polygamy at some of her father's wives, a number of whom were annoyed by her remarks. In addition to the political repression, the people of Swaziland have also endured abject poverty. The conditions are made worse by a system of forced labor in which people are made to work for the king without pay.

In 2021, the Swazi people became so frustrated with the poverty and unemployment in the country that they organized mass protests against the government. There was also growing frustration at police brutality. One notable case of this was that of a university student named Thabani Nkomonye, who was killed by the police. Nkomonye's murder sparked demonstrations on the part of the youth. The monarchy responded to the protests by killing and torturing the protesters. Journalists were also reportedly arrested and beaten as part of the crackdown against the protesters. Some Swazis have fled to South Africa to find opportunities, but they have faced attacks from South Africans who complain that Swazis are taking their jobs.

Paradoxically, the monarchy in eSwatini is one which is too deeply rooted in tradition to allow for the type of modernization which the country needs, yet it is also a nation in which the influence of colonialism does appear to have impacted certain aspects of how the country is ruled. Despite being ruled by the traditional monarchy, the Swazi monarchy has deployed certain colonial institutions—such as prisons and a standing police force—to terrorize and suppress its citizens. Mswati decided to change the name of his country from Swaziland to eSwatini, which essentially means the same as Swaziland. This was done in an attempt to rid the country of the colonial legacy, but the reality is that he has not gone far enough to rid his nation of the colonial legacy because he continues to benefit from the state of eSwatini. King Mswati is known for living lavishly as his people struggle.

25

THE SHINING PATH IN PERU

Following the capture of Abimael Guzmán Reynoso, Kwame Ture sent a letter to express his support for Guzmán and the Shining Path organization which Guzmán led. Ture explained that he supported anyone who was fighting against capitalism, whether he agreed with them or not. The Shining Path was formed in 1980. Guzmán declared: "Our labour has ended, the armed struggle has begun…" With these words, the Shining Path declared an armed struggle to overthrow the government of Peru. The war would cost Peru more than 10 billion dollars in damages and thousands of lives.

To understand the roots of Shining Path, one must understand Peru's history of conflict and unrest which dates back to the colonial period. Much as with the rest of the Americas, the history of colonialism in Peru is steeped in violence and misery. Disease wiped out much of the indigenous population in Peru. Pedro de Cieza de Leon wrote that when the Spaniards conquered the area there were more than 25,000 men. He doubted that there were even as many as 5,000 left. It is estimated that millions were killed within a short span of time.

The conquest of the Inca empire was a gradual one. The Incas maintained the largest and most powerful state in pre-colonial Peru. The greatest expansion of the Inca state occurred under the rule of Pachacuti Inca Yupanqui. His son Topa Inca Yupanqui continued this expansion. The political and economic organization of the Inca state was described as follows: "Although displaying distinctly hierarchical and despotic features, Incan rule also exhibited an unusual measure of flexibility and paternalism. The basic local unit of society was the *ayllu*, which formed an endogamous nucleus of kinship groups who possessed collectively a specific, although often disconnected, territory. In the *ayllu*, grazing land was held in common (private property did not exist), whereas arable land was parceled out to families in proportion to

165

their size. Since self-sufficiency was the ideal of Andean society, family units claimed parcels of land in different ecological niches in the rugged Andean terrain."

The Spanish conquest of the Inca empire coincided with political instability within the empire itself. There was a five year civil war from 1528 until 1532 between two of the former emperor's sons, Huáscar and Atahualpa. They each inherited half of the empire, but fought for control of the whole empire. The Spaniards also benefited from the support of indigenous groups which allied with the Spaniards to fight the Incas. It took several decades for Inca resistance to finally be crushed. The remnants of the Inca empire resisted until 1572. Túpac Amaru, who was the last reigning Inca ruler, was captured and beheaded.

The establishment of Spanish colonial rule could not quell the rebellions. There were eleven uprisings in the 1750s, twenty in the 1760s, and twenty in the 1770s. The most notable of the rebellions from this century was in 1780. A wealthy mestizo descendant of Inca ancestors named José Gabriel Condorcanqui raised an army. He assumed the name of Túpac Amaru II, after the last Inca ruler. Túpac Amaru II was eventually captured and executed along with his relatives in 1781, but the rebellion was not suppressed until the following year.

Peru became independent in 1824 after Simón Bolívar invaded. Peru quickly fell into instability after independence. Independent Peru faced the problem of how to replace the prior colonial system. Bolívar attempted to implement a system of governance, but he was forced to relinquish power, which created a political vacuum. There were rebellions and fights for power, including civil wars in Peru. It was not until the 1840s that Peru was finally stabilized. This stability would not last long, however. Following another period of civil strife, General Andrés Avelina Cáceres managed to establish control. Cáceres was elected president in 1886 and moved to crush a rebellion in Sierra.

There was further unrest in the early part of the 1900s. Peru experienced violent strikes on sugar plantations in 1910. In 1918 and 1919, Peru then experienced a wave of strikes and labor mobilization which was joined by student unrest over university reform. There was political unrest as well. President Guillermo Billinghurst clashed with Congress in Peru. Congress initiated impeachment hearings against Billinghurst in 1914. Billinghurst responded by threatening to arm workers and dissolve Congress. During this political chaos, the armed forces under the leadership of Colonel Oscar Raimundo Benavides seized power.

The formation of the American Popular Revolutionary Alliance brought yet more unrest in Peru. The American Popular Revolutionary Alliance was formed by Haya de la Torre in 1924. This was an anti-imperialist, revolutionary organization which advocated for revolution on the part of the working class. Torre's party contested the election in 1931 and he was defeated. Torre claimed that the election was a fraudulent one. In 1932, the American Popular Revolutionary Alliance rose up in a violent rebellion in which sixty army officers were executed. The army responded by killing hundreds of members and supporters of the American Popular Revolutionary Alliance. This was carried out through aerial bombings.

This history provides some of the background for Peru during the colonial period and the period following colonialism. This was a period marked by violence and unrest. The political developments which resulted in the emergence of Shining Path began in the 1950s and 1960s. This was a period in which Peru experienced economic stagnation, as well as strikes and protests. In 1963, Fernando Belaúnde Terry became the president of Peru. Belaúnde's presidency saw a period of reforms which attempted to diffuse the unrest in the country. The reforms were not enough to prevent further unrest in Peru, however. In 1965, a guerrilla movement known as the Movement of the Revolutionary Left arose. Belaúnde decided to call on the army to put down the guerilla movement. The guerilla movement was defeated, but public discontent towards Belaúnde's government continued. This resulted in Belaúnde being overthrown by the military in 1986. General Velasco Alvarad took power.

Velasco moved to implement a reform program, which included transferring arable land and dismantling the export model of development. This was the first time in Peru's history that the state assumed a major role in the process of development. These reforms did not provide a lasting solution to Peru's problems, however. Peru was also amassing debt because Velasco had borrowed heavily. Poverty remained a problem in Peru as well. A study in 1970 concluded that half of the families in Peru were below the poverty line. On August 29, 1975, Velasco was replaced by Francisco Morales Bermúdez Cerrutti. By the 1970s, military rule in Peru was becoming unpopular. This forced Morales Bermúdez to prepare for a return to civilian government.

In 1980, an election was held in which Belaúnde was elected. In the 1980s, Peru was experiencing an economic collapse which reduced the quality of life of its citizenships. Infant mortality rose, life expectancy for men dropped, and 60 percent of children under the age of five were malnourished. It was during this period that Guzmán founded the Shining Path.

Shining Path was initially successful at seizing territory in the country. The police in the area were poorly armed and poorly trained. Shining Path also received support from the peasantry, which had grown tired of the corrupt authorities. The peasant support for Shining Path helped to portray the image of Shining Path as being a "peasant rebellion". Women also played a significant role in the Shining Path organization. By 1990, a third of the members were women. Eight of the nineteen slots in the Central Committee were filled with women.

A cult of personality was formed around Guzmán or "President Gonzalo." The ideology of Shining Path became "Marxist-Leninist-Mao Zedong-Gonzalo Thought." Hymns, poems, and oaths celebrated the greatness of "President Gonzalo." Shining Path propaganda proclaimed that Guzmán was the "Fourth Sword of Marxism" and the "world's greatest living Marxist-Leninist."

Shining Path not only terrorized authorities who represented the Peruvian government, but also peasants who were seen as collaborators with the government. In 1983, eighty peasants were slaughtered on the charge of collaborating with the government.

Orin Stran noted that Peruvian scholars have framed Shining Path as being in the tradition of Tupac Amaru II. This is not how Guzmán saw Shining Path, however. Shining Path was not an indigenous led organization. Stran noted that Shining Path merely echoed "the standard Peruvian association of wisdom and leadership with the white, the urban and the educated." The leadership of Shining Path consisted mostly of white professionals.

Grant further noted that the leadership of Shining Path looked to Marx, Lenin, and Mao for inspiration, not Túpac Amaru II or any other indigenous rebel in Peru's history. Whereas José Carlos Mariátegui argued that Incan ethics of collectivism could be the foundation of Peruvian socialism, Guzmán displayed a noticeable disinterest in Peru's history and culture. As one report on Peru's history noted, for intellectuals "from José Carlos Mariátegui to Luis Guillermo Lumbreras, the path to development has continued to call for some sort of return to the country's pre-Columbian past of communal values, autochthonous technology, and genius for production and organization." This was not Guzmán's vision.

The Túpac Amaru Revolutionary Movement emerged as a rival Marxist-Leninist rebel group in Peru. The Túpac Amaru Revolutionary Movement was more obviously influenced by Peru's own history than the Shining Path was. The Túpac Amaru Revolutionary Movement declared that the people of Peru "are heirs to a very ancient and glorious past." The movement praised the "glorious anticolonial struggle of Túpac Amaru in 1780" and other struggles in Peru's history.

Gordon H. McCormick noted that the Túpac Amaru Revolutionary Movement was much less successful than the Shining Path despite the Shining Path's "evident extremism and purported lack of natural popular appeal." The problem was, as McCormick explained, the Túpac Amaru Revolutionary Movement "has chosen to pursue short-term operational goals, usually designed to keep the group in the headlines, rather than look to the future and gradually build the grass roots organization necessary to pose a long-term institutional challenge to the standing political order." McCormick also described the Túpac Amaru Revolutionary Movement as being more of a terrorist organization than a true insurgency. The Túpac Amaru Revolutionary Movement was also plagued with internal divisions which further weakened the party.

The government of Peru responded to the Shining Path with a brutal campaign which resulted in human rights violations being committed against the civilian population. This only helped the Shining Path to gain more recruits. Belaúnde was denounced by internal human rights organizations, but he continued the bloody campaign against the Shining Path. The Shining Path was willing to match the brutal violence of the military. In Guzmán's view, violence was a necessary part of the revolution. He argued that "violence is a universal law" and that "without revolutionary violence one class cannot be substituted for another, an older cannot be overthrown to create a new one." Civilians bore the burden of this conflict. In 1984 and 1985, thousands were killed. It is estimated that in the 1980s, nearly 20,000 people were killed as the result of political violence in Peru. Peru also ranked as the country with the highest number of disappearances in the world.

Unlike Lenin and Mao, Guzmán would not succeed in seizing power. Peasants in Peru grew wary of the conflict and peasant militias against Shining Path began to emerge. The villagers in Peru formed an alliance with the military to oppose the Shining Path. Guzmán was eventually captured along with more than half of the Central Committee. Peru in the 1980s was in desperate need of a revolutionary change, but revolutionary movements such as the Shining Path and the Túpac Amaru Revolutionary Movement were not able to offer much of an alternative. The brutality of these movements, combined with the brutality of the Peruvian government, merely caused more hardship and suffering for the Peruvian masses.

Further Reading:

Gordon H. McCormick, "Sharp Dressed Men: Peru's Túpac Amaru Revolutionary Movement

Orin Stran, "Maoism in the Andes: The Communist Part of Peru-Shining Path and the Refusal of History"

Rex A. Hudson (editor), *Peru: A Country Study*, 1993.

26

A PAN-AFRICAN DISCOURSE

Eddie Wilson sits at a table in the corner of his favorite coffee shop, reading a newspaper. Millard Grant, who has just finished his breakfast and is on his way out, notices Eddie Wilson sitting at the table. He recognizes Eddie as a regular guest at John Walks' talk show, where Eddie and John have very contentious debates over racism in America. Millard decides to engage with Eddie on the topic of Pan-Africanism.

"Excuse me," Millard says, "I don't mean to bother you, but I recognize you. You are Eddie Wilson."

"Yes, I am," Eddie replies.

"I recognize you from John Walks' program. I'm a big supporter."

"Of John or me?"

"John, but I do think that some of your views are interesting. I want to ask you about this Pan-Africanism that you espouse."

"Sure."

"I have a hard time understanding why anyone would embrace a doctrine like this. It seems to me to be a racist doctrine."

"Racist?" Eddie replies with surprise.

"Yes. I think it is racist to advocate for unity based on skin color. I also don't think that it is practical."

"Why do you think that?"

"Africa is a very diverse place with so many tribes. It just seems impractical to suggest that all of these people should unite simply because they are black."

"The history of African people demonstrates the practicality of Pan-Africanism."

"How so?"

"Marcus Garvey's organization established branches all over the world. When I speak of Pan-Africanism, I am not speaking of some ideal. Pan-Africanism has always had a very practical function in the struggle of African people because we have always worked together and organized on an international level. This is just a historical fact. The tribal differences that you speak of in Africa does not negate the history of the Pan-African struggle. It merely confirms the need for Pan-African unity."

"I understand, but I just don't think that anyone should center their ideology around race. It's too arbitrary. I mean to say, how do you even determine who is African and who is not. Would my biracial daughter be excluded?"

"No. Historically biracial individuals have been part of the movement towards liberation of African people. Pan-Africanism has never been about biological purity."

"What about someone who is ninety percent white and ten percent black? Where would such an individual fit into your ideology?"

"My question would be would such an individual identify as an African?"

"That person would have African blood. I may even have African blood. Would I be part of your Pan-African ideology if I did have African ancestry from several generations ago?"

"You may, but you don't know, so you cannot claim what you don't know. Assuming that you did have African ancestry, what would change. You are already opposed to Pan-Africanism as it is. Would your worldview or your understanding of race change if you discovered some distant African ancestry? Would you then identify as black?"

"My point is that race is a social construct. It's not real."

"It is a social construct, but social constructs are real. This language that we are speaking in is a social construct, but it's also a very real way to convey our thoughts to each other. The money that we spent at this establishment today is a social construct, but it is also real for conducting financial transactions."

"Race is different though. There is no such thing as race. We are all humans. There is no meaningful difference between me as a white man and you as a black man. There is no inherent difference between us. There is no inherent difference between myself and my biracial child or my black wife."

"As humans we each have our own unique cultures. As a white American man your culture is not the same as an Arab from Syria. Would you admit that?"

"Yes, but what does that have to do with race?"

"You are thinking of race in biological terms. You are thinking that the difference between us is merely based on our different skin complexions or hair texture. What I am suggesting to you is that there are cultural differences as well. This isn't just white and black. It's deeper. Your biracial child may not see the world the same way that you do because she comes from a different experience. As a white man, you probably have never experienced the feeling of being split between two cultures, but this is something biracial individuals often deal with."

"But isn't such an interracial union offensive to your Pan-African ideology which promotes racial unity?"

"Your interracial union is between you and your spouse. That has nothing to do with me."

"But would you support it?"

"I support African unity and black love. I should ask if that is offensive to you?"

"It is not?"

"So then there is no problem."

"But you did not answer my question."

"About my views on interracial unity?"

"Yes."

"That's your business."

"What is the Pan-African view on this matter?"

"There is no Pan-African view on the matter. Different Pan-Africanists have had different views on this matter. Some prominent Pan-Africanists were even married to non-black women, such as Kwame Nkrumah and C.L.R. James."

"Is that offensive to you?"

"That was their business, not mine. In the case of Nkrumah, it was not a particularly happy marriage and he may have been better off marrying an African woman who shared his zeal for Pan-Africanism. The Bible says that a married couple cannot be unequally yoked."

"Can white and black people be equally yoked in marriage?"

"Well, if you have a happy marriage then you would already know the answer to that. You would know better than I."

"Here is what I am struggling with."

"Okay."

"Race is a social construct which Western society created. From what I understand, Africans had tribal divisions. Africans did not see themselves as being one large Pan-African race. This whole idea that Africans are all one race came from the European colonizers, who developed this view—which is a racist view—to oppress African people. Is Pan-Africanism not an acceptance of a Western racial hierarchy which classifies people based on this arbitrarily defined category of race?"

"That is your view. I would argue that Pan-Africanism is something that we as African people created. When Robert Campbell and Martin Delany went to Africa, they were welcomed as family. That had nothing to do with any Western notions of race. That was simply family reconnecting. Family is an important part of African culture. Again, you seem to have a hard time thinking of this outside of the biological concept of race, which is a Western construct that was designed to justify Western imperialism against the non-white people of the world."

"If family was so important, why did Africans sell their own people into slavery? Why all of the destructive tribal wars?"

"Typically, Africans sold other people, not their own people."

"Yes, because of the tribal divisions. How do you reconcile that with Pan-Africanism?"

"I don't think I have to."

"What do you mean? Why don't you?"

"Because Pan-Africanism is about the unity of African people. It is a rejection of the very tribal divisions that you are referring to."

"So it is not a glorification of history?"

"Not particularly. I think all people have made important contributions to the development of human civilization which we can be proud of, but I am not particularly interested in the glorification of the past simply for the sake of doing so."

"But in your writings and speeches you do glorify certain aspects of African cultures which you seem to believe are worthy of praise. I think you had even praised Mansa Musa as a great African emperor."

"That is correct."

"But he was also a slave owner. How do you justify praising a slave owner even as you have been so critical of George Washington and Thomas Jefferson for doing the same thing?"

"I don't think I have to defend or justify it."

"What do you mean?"

"Do you reject the Founding Fathers because they held slaves?"

"I certainly do not condone that aspect of their legacy."

"But you don't reject them."

"I can't. They are the men who created this nation. I don't condone them owning slaves, but I have to admire them as great statesmen."

"What I am getting at is that I'm developing an African-centered worldview. Just as white people can recognize George Washington or Thomas Jefferson as great statesmen, I don't think that there is any problem when I identify Mansa Musa as a great statesman for African people. That's not something that I feel the need to defend or justify, particularly because Mansa Musa did not conquer or colonize Europe. He was not a leader who attempted to create any type of racial supremacy over another group of people."

"But he created supremacy over his fellow Africans."

"That's history. Just about all civilizations have had their conquerors who built empires at the expense of the ones that were conquered."

"And if you can accept Africans conquering other Africans, why is it you think Europeans doing the same is different?"

"Because Europeans did not do the same. Europeans did not build empires in Africa. They underdeveloped Africa. They also engaged in very brutal violence. There's a difference between war which is carried out for the purpose of territorial expansion or resource acquisition for empire building, and outright torturing and massacring colonial subjects just to keep them colonized."

"I disagree. I think that all acts of aggression and violence are wrong."

"But you think that America was correct to invade after the attack on the World Trade Center?"

"Yes, but we are not talking about empire expansion. That was a case of self-defense."

"So then you don't think all acts of violence are wrong?"

"I do, but what I'm saying is that I don't think you can compare fighting terrorists who kill innocent people with slave owning warlords who were building empires. Colonialism and slavery were wrong when Europeans did it and I think it was also wrong with Africans do it."

"I don't disagree. I'm just pointing out that Europeans generally don't throw away their whole history because colonialism and slavery happened in the past. Many say, 'we can't judge the past by modern day understandings of human rights.' Isn't that the usual defense of the Founding Fathers?"

"Yes, but do you reject that defense?"

"No. I'm in favor of it. The difference is that—again, coming from an African-centered perspective—I look at the past from the perspective of African people. Africans who were enslaved in the United States at the time did not like being enslaved, so they resisted. George Washington's own slave fought against him in the Revolutionary War. Harriet Tubman knew that slavery was wrong for her, so she ran away. I am not applying a modern understanding of human rights to the past. I'm looking at the fact that oppressed Africans did not like being oppressed, so they did something about it."

"Would you extend that to Africa as well. Was slavery in Africa just as wrong because Africans during that time hated being enslaved? I am sure slaves in Africa were not happy about their conditions."

"Slavery in African societies was typically not as brutal as slavery in America."

"Is that not an attempt to rationalize slavery?"

"Africans themselves knew that there was a difference. Read David Walker's appeal. In his appeal he states that slavery in the United States was worse than how the Spartans treated the Helots. Again, this is about whose perspective we are looking at."

"Is it not true that the perspective from which you speak of African history is the perspective of the ruling elite? You seem to focus on the perspective of tribal kings who conquered and enslaved people."

"My friend Tony Baker makes the same complaint, but I am not a Marxist-Leninist. I do not view history solely through the lens of class struggle. As such, I am willing to admit that the ruling class in pre-colonial Africa was one which—although at times brutal and exploitative—was also capable of providing effective leadership and state management, which is something that African people are lacking today. I am interested in understanding nation management and nation development."

"John Walks who has been a consistent critic of yours has accused you of ignoring things like human sacrifice in Africa."

"And I have accused him of exaggerating practices such as this. Those things did happen, but he tries to give the impression that it was a standard practice across all of Africa. He is very selective with how he treats this history."

"And you are not?"

"I try not to be. I don't think it makes me less of a Pan-Africanist to point out that pre-colonial Africa was not a utopia before the white man—before your people, I could say—arrived. I just think that colonialism prevented Africa from further developing our societies in constructive ways."

"I just don't think that anybody should be a Pan-Africanist."

"Why?"

Millard pauses before he answers. "I don't know. I just don't like this idea of an ideology which promotes unity around race. It's arbitrary and seems a bit divisive."

"I think it is no more divisive than the existence of national identities. You don't find being an American to be divisive, do you?"

"No."

"Yet being an American separates you from a Mexican or a Canadian, with whom you share a border with."

"I think that's different."

"Different how?"

"Nationalities aren't as arbitrary. Americans are defined by citizenship and shared values."

"It's still a social construct."

"I get that, but I'm just struggling with this idea of an ideology which promotes racial unity. I just don't think that anybody should be a Pan-Africanist."

"And that is your right as a white man, but my belief is that

African people should define our own realities."

"Do you think that there are any good white people?"

"Certainly."

"Where do they fit in your Pan-Africanism?"

"They don't have to fit. Just as I don't have to fit into their particular social or cultural identity. If you believe in diversity then you would understand what I am saying. For too long, Africans have been conditioned to think we have to act like Europeans to be accepted by Europeans. We have our own cultural values and you have yours."

"But that is the very type of racial division that I am opposed to."

"So it's racial division because you are not entitled to be included in something that African people have defined? I don't want any part of defining your history or your culture for you. I can respect you as a white man and you can respect me as a black man."

"Why can't we just respect each other as human beings?"

"We can do that as well, but everyone is a human being. That's not what makes us unique or diverse."

Millard nods as he states, "Fair enough. I appreciate you taking the time to have this discussion with a white man like me."

"I'm willing to have a discussion with anybody. I'm not a racist, contrary to what my critics might have you believe. I'm not interested in alienating anybody or making enemies out of anybody. I believe that the good white people that you were asking me about are the type of white people who would understand what I am saying and not feel offended by it."

Millard gets up and shakes Eddie's hand before he departs, leaving Eddie to enjoy the rest of his now cool coffee.

BREAKDOWN PARTY: THE PSYCHE OF THE OPPRESSED

An oppressed and colonized people must understand that they must seize control of their own destiny by struggling to liberate themselves. Unfortunately, some colonized individuals seek to find ways to cope with their condition rather than striving to change their condition. Black Stalin depicted this situation in Trinidad in his song "Breakdown Party." In it, he depicts Trinidad as a nation in which all of the major industries across the country are breaking down, but Trinidadians are content with singing songs and drinking rum. Black Stalin depicts Trinidadians as being more preoccupied with shopping and partying than with managing the country. Black Stalin also points out that those who leave the country to study overseas either decide to sell their talents to other countries or they return to Trinidad to participate in the breakdown of the country.

Black Stalin frames this situation as one in which Trinidadians have no pride in their country to the point where they forget the lines to the national anthem. In "Breakdown Party," Black Stalin plans the conditions of the country on Eric Williams (or "Mr. Divider"). Indeed, the neo-colonial ruling class which Eric Williams represented is to be faulted for creating this feeling of empathy within the population, but, as stated before, a colonized people must seize control of their own destiny by resisting this feeling of empathy and by becoming directly engaged in producing the necessary change.

THE REVOLUTIONARY BLACK ATHLETE

Sports provide entertainment through competitive displays of skill. This is something which is consistent throughout different cultures around the world, including in African cultures. In South Africa, stick fighting is a form of competitive sport. African people in Trinidad also engage in a similar form of competitive stick fighting. Sports is more than just entertainment, however. Sports can be political as well.

There have been athletes who have used their position to make very public political statements. John Carlos and Tommie Smith very famously engaged in protests at the Olympics. At the Olympics, Feyisa Lilesa displayed the x sign, which was the symbol of resistance against the Ethiopian government's poor treatment of the Oromo people. Colin Kaepernick famously protested against racism in America by refusing to stand during the national anthem. Gwen Berry engaged in a similar type of protest when she turned her back on the American flag during the national anthem. These are all examples of ways in which athletes have used sports to make public political statements about injustices confronting a particular group of black people. For the athletes that have been named, athletics became more than just a competitive endeavor to make money. They recognized that they could use athletic competition as a means to make a political statement about the conditions of their people.

The role of the athlete is not an inherently revolutionary one, although the black athlete certainly can become a revolutionary. By revolutionary, I am referring to an individual who recognizes that the existing system which exploits and oppresses black people needs to be changed and is willing to contribute to the process of producing the type of change which is necessary. I have written about Muhammad Ali as an example of an athlete who came close to transcending the traditional role of the black athlete, but Ali ended up encountering many of the problems which hinder professional athletes. In the first place, Ali stayed in the sport longer than he should have. His fight with Larry Holmes was so one-sided that it had to be stopped. Holmes later stated that during his fight with Ali, he tried to avoid hurting Ali and kept asking the referee about stopping the match. Holmes was in tears after the match. Ali returned for one more fight. This was a loss against Trevor Berbick in 1981. Whereas Holmes attempted to avoid hurting Ali, Berbick brutalized Ali in the ring. Berbick had a reputation of being a bully. Berbick was later murdered in Jamaica. When asked about this, Holmes stated that he did not feel bad for Berbick.

Ali was also in poor financial shape after he retired. Ali had poorly managed his money, and this situation was made worse by the number of divorces that he had. Ali also ran into issues within the Nation of Islam. He was stripped of his name by Elijah Muhammad, who disapproved of the fact that Ali continued boxing in order to make money.

In my view, what made Ali unique as a professional athlete was his association with the Nation of Islam. Unlike Malcolm X, Ali never developed beyond the Nation of Islam's teachings. Ali actually did the opposite. Ali's politics regressed in the years after Elijah Muhammad's death, but it is still significant that Ali was a member of a religious organization which promoted black empowerment, black self-determination, and which openly denounced injustices. Ali was not acting as an individual. He was part of a larger movement. He was part of an organization.

Taking an individual stand against injustice is something which should be celebrated and applauded, but being part of a collective effort is certainly a more effective way to bring about change. The Nation of Islam is an organization which has its flaws and contradictions. I have dealt with the problems within the Nation of Islam in several other writings, so I shall not recount them here. What I will state, however, is that the Nation of Islam under the leadership of Elijah Muhammad was an organization which helped to transform the lives of its members.

Ali's membership within the Nation of Islam meant that there was a collective movement behind his efforts. He was not acting as an individual. The revolutionary black athlete should understand the significance of movement and organization building. Public protests are a great way to bring attention to an issue, but that is merely the first step in resolving the issue. There must be a collective effort aimed at producing change. Here is where the revolutionary black athlete can play a significant role, especially given that athletes are typically able to amass wealth that the average black person does not have access to.

For black people, for oppressed and colonized people, athletes are seen as heroic figures because of their athletic skill and their ability to beat the colonizers in sports. This is demonstrated by cricket in the Caribbean. Cricket is a sport of British origin, which means that it is the sport of the colonizers, yet for people in the Caribbean cricket was not only a form of entertainment, but an act of resistance and self-determination. In 1950, the West Indies cricket team defeated England at a test match. Lord Beginner celebrated this victory in his song "Victory Test Match." He sang:

> Yardley wasn't broken-hearted
> When the second innings started
> Jenkins was like a target
> Getting the first five in his basket
> But Gomez broke him down
> While Walcott licked them around
> He was not out for one-hundred and sixty-eight
> Leaving Yardley to contemplate
> The bowling was superfine
> Ramadhin and Valentine
>
> West Indies was feeling homely
> Their audience had them happy
> When Washbrook's century had ended
> West Indies voices all blended
> Hats went in the air
> They jumped and shouted without fear
> So at Lord's was the scenery
> Bound to go down in history
> After all was said and done
> Second Test and the West Indies won

The victory of the West Indies team at the cricket World Cup was such a significant occasion that Maestro celebrated it with a song titled "World Cup." In the song, Maestro sang:

We beat Sri Lanka, Pakistan, Australia, and New Zealand
Them Australian play with zest
To press the champions from the West
Kallicharan, Richards, Lloyd, Roberts and Julien
Australia say dey go kill West Indies
Sobers eh dey, we go flop
New Zealand say we getting licks like peas
Dey eating we like a pork chop
It was a fantasy to see
Tiny little Kalli
Hit Thommo and Lillee
Boundary after boundary
Right on
Right on top
We end up with World Cup

In these lines, Maestro was referring to Alvin Kalicharran's masterful performance against Dennis Lillee and Jeff Thompson. Cricket became a significant aspect of Caribbean culture. This is reflected in the music of the Caribbean. For example, the Mighty Spoilers' "Picking Sense from Nonsense," recounts a conversation about cricket which Spoiler overheard. He sings:

Then I heard this one up at Arouca
It was about the cricket in Australia
A fellow say, "the boys from the West Indies
Can play cricket like they eating bread and cheese"
Another fellow said he too feel they are the best
But he don't know how the France they lose all the tests

The impression given by Spoiler here is that the West Indies cricket team is so skilled that the expectation is that they should win their test matches. For some in the Caribbean, cricket came to encompass something much greater than the sport itself. David Rudder expressed his view in "Rally Around the West Indies," in which he compared the resiliency of the West Indies cricket team to the leaders of the Haitian Revolution:

when the Toussaints go
The Dessalines come
We've lost the battle
But will win the war

Rudder explained that this went beyond just cricket:

This is not just cricket
This goes beyond the boundary
It's up to you and me to make sure that they fail
Soon we'll have to take a side
Or be lost in the rubble

Given the conditions of black people, sports have represented more than just entertainment. For the athletes involved, sports have offered an opportunity to make money and to escape poverty. For spectators, sports offer a sort of symbolic victory over white racism and oppression. The black masses are in a sense able to live vicariously through the victories and the successes of athletes. Supporting one team against another team is one of the central appeals of athletic competitions, but the connection is even deeper for black people who have been oppressed. One of the reasons why Joe Louis was such a prominent figure among the black community in the United States was that he was a black boxer who defeated white opponents during a period of time when black Americans lived under racial segregation. His successes seem to represent the collective resilience of the race. West Indians viewed the success of their cricket team in a similar manner.

One problem is the fact that many successful athletes do not even see themselves as being representatives of the black community. An example of this is Tiger Woods. Woods became caught in a scandal in which his extramarital affairs were exposed. It turned out that Woods was not only married to a white woman, but all of his mistresses were white as well. When asked if the scandal would hurt Woods' marketability, Stephen A. Smith argued that it would not because Woods was not specifically marketing his products to the black community. Woods was someone who was so disconnected from the black community that he would not even identify as being black.

It is not enough to merely win an athletic contest. The revolutionary athlete must commit himself or herself to the advancement of African people. This means taking political positions, no matter how controversial those positions may be. It also means recognizing that athletic competitions are ultimately a form of competitive entertainment for spectators.

29

THE SHADOW

One important aspect of Shadow's legacy was that Shadow's music urged the people of the Caribbean to celebrate and embrace their own culture. Take for instance Shadow's song "Pay De Devil," which served as a tribute to the Tobagonian masquerader Abyssinia. In the opening verse, Shadow presents Abyssinia as a heroic figure who masqueraded as the devil during carnival time:

> Long ago in Tobago
> The Carnival wasn't so, no
> Was plenty jab jab and devil
> They came down to Les Couteaux
> They came from Culloden, horns on their head
> One name is Vixen, eyes always red
> One Abyssinia, a hero of man
> Portraying Lucifer with a fork in his hand

The jab jab or devil masqueraders which Shadow sings about are part of the Caribbean's carnival traditions. Hollis Liverpool gave the following description of jab jab masqueraders: "Africans displayed disguises such as the 'Devil' whereby they dressed in tattered clothes, painted themselves black or blue, and wore horns on their heads to symbolize Satan and all his works and pomps. At times, they poured molasses over their bodies (Jab Molassie) to indicate that, having produced it with their sweat, they were not paid for their labour." This is the tradition which Shadow was honoring by honoring Abyssinia.

In the second verse, Shadow gives the listener an image of what it was like when Abyssinia came into town during carnival. Shadow sang:

> The children begin to tremble
> Abyssinia coming down
> The crowd start to scatter

Place getting warm
Fall in the gutter
They don't care a damn
Man start to free up
Spirits are high
The crowd start to jump up
Like they learning to fly

In the final verse Shadow reminisces about his own experiences during this period:

I used to love the rhythm
When I hear dem coming down. Oh lord, oh
Oh, what a sweet vibration
I want to play the drums
But I can't find the drummer and I have to go now
To help my grandfather look after the cow
And I can't find a helper, not even a thief
And I can't find a butcher to turn them to beef

Obeah was yet another tradition which Shadow sang about. In his song "Whap Cocoyea," Shadow tells the story of a man who goes to the obeah man to get back his lover. In this song, Georgie goes to the obeah man to cure his "tabanka," which is a Caribbean Creole word which refers to the feeling of loving someone who does not love you back. Turning to obeah is one of the ways in which this feeling is dealt with in the Caribbean because it is believed that the obeah man can use his supernatural abilities to win over an individual's love. Shadow sang:

Me good partner lost his lover
He looking for obeah man
He want to get back his lover
He looking for obeah man
He went to Sangre Grande
He went up to Sans Souci
There he met a old Bad John

Who say he's a obeah man

In "Jumbies," Shadow tells the story of singing calypso in the middle of the night. Some jumbies overheard Shadow's melody and decided to join him. Shadow sings:

I was alone
Away from home
Quite in Toco
Making calypso
And in the middle of the night
Jumbies came out in the bright
They heard the melody
So they come to jump with me

The jumbies tie up Shadow and demand that he play more calypso for them, threatening to turn Shadow into a jumbie as well if he stopped playing. During the course of the song, Shadow is joined by his personal bodyguards from hell and later by Farrell, Shadow's bass man from hell. Shadow describes the scene as follows:

Then Mr. Farrell
My bassman from hell
He came with a bass
Trouble in the place
And when Farrell start to jam
Bass warm like tiger balm
I want to join them in the dance
But I trembling in me pants

Shadow also sang about the connection to Africa and the importance of unity among African people. In "Unite African," Shadow urged Africans who were dispersed throughout the Americas due to the slave trade to unite with each other, singing:

The ships came down
On the open sea
And brought us here

Into slavery
They send some here
And they send some there
Time for unity
With your family

In "Free South Africa," Shadow laments the plight of black people in South Africa and calls for the liberation of South Africa:

The devil in South Africa
He change his name to Botha, yeah
The devil and his followers
Distributing horrors
It's pressure down there
Pressure everywhere
The devil doing well
But the black man in hell

One of the challenges which the Caribbean faced following the period of decolonization was the lasting psychological impact of colonialism which has caused the people of the Caribbean to view their culture as being inferior to the culture of the European colonizers. Shadow was part of a generation of calypsonians who challenged this psychological colonialism by using his music to highlight and celebrate Caribbean culture, while also reminding his listeners about the importance of Pan-African unity.

30

ANCIENT RHYTHM: THE MIDDLE PASSAGE IN SONG

Music has been one of the ways in which Africans in the Diaspora have maintained their connection to Africa. Artists in the Diaspora have served as griots who remind African descendants of their historical connection to the African motherland. One example of this is "Nous Travay Pou Ayen" ("We Work For Nothing") by Exile One. This song recounts the hardships that Africans endured on the slave plantations after they were stolen from their homeland:

> There were forty of us
> Well chained in a small boat
> Day and night we were squeezed
> We crossed the ocean
> No question of seeing Africa again
> We are in captivity
> That is nothing that is fantastic
> We unloaded on a country that has sun
> Is a little bit like our home, but is not the same
> They greased me, they exposed me
> With pig fat and like a commodity
> They sold me
> I work for nothing
> They treated me worse than a dog
> I ask to whom did they sell my brother

Calypso Rose's song "Back to Africa" was composed in honor of her great-grandmother who was taken from Africa and enslaved in Tobago where she died. Calypso Rose intoned:

> Sitting on another man land, I only suffering
> Toiling up another man land
> I getting nothing

My culture, creed, and race
Wherever it was placed
I'm going to find it
Oh yes
I'm going to find it
Because I want to go
But the land too far
I want to go
And I begging Jah
Over yonder
Where there's many, many moons yonder
I want to go
Back to Africa

In her song "Ancient Rhythm," Singing Sandra proclaimed:

From across the continent that some once described as dark
Oh ho
I feel a vibration, feel a rhythm, feel a spark
Oh ho
When my spirit is feeling low, this natural mystic lifts me so
Like a bongo or Orisha drum, deep in the Congo calling me,
"Sandra, come!"

[…]

Now I'm free as a bird, liberty is the word
West Indian, Caribbean, African, Nubian queen
My skin they may spurn, with crosses they burn
No, I won't be denied, there is beating inside

I mention these three songs as examples, but there are many other examples of how artists in the Diaspora have used their music to remind listeners that the Middle Passage was an event which physically displaced African people, but it did not sever the cultural connection to Africa.

31

ON JILL STEIN AND THE GREEN PARTY

During the 2016 election campaign, I was one of two members from Speak Up Florida who were invited to speak at a Green Party campaign rally in Orlando, Florida. Jill Stein spoke at this rally as well. At the event, Jill Stein expressed her vision for America. She spoke about providing well-paying jobs for America and bailing students out of debt. She also spoke about renewable energy and police review boards so that the community can oversee the police.

I agreed with everything Jill Stein stated in theory, but in 2016 was also made to confront the reality of electoral politics in America, particularly what electoral politics means for black people. I will defend the right of the Green Party to exist and the right of people to vote for the Green Party. The two major parties are not entitled to support from the voters. This support must be earned through promoting policies which will improve the lives of their supporters. At the same time, I also recognize the challenges which confront third parties such as the Green Party. This became very apparent in 2016.

To be clear, the two individuals who were running for office were not great candidates at all. Hillary Clinton faced controversies such as switching her position on the TPP or violating protocol by using her own personal email address on a private server while she was serving as Secretary of State. Clinton had also infamously referred to young criminals as "super predators." This was viewed by some as racially charged language. When asked about using the term, Clinton stated that it was a poor choice of words and that she would not use the term again, but this was not enough to truly address the harmful impact of aggressive policing of black communities.

As bad as Clinton was, Donald Trump was even worse on racial matters. He openly supported stop-and-frisk, a controversial policy which was ruled to be unconstitutional in New York. Trump's campaign was also supported by Rudy Giuliani, the former mayor of New York. Giuliani proudly proclaimed that Trump would do for America what he had done for New York. This was something which concerned me. As the mayor of New York, Giuliani's tenure witnessed several high-profile incidents of police brutality against black people. This included the shooting deaths of Amadou Diallo and Patrick Dorismond. Dorismond was the brother of the artist known as Bigga Haitian. Bigga Haitian recorded a song to honor his slain brother. There was also the case of Abner Louima, who was brutally tortured by police officers in New York. All of this happened while Giuliana was mayor in New York.

The death of Diallo was an especially significant event because the officers were acquitted, which resulted in massive protests in New York. Al Sharpton held a rally in Harlem in which he claimed that they would fight for justice. Giuliana claimed that the police in New York needed to improve, but these remarks could not quell the anger that people felt over what had happened to Diallo. This is what Giuliani had done for New York and he was now proclaiming that Trump would do the same for America.

The principle upon which the Green Party stood was that Americans should vote for the greater good rather than the lesser evil, but the obvious concern was what if the greater evil was elected? In this situation, the greater evil would have been Trump. To be clear, Americans were suffering greatly during Obama's presidency and Clinton was not offering anything which appeared to be a radical improvement from Obama, but what Trump was offering could have potentially made life more difficult for black people in America and around the rest of the world.

In the end, Trump did win the 2016 election. The Green Party had little hope of winning, so their defeat was no great surprise. It also was no great surprise that during the campaign the Green Party was forced to confront this notion that the Greens are "spoilers" for the Democrats. I reject this notion. The Green Party is a legitimate party, although it may not have the same size and following as the Democratic and Republican Party. The issue for me is not so much that the Greens are spoilers, but that the Greens are powerless.

Trump was elected and the Green Party could only watch as Trump's administration engaged in policies which they opposed.

The Green Party's position on the migrant crisis especially caught my attention. The Green Party condemned the policy of separating families at the border and then locking those families up in cages. Would this crisis have happened if Clinton had been elected president? I doubt it. I am not suggesting Clinton would have supported comprehensive immigration reforms, but she also did not campaign on the claim that a large number of illegal immigrants were threatening the lives of peaceful citizens. Trump did campaign on this idea and the poor treatment of asylum seekers was the logical outgrowth of the very thing that Trump campaigned on.

In the American political system, there is very little space for third parties to operate. I admire what Jill Stein and the Green Party stood for in 2016, but I also think that the Green Party has not done enough to make itself a viable third option, especially among voters who are concerned that the outcome of a particular election could very well bring the greater evil into political power.

32

GANDHI'S RACISM

The relationship between Africans and Indians has been a very complex one. Both are non-white groups that have victims of European colonialism, yet this common experience of being oppressed under colonial domination has not truly created a sense of solidarity among the two groups. The relationship between the two has been marked by competition and in some instances violent confrontation. Mahatma Gandhi demonstrates the complexity of this relationship.

Gandhi was a leading anti-colonial figure in India. Gandhi was also an individual who was admired by African leaders who were also struggling against racism and colonial oppression. The Jamaican leader Marcus Garvey expressed his support for Gandhi's struggle in India and saw India's struggle for liberation as being connected to the global struggle for freedom on the part of the colonized dark-skinned races of the world. Martin Luther King was influenced by Gandhi's nonviolent philosophy.

Gandhi was a leading figure in India's struggle for independence, but he was largely indifferent towards the struggle of Africans in South Africa. What is worse is that Gandhi often accepted the racist stereotypes of African people as being a savage and uncivilized people. In an article titled "Was Gandhi a Racist?" Nishikant Kolge attempted to defend Gandhi against the charge of racism. Kolge admitted that it "is true that Gandhi never made an attempt to form an alliance with the blacks and he emphasised the Aryan connection of Indians to argue for equal treatment of British Indians in South Africa." This alone should disqualify Gandhi from being viewed as a heroic figure where African people are concerned, but there is more. As Kolge also admitted Gandhi's writings on Africans—whom he referred to as Kaffirs—were less than flattering. For example, Gandhi wrote: "Some Indians do have contacts with Kaffir women. I think such contacts are fraught with grave danger. Indians would do well to avoid them altogether."

There are more writings such as this, which Kolge acknowledged. Gandhi also wrote: "It was a gross injustice to seek to place Indians in the same class as the Kaffirs." He also expressed the view that "Kaffirs" are uncivilised: "Kaffirs as a rule are uncivilised—the convicts even more so. They are troublesome, very dirty and live almost like animals."

Kolge stated that it "is a basic tenet of the practice of writing history not to judge the past by present-day standards." This is true, but this is also hardly a defense of Gandhi, especially since Gandhi's conduct was the very thing that African leaders such as Robert Sobukwe and Anton Lembede complained about. They viewed Indians as a merchant class which was not concerned about the struggles which Africans in South Africa were engaged in. Kolge could not deny the reality of Gandhi's indifference to the struggles of African people, although Kolge does note that Gandhi did come to criticize certain colonial policies. In 1905, Gandhi complained about a proposed by-law in which every African, holding a cycle permit, was mandated to wear a numbered badge along with the permit.

By 1908, Gandhi had apparently also changed his views on segregation, writing that he did not object to Asiatic prisoners being classed with the natives. In 1910, Gandhi wrote that sincere well-wishers should welcome the rise of native leaders and that the more leaders Africans had would be better. That same year, Gandhi also sent a letter in which he stated: "I shuddered to read the account of the hardships that the Kaffirs had to suffer in the third-class carriages in the Cape and I wanted to experience the same hardships myself." In 1924, Gandhi wrote that "it is only vanity which makes us look upon the Negroes as savages. They are not the barbarians we imagine them to be."

The image which emerges here is one of a man who was beginning to express more sympathy towards Africans and a man who softened his views, although it is difficult to determine if Gandhi completely abandoned his prior racist views since Gandhi never explicitly repudiated those views in his writings. As Kolge noted, Gandhi's "writings seem to be contradictory rather than evolutionary." Kolge explained that in these writings we encounter two Gandhis, "one the visionary Gandhi who is cordial and respectful towards black Africans while writing about them and two, the narrow racial pleader Gandhi who appears to be frankly racist."

Kolge argued that Gandhi's remarks "should be taken as part of his political strategy rather than a byproduct of his racist outlook." The political strategy was to argue for civil rights for Indians in South Africa. In defense of Gandhi, Kolge quoted Nelson Mandela, who stated that "all in all, Gandhi must be forgiven those prejudices and judged in the context of time and the circumstances." Indeed, Mandela was a forgiving individual, but forgiving Gandhi for the racist remarks which he made does not negate the fact Gandhi's remarks demonstrate the very reason why tensions existed among Indians and Africans in South Africa.

33

THINGS FALL APART: THE FRAGILE NATURE OF AFRICAN STATES

In 1966, Nigeria experienced an incident in which Prime Minister Abubakar Tafawa Balewa was executed. This was part of an attempt to organize a revolution in Nigeria. The attack was led by Major Chukwuma Nzeogwu. Nzeogwu declared martial law over the northern provinces of Nigeria and decreed the death penalty for corruption. General Johnson Ironsi seized power through the chaos caused by the coup. This event signaled the beginning of years of political instability and ethnic strife in Nigeria.

There was some suspicion in the North over the motives of the coup. Most of the participants in the coup were Igbo (Ibo) officers and no Igbo politicians had been killed. Northerners saw the coup as an attempt by the Igbo people to gain control in Nigeria. General Ironsi made matters worse when he declared a new constitution. With Decree number 34, he abolished the federation and declared Nigeria to be a united state. Those in the North reacted by staging protests which targeted the Igbos. Ironsi himself was killed in a counter-coup which was led by Northern officers. Igbo people were targeted as well, with several hundred Igbos being killed.

During the chaos, Yakubu Gowon seized power and rescinded Decree number 34. Lieutenant Colonel Emeka Ojukwu refused to accept Gowon's position as supreme commander, however. Ojukwu favored the creation of an independent Igbo state known as Biafra. To rally support for the cause, Ojukwu played on the fear of genocide by warning that worse violence was to come.

There were ethnic tensions in the East. Minority groups such as the Ibibio, Ijaw, and Efik resented the influence which the Igbo people held in the region and had even campaigned for their own separate states. These groups were also targeted in the attacks against the Igbo people. These groups were not enthusiastic about secession, since this would leave them under Igbo control. Ojukwu continued with his plans for secession, however. He declared

Biafra to be an independent state in Nigeria, which resulted in a civil war to keep the nation together.

The civil war lasted two and half years. Biafra was poorly equipped for waging a war, but Ojukwu continued with his plan anyway. Martin Meredith noted that "despite the appalling suffering of Biafra's population, Ojukwu doggedly held fast to the notion of independence, spurning all attempts at international mediation." Ojukwu was eventually forced to recognize that he was fighting a losing battle. Biafra surrendered in 1970 and Ojukwu went into exile.

The Nigerian musician Fela Kuti did not like the war and supported the right of the Igbo people to secede from Nigeria. He stated: "I thought the Nigerian government was wrong. I thought the Biafrans were right. The Yoruba are not Ibo. I thought the Ibos were right." Kuti added: "From secession we could come together again. But by not seceding, we're put together *by force*." Kuti's point here is a profound one. He believed in African unity, but he did not believe that it should be forced. He supported the right of the Igbo people to secede from Nigeria, with the understanding that such secession may lead to a more constructive form of unity instead of forcing the various ethnic groups to live together. Similar issues emerged in Côte d'Ivoire, which has also experienced secession efforts and civil war.

There was no centralized state which controlled the territory which would become Côte d'Ivoire. Instead, there were several different states, such as the Kong Empire which was a Muslim kingdom. The Kong Kingdom was a center of agriculture, trade and crafts. The city of Kong was eventually destroyed by Samori Touré in 1895. There was also the Abron kingdom which was established by the Abron Akan who fled the Asante confederation. Other Akan groups which were fleeing the Asante established kingdoms as well, including two Agni kingdoms and Sanwi. Boubacar N'Diaye, Sonja Theron and Nayanka Perdigao identified six main political formations in pre-colonial Côte d'Ivoire. These were the Malinke Empire of Samori Touré; the Kong Kingdom; the Agni-Ashanti Kingdoms of Bondoukou, Indenie, and Krindjbo; and the Sakasso Kingdom. N'Diaye, Theron, and Perdigao explained that "these were autonomous and evolving at their own pace when that natural evolution was cut short, often violently, by colonial superimposition of foreign political, military, and cultural rule. This superimposition of alien agendas and methods was to have serious damaging consequences for the state building conversations that were to emerge over time."

Côte d'Ivoire became an independent state in 1960 under the leadership of Felix Houphouët-Boigny. Not everyone acknowledged the authority of this new state. The Agni of Sanwi attempted to secede from Côte d'Ivoire to create an independent kingdom, claiming that the kingdom had become part of Côte d'Ivoire without the consent of the Sanwi people. The Sanwi king led a separatist revolt in 1969, but the rebellion was swiftly suppressed by the military. This was a clear rejection of the borders which the Europeans had created and an attempt to bring about the restoration of a pre-colonial state. This was not the only rebellion which Houphouët-Boigny confronted. In 1970, a Bété leader, Gnagbé Niabé (also known as Gnabé Opadjelé) proclaimed himself grand chancellor of Côte d'Ivoire. He also led a rebellion which was suppressed by the military.

Côte d'Ivoire was held together by an autocratic one-party state led by Houphouët-Boigny. The death of Houphouët-Boigny was the first in a series of events which would lead to political instability in Côte d'Ivoire. Henri Konan Bédié became the next president of the country, but he was overthrown in a coup in 1999. A new government of national unity was formed and open elections were promised. A new constitution was formed. This constitution stipulated that anyone who wished to run for president must be born in Côte d'Ivoire. It was believed that this was implemented to bar Alassane Dramane Ouattara from running for president. Ouattara had previously served as the prime minister of the nation.

Laurent Gbagbo won a contentious election in 2000. By the next year there was a coup attempt. In response to the attempted coup, government security forces raided shantytowns searching for weapons and rebels. In the process, a number of the shantytowns were destroyed, which displaced more than 12,000 people. The instability in the country led to a rebellion which divided the country in two. Rebel movements came to control the northern half of the country.

There was a short-lived period of peace after the civil war, but this was followed by yet another conflict in 2010 when an election was held. This election was contested by Laurent Gbagbo and Alassane Ouattara. The results showed that Ouattara won the election, but Gbagbo refused to step down as president. This led to a violent clash between the supporters of Ouattara and Gbagbo. Hundreds were killed in the fighting, including children and pregnant women. After months of fighting, Gbagbo was arrested and Ouattara became the new president.

Colonialism disrupted local development in Africa by creating nation-states which were imposed on those who were colonised. This problem has been worsened by the political elite which has not only been authoritarian and corrupt, but has also fueled ethnic tensions for their own purposes. Independent African nations have generally been very hostile towards secession movements, but perhaps Fela Kuti was correct when he expressed the view that ethnic groups should not be made to live together by force. This is not to suggest that secession itself is necessarily an answer to the problem, but having different ethnic groups feeling forced to live within a nation which was created by European colonialism has not been an ideal situation either. Nigeria and Côte d'Ivoire offer two examples of how difficult it has been for post-colonial African nations to hold together the entities which the colonisers created.

References:

Boubacar N'Diaye, Sonja Theron and Nayanka Perdigao, "Reframing Narratives of Statebuilding and Peacebuilding in Africa"

Martin Meredith, *Fate of Africa*

Raisa Simola "The Construction of a Nigerian Nationalist and Feminist, Funmilayo Ransome-Kuti," *Nordic Journal of African Studies* 8(1): 94-114 (1999).

Robert E. Handloff (editor), *Côte d'Ivoire: A Country Study*, Washington: GPO for the Library of Congress, 1991.

34

THE FALLACY OF NOT SEEING COLOR

A black man named Corey Jones was shot and killed by a police officer as he was waiting for a tow truck to arrive. What was notable about this particular situation was the response from Jones' brother, Clinton Jones. In a press conference, Jones' brother proceeded to tell the audience that his brother's killing was not "a black thing." He stated that "all lives matter." Most curiously was that he insisted that he and his brother did not see color. He then continued to introduce his wife to the audience, letting the audience know that his wife is white. If he did not see color, how is it that he could easily see that his wife was white? Clearly, Jones could see color. Perhaps more significantly is the fact that not seeing color did not protect his brother from being killed by the police.

The problem with this colorblind approach is that it is very disingenuous. Humans have different skin colors and complexions, and there is nothing wrong with recognizing this. Jones saw color. He saw that his wife was white. If he was being more honest, he would have stated that he did not want to see color because he did not want to deal with the world as it is. He did not want to confront the racism of the world. He did not want to recognize the reality of a society in which an unarmed black people can be shot down by the police.

The colorblind approach fails to address the actual problem of racism itself. The problem of racism is not simply a problem of color, for race itself is more than an individual's color. Race is a social construct which encompasses a person's physical appearance, as well as cultural traits. This is why one aspect of European colonialism has been to impose European culture on African people. The justification for the oppression of African people is not that our dark skin makes us inferior, but that we are an inferior people because of our culture. The European slave masters and colonizers portrayed Africans as a savage and heathen people who lacked civilization. This is why the struggle over cultural identity has been a very important aspect of the global African liberation struggle. Racism is not merely about color, although color is certainly a major feature of racial exploitation and domination.

Those who only understand racism and race in terms of color often fool themselves into believing that somehow not seeing color is a virtue, although, as Clinton Jones demonstrated, those who claim that they do not see color are actually perfectly capable of seeing color. The reality is that such individuals see color, but they pretend not to see racism. This is why Clinton Jones could insist that all lives matter. Clearly Corey Jones' life did not matter to the police officer who killed him. Not seeing color was not enough to save his life.

35

JOHN HENRIK CLARKE: THE LIFE OF A PAN-AFRICAN HISTORIAN

The history of Pan-Africanism is the history of how interconnected the struggles of African people around the world have been. We are a people who have been forcibly separated due to historical events such as the Trans-Atlantic slave trade which stole millions of Africans from their homelands and colonialism which drew up borders in Africa which separated members of the same ethnic group. Pan-Africanism as a movement has largely been aimed at unifying African people beyond the national identities which were imposed on us via slavery and colonialism.

The Pan-African movement is not merely a movement that promotes a sense of abstract unity among African people. Rather, the movement has been rooted in the self-activity of African people around the world. This can be demonstrated in the life of John Henrik Clarke, who was a proponent Pan-Africanist.

John Henrik Clarke was a historian and a teacher. Clarke lived and experienced much of the Pan-African history which he wrote about. Clarke was born on January 1, 1915. He described his parents as being poor landless peasants. Clarke explained that his father dreamed of owning land, but he never lived to accomplish this dream. Clarke explained that the only free land his father ever knew was the grave in which he was buried.

Clarke's early interest in history came from his great-grandmother, who was known as Mom Mary. Mary had witnessed the last set of slaves who arrived directly from Africa. She recalled that they had a hard time learning the English language. Mary's husband was sold to a slave-breeding farm in Virginia. After slavery was abolished, Mary went to Virginia to try to find him, but she was unsuccessful.

Clarke explained that he experienced colorism while he was in school. The light-skinned children would not let him participate in the program during the school assembly. Clarke began to organize against the light-skinned children. He organized what he called the

"Black Brigade."

At a young age, Clarke began having questions about the role of African people in history. He learned to teach junior class in Sunday school. He could not find any images of his own people in the Bible. Clarke had been told by his great-grandmother that everything in the Bible was true and should not be questioned, which placed him in a dilemma. He loved his great-grandmother and did not want to be in conflict with her, but he also could not find his people in the Bible.

There was another experience which shaped Clarke's interest in history. Clarke explained that his teacher was special to him, so he wanted to do something for her. He wanted to speak on the history of African people in ancient times. Clarke went to a white man that he worked for. This white man had a library, but Clarke explained that he never saw the white man read any of the books in the library. One day, Clarke asked for a book on African people in early world history. The white man told Clarke, "I'm sorry John, but I don't have such a book. You came from a people who have no history."

Clarke left home at the age of fourteen. He lived in Georgia until he was eighteen. Clarke explained that there were lynchings every year in Georgia. This encouraged him to leave. Clarke decided to go North. He was inspired to do so by the stories he heard from a comedian called Sloppy Henry. Clarke explained that Henry was the best-dressed man in town, so to ridicule him he was called Sloppy Henry. Sloppy Henry told Clarke about his adventures in New York. Clarke would later learn that much of what Sloppy Henry told him was a lie, but those stories made Clarke dream and hope. Clarke eventually did move to New York.

One day, while doing chores at a high school, Clarke came across a book called *The New Negro*. In that book was an essay titled "The Negro Digs Up His Past" by a Puerto Rican author named Arthur Schomburg. That essay began with the following sentence: "The American Negro must remake his past in order to make his future." In the essay, Schomburg spoke of the importance of understanding the history of African people. Schomburg explained that "as the study of the Negro's past has come out of the vagaries of rhetoric and propaganda and become systematic and scientific, three outstanding conclusions have been established". The first conclusion is that "the Negro has been throughout the centuries of controversy an active collaborator, and often a pioneer, in the struggle for his own freedom and advancement." Second is that "Negroes of attainment and genius have been unfairly disassociated from the group, and group credit lost accordingly." Third was that the racial origins of the Negro "are of vital and general interest because of their bearing upon the beginning and early development of culture." Schomburg ended the essay by writing: "Already the Negro sees himself against a reclaimed background, in a perspective that will give pride and self-respect ample scope, and make history yield for him the same values that the treasured past of any people affords."

Clarke described reading "The Negro Digs Up His Past" as a key moment in his life. It was at that moment that he decided that black people did have a history. Reading Schomburg's essay was the first time that Clarke read anything on the history of African people.

Clarke would eventually meet Schomburg. Clarke explained: "He taught me the comparative approach to history. How to compare Afrikan history with other history. He taught me to read European history. He said by doing that, 'You're going to understand Afrikan history better. The more world history you know, the better. You can put Afrika into proper focus if you have a good knowledge of world history.'"

Clarke arrived in New York in the 1930s and participated in the youth group of Marcus Garvey's movement. Clarke recalled that Garvey would send his papers and messages from London, where Garvey was living at the time. Clarke explained that Garvey's supporters would wait by the boat to come in to receive copies of the *Black Man Magazine*. Clarke explained that Garvey did not send a lot of copies to the United States and the Garveyite group that he was involved in would buy up all of the copies before it ever got to the newsstand.

In Clarke's view, the three greatest Pan-Africanists were the Trinidadians: Henry Sylvester Williams, George Padmore, and C.L.R. James. Clarke never met Williams, but he did know Padmore and James. Clarke described James as a friend and a colleague. Despite praising them as great Pan-Africanists, Clarke did note a particular contradiction among the three men. All three of them had children with a black woman that they did not marry and that none of the three had established a long relationship with a black woman. Clarke confronted Padmore about this, asking Padmore where was his Pan-Africanism when the door is closed and the bed is ready. Padmore told Clarke to stop meddling in his personal business.

John Henrik Clarke also developed a friendship with Pan-Africanists such as Malcolm X and Walter Rodney. Clarke explained: "Malcolm had a shadow non-Muslim cabinet, and that was his great strength. People who were not Muslims, and were not even involved in the politics of being Muslim. People who would furnish him with basic information. The idea was that Malcolm must never be caught wrong, no matter what you did with the facts, make sure you get your facts straight." Clarke was the one responsible for providing Malcolm with information about history. Clarke stated that he placed Malcolm over Martin Luther King in "in the long range significance of leadership." In Clarke's view, King had a dream, but he did not have a plan.

Clarke described Rodney as being a "beautiful friend", although he noted that the two disagreed on whether or not Marxism was applicable to African people. Clarke considered himself to be a socialist, but he did not follow Marxism. Clarke explained: "When I say socialism, I'm just not talking about what Karl Marx was talking about. I was not following the European invention of socialism."

Clarke also considered himself to be a nationalist and he was unapologetic about his position. This came up in a debate between Clarke and Cornel West. West raised a point about peoplehood versus nationhood. West expressed the view that people of African descent are a distinct people, but that nationhood thought does not necessarily follow from distinct peoplehood. Clarke simply responded with, "You wouldn't say that to an Israeli." Clarke was not particularly fond of Cornel West. He explained that black conservatives such as West, Skip Gates, and others "are no different from the Afrikans who participated in delivering the Afrikans to the beach, to be put on the boat to become slaves. They're the new slave traders."

Clarke's own personal travel also reinforced this global connection among African people. He spent some time in Ghana in 1958. There he observed a wake among the Ga people. He noticed that the widow was cared for and supported throughout the grieving process. He explained that whenever she cried, there were mourners who cried with her. Her house was also cleaned for her. Clarke explained that he's seen the same traditions in Alabama, Georgia, and New Orleans.

In Cuba, Clarke observed that the Yoruba culture was very predominant. He explained: "I visited Cuba in the early 1960s, and there were still Afrikans in the Sierra Maestra who had not gone to Havana. Havana was maybe two and a half hours away by a fast moving train. Yet, they were obviously Yorubas. They still spoke Yoruba. They still ate Yoruba type food and engaged in Yoruba type ceremonies."

Clarke traveled throughout the African world, meeting and working with some of the most prominent Pan-Africa figures of his day. His passion for Pan-Africanism was something which Clarke taught in his classroom. He explained that on one occasion he noticed that his African, African American, and Caribbean students were arguing among themselves. To settle this argument, Clarke selected some of his students to try to get a taxi cab. He asked them to count how many cabs passed by before one stopped to pick them up. On average, twenty-one cabs passed by before one stopped. Clarke's message to his students was that they are all African people in the eyes of bigoted cab drivers. His message to his students that they are one African family.

36

THE ROLE OF IDEOLOGY IN SHAPING NORTH KOREA

In 2002, President George W. Bush declared that North Korea was part of the "Axis of Evil" along with Iraq and Iran. This speech was a very clear public indication of Bush's aggressive policy towards North Korea. Bush's remark came weeks before a scheduled trip to South Korea where Bush would meet with President Kim Dae-jung. Bush's objective was to get South Korea to adopt a more confrontational policy regarding North Korea. The policy pursued by President Bush placed a strain on America's relationship with South Korea. When Bush visited South Korea in 2002, Kim Dae-jung reminded Bush that the South Korean people would pay the price if the Korean War resumed. South Korea opposed America's pursuit of regime change in North Korea.

The Bush administration was also concerned with preventing North Korea from developing nuclear weapons. North Korea became concerned that the Bush administration was working to destroy its government. This in fact was the objective of the administration, as admitted by John Bolt who slapped a book titled *The End of North Korea* on a table. "That," Bolton explained, "is our policy." This policy only emboldened the regime in North Korea which expanded its nuclear arsenal during Bush's presidency. In 2003, North Korea expressed a willingness to halt its nuclear weapons program if the United States agreed to sign a non-aggression treaty, but this proposal was rejected by the United States.

North Korea would have a similarly tense relationship with Bush's successor, Barack Obama. The tension between the two nations was demonstrated by an incident involving a movie titled *The Interview*. The movie was a parody film produced by Sony which depicted the assassination of North Korea's leader, Kim Jong-un. The government of North Korea was not pleased by this film. North Korea sent a letter to the United Nations which described the film as an "act of war". There was some consternation about the film within Sony, but Sony decided to move ahead with releasing the film.

North Korea responded by launching a cyberattack against Sony. The attack was carried out via phishing emails which were sent to employees at Sony. The attackers established phony websites to harvest credentials which allowed them to gain access to Sony's systems. The attack was carried out by a group calling themselves the Guardians of Peace. This group not only managed to hack its way into Sony's system, but they also exfiltrated Sony's protected contact. Some of this information—which included unreleased movies and scripts, as well as social security numbers and employee medical records—was leaked publicly. The attackers did more than steal data. After the data had been exfiltrated, the attackers modified Sony's computers and servers. This included corrupting the system's disk drivers by removing low-level information needed for booting up. Michael Lynton explained: "The folks who did this didn't just steal practically everything from the house; they burned the house down."

The Guardians of Peace demanded that theaters pull the film and suggested that theaters that refused to do so should "remember the 11th of September 2001." Theaters did begin pulling the movie. President Obama publicly stated that the American government was able to confirm that the attack was carried out by North Korea. This was followed by sanctions against North Korea. Critics argued that the sanctions were ineffective and weakly implemented. North Korea also experienced the internet going down for eight hours. The American government did not admit any involvement in North Korea's internet going down, though there was speculation that this was a denial-of-service attack by the American government as a form of retaliation.

From the American perspective, North Korea is part of what Bush called the "Axis of Evil." North Korea is a nation which has been run by a brutal and oppressive dictatorship. North Korea has been described as "a failing Stalinist dictatorship held together only by the ruthless repression of a mad ruler who dreams of firing nuclear weapons at Los Angeles." American foreign policy towards North Korea is one which has generally viewed North

Korea as a threat to be isolated and eliminated. It is true that the regime in North Korea has been a brutal one centered around a dynastic personality cult which has sanctioned human rights abuses, such as kidnapping Japanese citizens. Even so, the American depictions of North Korea have tended to overlook how North Korea's historical experiences and its ideology has shaped both North Korea's domestic policies and its relationship with the rest of the world.

In the first place, one must understand the history of how foreign powers have shaped the politics of Korea. Grace Lee provided a short summary: "Strategically located at a peninsular tip of the East Asian continent, Korea has long been a pawn of contention between its two powerful neighbors, China and Japan. From the earliest recorded history, the Korean people have fought fiercely to maintain their independence in the face of multiple invasions by Mongols, Manchurians, Han Chinese and Japanese pirates and samurais. The sum total of these invasions may qualify Korea as the most oft-invaded territory in the world. Under the Yi Dynasty, which ruled Korea from 1392 until the Japanese annexation in 1910, Korea became a highly defensive state with a foreign policy of isolation towards the outside world. When Kim Il Sung came to power in North Korea in 1945, he arguably reverted to the highly isolationist policies of pre-modern Korea."

North Korea was founded by Kim Il Jung. Kim Il Sung promoted an ideology known as Chuche (or Juche). This was an ideology which was rooted in Korean culture and ideas, such as Confucianism. Kim Il Sung had described the ideology as follows: "Establishing *juche* means, in a nutshell, being the master of revolution and reconstruction in one's own country. This means holding fast to an independent position, rejecting dependence on others, using one's own brains, believing in one's own strength, displaying the revolutionary spirit of self-reliance, and thus solving one's own problems for oneself on one's own responsibility under all circumstances."

Chuche is an ideology which promotes the idea that the Korean masses are the masters of their country's development. As such, Chuche promoted self-reliance. A curious contradiction of the regime in North Korea is that Kim Il Sung promoted self-reliance, even though the North Korean government was heavily dependent on aid from other socialist countries. This aid was not officially recognized, however.

A report from the Embassy of Hungary in North Korea to the Hungarian Foreign Ministry noted: "Comrade Puzanov said that the Soviet Union does not need constant expressions of gratitude for its help, but the Korean comrades are displaying too 'modest' behavior concerning the assistance, and they try to hush it up." The report noted that Kim Il Sung personally requested assistance with his Five-year plan. Such aid to North Korea was considered important not only because of what it "can mean for the development of a previously backward and colonial country," but also because of the achievements which resulted from the American aid to South Korea.

The same report from the Embassy of Hungary also noted that North Korea's attempt to conceal the aid would ultimately be unsuccessful, stating: "It could be that they wish to emphasize to South Korea the independence of the DPRK in all respects, or that they have some other ideas. Comrade Kohousek remarked that any bourgeois economist can easily calculate that the DPRK was unable to reach its achievements on its own, and it is similarly unable to provide the economic aid it recently offered to South Korea from its own resources. In his opinion, the Korean comrades will achieve just the opposite with this, and their proposals can be more easily labeled 'Communist propaganda.'"

In the 1990s, it became undeniable that North Korea's economy was dependent on foreign support. It was expected that the collapse of the Soviet Union would result in a collapse of the regime in North Korea. This was not the case, though the fall of the Soviet Union did result in North Korea suffering a devastating economic blow. The Soviet Union had subsidized organizations which traded with North Korea, but this policy changed in the 1990s when Russia demanded that North Korea pay international market prices for Russian goods and services. China adopted a similar policy toward North Korea as well.

The economic disaster impacted agriculture in North Korea. North Korea's agriculture was heavily dependent on cheap oil and spare parts from the Soviet Union to run electric pump irrigation systems. Without the Soviet aid, North Korea faced an energy crisis which reduced agricultural production. The energy crisis combined with floods led to a famine in the country. The precise number of those killed is not known, though it is estimated that the number of those killed ranges from 500,000 to 3 million.

The economic collapse has led to other issues as well, such as the rapid increase of corruption in North Korea in the 1990s. Prior to the 1990s, strict regulations made private business impossible since items such as apartments and cars could not be purchased with cash, but these restrictions were no longer enforced. This led to officials taking bribes. In some cases, low ranking officials faced starvation themselves.

The economic hardships which North Korea experienced following the fall of the Soviet Union clearly demonstrated why self-reliance was necessary. Self-reliance was something which Kim Il Sung promoted, but which he was not able to successfully achieve for North Korea.

North Korea relied heavily on aid from socialist nations and had presented itself as a socialist nation, although following the economic struggles which North Korea faced in the 1990s, the limits of socialism in North Korea had been clearly exposed as Andrei Lankov explained: "The commonly held notion of North Korea as the only remaining Communist (or Stalinist or socialist) dictatorship on the planet is largely outdated. At the moment, North Korea looks like a poorly developed market economy characterized by extensive government intervention and heavy but inconsistent regulation."

North Korea described Chuche as Kim Il Sung's application of Marxist-Leninist principles to the political realities in North Korea, but there is certainly more to Chuche than this. After all, despite the fact that North Korea is officially known as the Democratic Republic of Korea, there is little that is democratic about it. Kim Il Sung established a family dynasty, which is quite unusual for a Marxist-Leninist state, especially considering that family dynasties were an aspect of the previous feudal Choson Dynasty which ruled Korea. Nicolas Levi explained that even "after the demise of the 500-year Choson Kingdom in 1910, North Korea still adheres to a dynastic system."

Chuche not only promoted self-reliance, but political and

ideological independence. This meant political and ideological independence from the Soviet Union and China. Kim Il Sung stated that North Koreans must "resolutely repudiate the tendency to swallow things of others undigested or imitate them mechanically." In time, Kim Il Sung would accuse both China and the Soviet Union of abandoning the principles of Marxism-Leninism, which demonstrated his ideological independence from both nations. Of course, such remarks were ironic coming from Kim Il Sung, whose ideology deviated greatly from Marxism-Leninism.

Kim Il Sung was apparently greatly influenced by the ideas of Mao Zedong, though this is something which Kim Il Sung never acknowledged publicly. Kim Il Sung was trained in the Chinese communist guerilla army from 1935 to 1941. Many scholars have suggested that Kim was also a member of the Chinese Communist Party. Despite the early Chinese influences on Kim Il Sung, the influence of Confucianism in North Korea demonstrated a very significant difference between the ideology of Kim Il Sung and that of Mao.

Nicolas Levi explained: "Confucianism had been both the religion and ideology of the state for centuries. Choson Dynasty Confucianism was not only a philosophical and ethical system but also a cult of the family. Everyone was expected to show filial piety towards their parents, ancestors and the king. Participation in family sacrifices helped link the individual to the monarch, who was considered the 'father' of the national community." In China, Confucianism became one of the targets of the Cultural Revolution. In North Korea, however, Confucianism remained an important part of the political and social organization. Confucianism is based on the relationship among family members. Sons are expected to obey their fathers, daughters obey their mothers, younger siblings obey older siblings, and wives obey their husbands. In the realm of politics, Confucianism meant that villages followed the leadership of venerated elders. Citizens were also expected to revere the ruling king, who was seen as the father of the state. Kim Il Sung was venerated as the father of the country. When Kim Il Sung died, he was succeeded by his son

Kim Jong Il.

Mao's opposition to Confucianism was based on the view that Confucianism is a reactionary doctrine which sought to restore slavery in China during a period in China's history when the country shifted from slavery to feudalism. Ling Hsiao explained: "Except for the revolution led by the proletariat, only the replacement of the slave system by the feudal system actually constituted a social change in China's history which saw the dictatorship of one class replaced by that of another class in its full sense. The struggle between the Confucian and Legalist lines took place during that social change."

Ling Hsiao argued that "Mencius (390-305 B.C.), a representative of the Confucian school, came out with the theory peddling 'benevolent rule' in an attempt to negate and overthrow the political power of the new emerging landlord class and restore dictatorship of the slave-owners." Ling Hsiao continued to note that the representatives of the Legalist school refused the theory of benevolent rule by pointing out that it was aimed at "deceiving and keeping the people ignorant" and that it opposed reform.

Chin Shih Huang, the emperor who unified China under a centralized authority, adopted the Legalist line. Chin Shih Huang implemented a policy of repressing Confucianist thought in China. He burned books and buried Confucian scholars alive. Ling Hsiao regarded such measures as "revolutionary measures" because these measures were aimed at smashing the attacks being made by the slave-owners' restorationist forces. Following Chin Shih Huang's death, Chao Kao seized power in an attempt to restore the previous social order. This was followed by a peasant uprising which was led by Chen Sheng and Wu Kuang. This uprising was a blow to the attempts to restore slavery. Ling Hsiao explained that the masses "were the main force in fighting against restoration." The peasant uprising created the space for the emerging landlord class to come into being. Ling Hsiao explained that the clash between the declining slave-owning class and the landlord class continued after the formation of the Western Han Dynasty.

Ling Hsiao noted that with gradual disappearance of the danger of the restoration of slavery after the Western Han Dynasty, the landlord class began to detest the Legalist ideas and found that a modified version of Confucian ideas suited its needs. At this point, the contradiction in Chinese society was not between slave-owners and slaves, but between landlords and peasants. At this point, Confucian doctrines became the dominant ideology of the landlord class and Legalists ceased to represent the newly emerging class. Ling Hsiao noted that it became "impossible for the Legalists to solve the daily sharpening basic contradiction in feudal society and find a way out for the feudal system." In the view of Maoists in China, Confucianism was an ideology which represented the interests "of the most reactionary and darkest forces" and that Confucianism always hindered social change and social progress.

Kim Il Sung held a different view of Confucianism. He utilized the ideals of Confucianism as part of his effort to create a personality cult. In this regard, Confucian culture became a powerful propaganda tool for Kim Il Sung, who was presented as the head of the "Korean family". In North Korea, Kim Il Sung was presented as a political figure who was superior to the great religious leaders in history. The ruling party in North Korea openly proclaimed that Kim Il Sung was "superior to Christ in love, superior to Buddha in benevolence, superior to Confucius in virtue and superior to Mohamed in justice."

This emphasis on Kim Il Sung being a great individual leader was a clear break with the principles of Lenin, as Grace Lee pointed out: "*Juche* also diverges from Lenin's focus on the educating and organizing functions of the elite revolutionary vanguard. Authoritarianism is inherent in the *juche* ideology because the guidance of an 'exceptionally brilliant and outstanding leader' is considered essential to the mobilization of the masses of the working class."

Nicolas Levi explained: "The first stage of this socialist reform used many ideological slogans calling for the abolition of established feudalistic institutions but did not directly challenge the basic ideological roots of Confucianism in Korea." Kim Il Sung did not challenge the ideological roots of Confucianism in North Korea because those roots proved to be very effective in maintaining his regime.

It is also worth noting that under the leadership of Kim Il Sung, North Korea was viewed as a model for others around the world.

Eldridge Cleaver stated in a pamphlet titled "On the Ideology of the Black Panther Party" that Kim Il Sung and Mao Tse-tung had injected something new into Marxism-Leninism. The Black Panther Party looked to North Korea and China as models of socialist revolutions which were led by non-white leaders such as Mao and Kim. In 1976, President Moussa Traoré of Mali visited North Korea. During the visit, he spoke about the achievements of the struggles in Indochina and Africa. President Traoré also expressed praise for Kim Il Sung and the Chuche ideology. He referred to North Korea as "a model for the developing countries."

North Korea certainly became a model to Guyana, which was led by Forbes Burnham at the time. Burnham came to power in Guyana with the support of the United States, but Burnham's relationship with the United States cooled after Burnham came to power and began promoting the ideology of "co-operative socialism." Despite claiming socialism, Burnham's relationship with other socialist nations came with challenges. The Soviet Union recognized the People's Progressive Party—one of the major opposition parties in Guyana—as a Marxist-Leninist party. This was hardly surprising given that Burnham came to power with American support and Burnham had denounced the "Soviet threat" in Guyana. The Soviet Union was clearly more favorable towards the PPP, even rejecting Burnham's bid to have his People's National Congress party join the Communist International.

Cuba was more supportive of Burnham's government in Guyana than the Soviet Union was. Cuba provided medical personnel, scholarships, and military aid. The problem for Burnham was that Cuba was also aligned with the PPP opposition party. Burnham was also concerned about the relationship between Cubans and the Work People's Alliance, which was another opposition party in Guyana. Five Cuban diplomats were expelled from Guyana for allegedly providing guerrilla training to members of the Working People's Alliance.

North Korea proved to be a more reliable socialist ally for Burnham. Whereas Cuba and the Soviet Union promoted orthodox Marxism-Leninism, which the PNC did not practice, North Korea praised the co-operative socialism of Burnham. North Korea saw similarities between Burnham's socialist ideology and the Chuche concept which was promoted in North Korea by Kim Il Sung, particularly because the two ideologies promoted self-reliance.

Throughout the 1970s, Guyana and North Korea developed close relations. North Korea provided aid to Guyana to assist with Guyana's goal of reaching self-sufficiency. North Korea also influenced the policies of the PNC government in more direct ways. In 1979, the PNC announced Mass Games in Guyana, which were to be held on February 23, 1980. Mass Games refers to a display of arts and gymnastics.

In September 1979, a team of seven members were sent to Guyana to help prepare Guyana for Mass Games. These seven individuals were headed by Kim Il Nam, who was personally selected for the mission by Kim Il Sung. The team spent several months familiarizing themselves with the history and culture of Guyana. Mass games were held by the government of Guyana throughout the 1980s under the direction of the Ministry of Education's Mass Games Secretariat.

Mass Games in Guyana was denounced by the opposition, who argued that it would "serve no educational purpose but merely to divert attention from the general economic and social situation of the country." The Working People's Alliance called on parents and teachers to boycott the event. Despite these objections, Guyana held Mass Games throughout the 1980s. By 1982, Mass Games training was incorporated into the public school system's physical education curriculum and by the mid-1980s the Guyana Defence Force was incorporated into Mass Games.

Much like in North Korea, Mass Games in Guyana was used to highlight the government and the nation's president. Mass Games in Guyana reflected the culture of Guyana, however. Yolanda Marshall, a writer and poet who performed in the 1986 Mass Games as a dancer, explained: "Our Mass Games resembled some type of an African celebration from slavery with a mixture of militancy and blending of cultures. I personally feel my Guyanese Mass Games was more fun, after all, most Guyanese love to dance to good music." Moe Taylor gave the following description of the type of influence that Kim Il Sung had on Guyana as follows: "In the 1970s when North Korea was presenting itself as a model for Third World development, Kim Il Sung's message for countries like Guyana was that cultural development and educational reform were of even greater importance for them, as they faced the double burden of building the objective conditions of socialism and freeing themselves from the psycho-cultural legacy of colonialism."

The appeal of North Korea under the leadership of Kim Il Sung was that North Korea was a socialist nation which freed itself from Japanese imperialism and withstood the onslaught from American imperialism during the Korean War. The end of the Cold War was a period of transformation for North Korea. The regime in North Korea was forced to change in order to survive in power. As noted previously, North Korea adopted a market economy in an attempt to bolster its struggling economy. In 2001, North Korea began pursuing economic ventures with South Korea, which seemed to contradict the principle of Chuche.

The economic situation in North Korea forced certain economic reforms, but one aspect of Chuche which remained consistent under the leadership of Kim Jong Il and Kim Jong-un has been North Korea's its desire to protect itself from outside threats. Cha and Kang explained that emotion and ideology "have often interfered with the reasoned study of North Korea, and this has led scholars and policymakers to consistently overestimate the North Korean threat and to misunderstand the motivations behind North Korea's actions." That motivation has been survival in the face of a superior adversary.

References:

Andrei Lankov, "The Resurgence of a Market Economy in North Korea," January 2016.

Antonio DeSimone and Nicholas Horton, "Sony's Nightmare Before Christmas: The 2014 North Korean Cyber Attack on Sony and Lessons for US Government Actions in Cyberspace," The Johns Hopkins University Applied Physics Laboratory LLC., 2017.

December 08, 1960 Report, Embassy of Hungary in North Korea to the Hungarian Foreign Ministry

Grace Lee, "The Political Philosophy of Juche," *Stanford Journal of East Asian Affairs*, Volume 3, no. 1, 2003.

James I. Matray, "The Failure of the Bush Administration's North Korea Policy: A Critical Analysis," *140 International Journal of Korean Studies*, 2013.

June 02, 1976 Hungarian Embassy in the DPRK, Telegram, 2 June 1976. Subject: Visit of the president of Mali in the DPRK.

Liang Hsiao, "Study the Historical Experience of the Struggle Between the Confucian and Legalist Schools," *Peking Review*, January 10, 1975.

Moe Taylor, "'Only a disciplined people can build a nation': North Korean Mass Games and Third Worldism in Guyana, 1980-1992," *The Asia-Pacific Journal*, Volume 13, Issue 4, no. 2, Jan. 26, 2015.

Nicolas Levi, "The Importance of Confucian Values to Kim Jong Il's System: A comparison with Kim Il Sung's System," 2012.

37

THE POLITICS OF LEBRON JAMES

LeBron James is unique among professional athletes not simply because of his success and longevity as a professional basketball player, but also because of his willingness to speak on social and political issues which affect America. Throughout his career, James has been known for taking political positions and often has received backlash for doing so. For instance, Laura Ingram tried to present James as an uneducated jock who just needed to "shut up and dribble." Her point was that James' attempts to make political statements have not always been very articulate or even accurate. Even so, the tone which Ingram expressed was very condensing and attempted to demean James. The implication was that James should simply play basketball and remain silent on political issues.

James' initial reaction to Ingram's remarks was to laugh at the report. He also stated that he did not know who Ingram was. James felt that her reaction simply demonstrated that everything he was speaking about was correct. He also stated that he would not "shut up and dribble" because he means too much to society and to children who feel that they do not have a way out. James further added that he wished Ingram did some fact-checking because she incorrectly stated that he did not finish high school.

James has been a controversial figure for much of his career, not only because of his willingness to speak on social issues, but for some of his actions as a basketball player, especially his decision to leave the Cleveland Cavaliers to play for the Miami Heat. The manner in which James handled the decision to switch teams did little to win him support. At a rally to celebrate James' arrival in Miami, James declared that the team would win as many as eight championships. He explained that he really believed what he said. James certainly could not be faulted for having such confidence in the newly formed team, though in hindsight the remarks were ill-advised. By the end of the next season, James would be humbled when his team was defeated in the finals.

Following the loss, James' response to his critics who wanted to see him fail was that they have to wake up to their personal problems the next day. This is true. Win or lose, the outcome of a basketball games typically does not have much of a direct impact on the lives of ordinary fans who cheer for or against certain teams and players. Even so, the ability of James and other players to earn as much money as they do from the game of basketball rests on the fact that spectators are so emotionally invested in the sport that they are willing to pay money to see the players perform. In some cases, they are also willing to watch the sport to see players fail, as was the case with James. Had James expressed more humility after deciding to play for the Heat he probably would not have faced such scrutiny, yet one cannot also fault a young player who is in the prime of his career for expressing such confidence in his team's ability to win championships.

After four years and two championships, James decided to return to Cleveland. He explained that he would have handled leaving for Miami differently, but the experience helped him to grow. He stated: "If I had to do it all over again, I'd obviously do things differently, but I'd still have left. Miami, for me, has been almost like college for other kids. These past four years helped raise me into who I am. I became a better player and a better man." What James stated about Miami being like college for him was interesting given that James himself did not go to college. He went from high school to being a professional basketball player.

One of the ways that James grew is that he became more outspoken on social issues. Following the killing of Trayvon Martin, James and the rest of the Miami Heat team sent a very simple, yet powerful message by taking a photo in which they were all wearing hoodies. This was meant to express their support for Trayvon Martin who was killed while he was wearing a hoodie. James would take a similar stand following the death of Eric Garner by wearing a t-shirt with the words, "I Can't Breathe." These were the words of Eric Garner as he was being choked to death by a police officer.

One has to remember that although James has been more outspoken on political and social issues than many athletes of his status have been, James is not a political activist, nor does he attempt to present himself as one. Following the shooting death of

Tamir Rice, James responded by stating that he was not knowledgeable enough on the situation to make a statement about it. This did not appear to be an attempt by James to avoid speaking out on the situation because he had done so in the past and he would later address similar situations in the future. It seemed that James really had not followed the situation and therefore did not want to speak on it. This was understandably disappointing to those who wanted James to speak out. Shaun King commented that 400 days after Tamir Rice was killed, "James could at least form a coherent, mildly courageous statement on Tamir." Some activists even called for James to sit out games until the officers that killed Tamir Rice were brought to justice. Kwame Rose wrote: "We wouldn't have to tweet Muhammad Ali."

I think James' critics may have been expecting too much from him in that situation. Muhammad Ali was stripped of his title and prevented from fighting for refusing to go to Vietnam to support the war there, but Ali never refused to fight in order to make a political statement. In fact, Ali's decision to continue boxing after he was reinstated created some tension between him and Elijah Muhammad, the leader of the Nation of Islam. James would not sit out games to protest police brutality and one is not certain if doing so would truly have pressured the city of Cleveland to take action.

It would have been great if James did have something to say on the matter, but the fact that he did not do so demonstrated that James was not making the effort to inform himself on high-profile incidents of police brutality against black people because that was not a priority for him. James demonstrated that he is a basketball player who will make a statement on such issues when they catch his attention, but that informing himself on these issues is not a priority for him.

In certain situations silence is a better option than making the wrong statement. This was the case when a sixteen-year-old was shot and killed by a police officer. James reacted by tweeting "you're next". His tweet also included an image of an hourglass. The tweet incited a backlash, which caused James to delete the tweet. He explained: "I'm so damn tired of seeing Black people killed by police. I took the tweet down because it's being used to create more hate." He explained that he was angry at the situation, but that anger doesn't do any good. Anger can do good if it is used as a catalyst for change, but in James' situation anger led him to react with a cryptic tweet which caused a lot of backlash against him.

James also came under criticism for remarks that he made regarding China. Daryl Morey, the manager of the Houston Rockets, expressed support for anti-government protests in Hong Kong. This created tensions between China and the National Basketball Association. James responded by claiming that Morey was not educated on the situation. James seemed more concerned about the Association's relationship with China than with the actual political situation in Hong Kong. In response to some of the criticisms which he received, James simply replied that Morey could have waited a week to send his tweet. News outlets did report that there was a financial incentive for James given that he had a deal with Nike which sells shoes in China, as well as James' upcoming movie which was set for an international release.

Senator Josh Hawley suggested that James should go to Hong Kong to meet with the protesters. Dan Wolken described James' remarks as being his most disgraceful moment. Jared Max stated that if James was not a talented basketball player, no one would care about what he had to say, which was a similar point to the remark that Ingram had made when she told James to shut up and dribble. The most dramatic display of criticism for James' comments were the fact that protesters in Hong Kong burned his jerseys as a reaction to James' comments.

This was perhaps another situation where silence would have been better for James. Instead, he put himself in a position where some in the media viewed him as a self-serving hypocrite who supported Colin Kaepernick's protest, but would not support the protests in Hong Kong because any tension between the National Basketball Association and China would hurt James financially. James' remark that Morey was not educated about the situation was also interesting given that there was no indication that James himself had taken the time to understand the situation which was taking place in Hong Kong.

James has also expressed an apparent disinterest in seriously studying the historical struggles of black people in America. For example, when asked about Malcolm X's autobiography, James' response was that Malcolm "was a very smart man" and that Malcolm was a very powerful-minded gentleman. James stated that he had been reading the book for a couple of days, but he did not offer much insights about what he read or what his thoughts were. In his response James noted that Malcolm used the word "Negro" a lot and he stated that he wished he could have met Malcolm, but at no point in his response did James actually speak to Malcolm's political views or Malcolm's analysis of the race problem in the America. A skeptic could conclude that James was not truly reading the book, since nothing that James said about Malcolm pertained to the contents of the book.

Given that James stated that he had only been reading it for a couple of days, one could generously conclude that James perhaps did not get to the part of the book where Malcolm joined the Nation of Islam, but even so the early part of Malcolm's life did play a role in shaping his views on race in America. At the very least James could have spoken about the racism that Malcolm and Malcolm's family experienced, but James gave no indication in his response that he was seriously reading the autobiography.

There is also the fact that although James is a black man in America, his fame and wealth means that his experiences are not the typical experiences of the average working class black person. This is not to suggest that James has not experienced these things. After all, James grew up in poverty and was raised by a single mother. James was able to work his way out of poverty because of his skills as a basketball player. Poor black youth who do not have the type of athletic skill that James has may be able to find some other means to lift themselves out of poverty, but the opportunities are very limited. Most impoverished black youths certainly can never hope to become as rich and famous as James became.

To James' credit, he has not been under any illusions that his success shields him from racism. This was very apparent during an incident in which James' $20 million mansion was vandalized. His gate was spray painted with the word nigger. James explained: "No matter how much money you have, no matter how famous you are, no matter how many people admire you, being black in America is tough." Even so, James' fame and his money have given him platforms that have not been available to other black people. This access to political power has also shaped the way that James has engaged in American politics.

During the 2016 election, James did not hide the fact that he was supporting Hillary Clinton over Donald Trump. James openly expressed his support for Clinton, writing that "we need a president who brings us together and keeps us unified. Policies and ideas that divide us more are not the solution." James also appeared at a rally for Hillary Clinton where he referred to her as the next president of the United States. This was later used by Ingram to mock him on Fox News after Clinton lost the election and Donald Trump became the next president.

James' position here can be contrasted with Colin Kaepernick. During the 2016 presidential race, Kaepernick was critical of both candidates. Kaepernick also received some criticism in the media over the fact that he did not vote in the 2016 presidential election. This was typical of the bourgeois understanding of politics. Kaepernick did not like either candidate so he simply refused to vote, rather than voting for the sake of doing so. If Kaepernick had voted, then what? Kaepernick started his protests during the presidency of Barack Obama, so there was already a Democrat in the White House. What would the election of another Democrat have done to change the things that Kaepernick was protesting over?

Kaepernick's refusal to vote raised questions about the political system itself, but certain pundits did not see it that way. Stephen A. Smith suggested that Kaepernick's refusal to vote was disrespectful to those who fought and sacrificed for the right to vote, as if voting was the only thing that black people fought for in America. Smith demonstrated a very swallow understanding of the political history of the black struggle in America by reducing it to a struggle for voting rights.

Kaepernick made it very clear that he was influenced by Malcolm X and unlike James, Kaepernick seemed to have actually studied Malcolm and was applying some of Malcolm's ideas, such as Malcolm's criticism of both major political parties. I am certain that Stephen A. Smith was not thinking about Malcolm's "Ballot or Bullet" speech when he criticized Kaepernick for not voting.

James' politics are typical of the type of bourgeois understanding of politics displayed by Stephen A. Smith. This is the type of approach to politics which views politics as simply being a matter of going out to vote, regardless of who is running or what issues are on the ballot. This is an approach to politics which suggests that black people should vote for the sake of voting simply because the right to vote was something that black people had to fight for. Those who adopt this type of thinking regarding politics do not think about how the actual policies of these political leaders directly or indirectly impact the lives of ordinary Americans, particularly black Americans who have historically been neglected by both political parties. Kaepernick understood this, so he decided not to vote.

This is not to suggest that Kaepernick's approach was correct and that James' approach was incorrect. James rightfully understood that Trump was a divisive figure and ill-equipped for the role of being the president of a country. For this reason, James threw his support behind Trump's opponent. The limitation of his understanding of politics is displayed by the fact that James campaigned for Hillary Clinton, but he did not advocate for any particular policies to be implemented. In his view, defeating Trump was enough. In the eight years that Obama was president, James offered no critique of Obama's policies. It is likely that James had not even been following Obama's presidency closely enough to have a particular critique of Obama. James' approach to politics has been a very superficial one in that regard. Simply electing a president into office is meaningless if there is no attempt to shape policy. James' wealth and fame offer him more influence in this regard than the average black citizen in America has, yet James has not truly used his position to advocate for political change beyond a few symbolic gestures to express support for black victims of police violence.

Interestingly, James referred to Bill Clinton as the first black president. James was referencing Toni Morrison's remarks about Clinton being the first black president. There are problems with this narrative, however. Aside from the fact that Bill Clinton is not black, the other problem with this narrative about Bill Clinton being labeled as the first black president has been his policies which impacted the black community in very adverse ways. For example, Clinton himself also acknowledged that his policies in Haiti played a role in destroying Haiti's rice industry.

James wrote, "We appreciate you still to this day!" One is left to question who this "we" is, especially given the backlash that the Clintons have experienced for some of their policies. The Haitians who protested the Clinton Foundation certainly did not express any appreciation for Bill Clinton. When James said "we" he was not referring to the collective masses of black people, but to black people of his particular social class and political orientation. The Haitians who protested against the Clintons certainly did not seem to have much appreciation for Bill Clinton, but James can have such appreciation not only because he has not been directly harmed by any of Bill Clinton's policies, but also because Bill Clinton attended a basketball game to watch James play. The average black person cannot say that they have ever had a former president show up at their workplace to take a photo with them, but that is the type of access to politicians that James' fame affords him.

Perhaps if James had made a serious effort to read Malcolm X's autobiography, James would have developed a more complete understanding of racism and politics in America, but that unfortunately was not the case. As such, James' efforts have not been aimed at producing real systemic changes. James has undertaken initiatives such as opening a school for at-risk students and helping to launch the "More Than a Vote" initiative which was designed to protect the voting rights of black Americans. These efforts are commendable, but none of these really get to the root of the problem of racial inequality in America. For example, protecting voting rights is critical to ensuring that black Americans are able to participate in the political process, but it is also equally important to ensure that political leaders are held accountable to their voters. As stated before, this is not something that James has typically done. With the wealth and influence that James has, he could easily launch initiatives that could have a more direct impact on the political process, such as lobbying for particular causes.

Michael Jordan is infamously stated to have remarked that Republicans buy sneakers to defend his decision not to endorse the campaign of a black candidate who was running against Senator

Jesse Helms. James could have easily taken this route and decided to remain silent on certain issues, but he did the opposite. In some respects, James' political views are typical of a multi-millionaire athlete who is removed from many of the struggles that ordinary people face, but what has made James unique is that he has tended to be more vocal on political and social issues than most athletes in his position have been. As such, James' attempts at activism often have not gone far enough to help produce impactful political change, yet his efforts have gone further than millionaire athletes who have refused to engage in any type of activism.

38

CHRISTOPHER HITCHENS AND THE IRAQ WAR

The support which Christopher Hitchens provided for the Iraq War was somewhat surprising to some who had viewed Hitchens as someone who had been very critical of imperialism. Interestingly, Hitchens attempted to frame his support for the Iraq War as support for an anti-imperial war. Hitchens argued that everything that the United States did in Iraq since 1968 was imperial. He noted that the United States helped to install the Baath party of Saddam Hussein, that the United States had promised support to the Kurds only to sell the Kurds out, and that Hussein was given a greenlight by Jimmy Carter to invade Iran. Hitchens explained that the war between Iraq and Iran resulted in at least one million and a half casualties. Given this history, Hitchens argued that it would have been an act of imperialism not to intervene and to leave Iraq as it is. Hitchens explained that the intervention in 2003 was the first time that he was aware of in which the United States intervened in Iraq on the right side and Hitchens explained that he was proud to have supported such an intervention. Hitchens' argument was that the United States had consistently done the wrong thing in Iraq since the 1960s and that the intervention to overthrow Hussein was the right thing to do.

It is true that Saddam Hussein was a brutal dictator who was helped into power by the United States. Even if removing him from power was the morally correct thing for the United States to do, the invasion itself was managed very poorly. In the first place, the invasion of Iraq was not presented as merely being a mission to topple a brutal dictator. The invasion of Iraq was justified under the pretense that Saddam Hussein had weapons of mass destruction.

It turned out that there were no weapons of mass destruction. Colin Powell, who delivered a speech before the United Nations in 2003 in which he made the case for the American intervention in

Iraq, later expressed regret over giving the speech. Powell explained that he spent four days at the CIA to make sure all of the intelligence was correct. He was given assurances that the information was correct, but it turned out that the information was wrong.

That the invasion was justified by inaccurate information did not seem to bother Bush. In fact, Bush publicly joked about the missing weapons of mass destruction, even displaying photos of himself looking for the weapons of mass destruction in the Oval Office. The joke was met with applause and laughter from the audience. Thomas Young, a veteran of the Iraq War, did not appreciate the joke. He described the joke as being callous. It indeed was callous for Bush to make light of the fact that American soldiers were sent to fight and die over a claim which turned out to be false.

Yet another problem with the invasion of Iraq was that the United States and its partners did not have a real plan for what to do after removing Saddam Hussein from power. This was the view expressed by Iraqi satirist Ahmed Albasheer. Albasheer explained that the invading countries' policies towards Iraq were a disaster. Government positions were allocated based on identity rather than merit. The Iraqi army was disbanded, which left hundreds of thousands of men in poverty. Moreover, people with no government experience were put in charge. During this time, Albasheer experienced a number of tragedies. A mortar fell on his house, killing his brother. He explained that the family had to scrape his brother's remains from the wall in order to have something to bury. Albasheer's father was tortured by Al-Qaeda and died a year later. Albasheer's cousin was also killed after stepping on an IED.

Whereas Hitchens felt a sense of pride over the American decision to overthrow Saddam Hussein, Albasheer, who had to live with the consequences of this intervention, concluded that the attempt to save Iraq in 2003 did not go so well. That the intervention did not go so well was a product of the fact that the intervention was poorly planned. Following the 9/11 terrorist attacks, President Bush wondered if Saddam Hussein had been involved. No link between Iraq and the attack had been uncovered. In reality, Osama bin Laden resented Saddam Hussein's regime.

Even so, it seemed that the United States was eager to see the removal of Saddam Hussein and the claim about weapons of mass destruction provided a pretense to support the invasion. Hitchens, who was also eager to see the fall of Hussein's dictatorship, supported this invasion. One may grant that Hitchens' reason for supporting the invasion was correct. Saddam Hussein was a brutal dictator who needed to be removed, but the invasion was carried out by an administration which was relying on false information and appeared indifferent to the devastating consequences of the war. Hitchens correctly noted that America had consistently gotten it wrong with Iraq. The invasion of Iraq demonstrated that even when America did do the right thing in Iraq, it was done for the wrong reason and carried out in the wrong manner. Hitchens attempted to suggest that his support for the Iraq War was an anti-imperial position, but he was ultimately simply attempting to defend and rationalize yet another failure on the part of the American empire.

39

END SARS IN NIGERIA

The Special Anti-Robbery Squad (SARS) was a police force unit which was formed for the purpose of addressing certain crimes in Nigeria. SARS became a controversial police unit for the abuses which officers committed. This resulted in complaints, but no action was taken. This is demonstrated by the fact that prior to the protests in 2020, SARS had been previously disbanded several times throughout the years. The situation was different in 2020, however.

In October of 2020, a video of a SARS officer shooting a man surfaced. This incident was followed by a Nigerian musician being killed. This led to the End SARS hashtag, which gained global attention. By October 8, Nigerian citizens took to the streets to protest for the end of SARS. Obianuju Catherine Udeh (also known as DJ Switch) was among those who joined the protests. She was there for the infamous Lekki shooting which took place on October 20 when soldiers decided to open fire on the protesters. Udeh herself was almost shot. As she laid on the ground, Udeh was covered by a man who was subsequently shot in his lower back while he was covering her in an attempt to protect her from being shot. Udeh recorded some of the shootings on social media. The soldiers blocked the roads to prevent ambulances from arriving on the scene to treat the wounded. The protesters had to perform surgery on each other, using firelighters to sterilize the blades that they were using.

After the shooting, some wounded were taken to a hospital and others were taken to a church which offered refuge. The next day, the hospital was raided by soldiers who were looking for Udeh. Udeh's boss also received threatening phone calls. Udeh also could not go home because men were seen lurking around her apartment complex. This was apparently all because Udeh had shared a live video feed of the shooting. Prior to the shooting, security cameras were apparently cut. This would suggest that the Nigeria military had been planning to shoot at protesters and were ensuring that there would be little evidence of such an attack.

This was a shooting which the government of Nigeria attempted to dismiss. Lai Muhammad, the minister of information, stated that the shooting was nothing more than a fabrication. Udeh was accused of spreading fake news in an attempt to tarnish the image of Nigeria. The military even went so far as to suggest that Udeh had used a green screen to produce a video of the shooting.

The attempt to dismiss the shooting as a fabrication failed. Instead, the world was made aware of the fact that the Nigerian government had responded to these demands for change by killing its own civilians. What made the whole ordeal worse was the realization that the government of Nigeria was more forceful in its response to these citizens who were protesting for change than it had been in its response to Boko Haram, which has been terrorizing and killing citizens in Nigeria. In response to the massacre, there was a petition being circulated which demanded that President Muhammadu Buhari be charged by the International Criminal Court for his role in the massacre.

Military violence against civilians is certainly nothing new in Nigeria's history. In her speech before the Oslo Freedom Forum, Udeh mentioned "Zombie" by Fela Kuti. In that song, Fela Kuti presented the Nigerian military as being mindless zombies who simply followed orders. Fela Kuti himself was a victim of state repression in Nigeria. His home was subjected to numerous raids by the security forces in Nigeria. During one of these raids by the army, Fela's house was burned down. Fela's mother was severely injured during the raid and Fela would later blame President Olusegun Obasanjo's soldiers for killing his mother.

The massacre which took place on October 20 was an example of brutality being inflicted against Nigerian civilians on behalf of the Nigerian state. In the larger Pan-African context, the massacre which took place on October 20 was yet another example of how the military has been utilized to oppress civilians in African politics. This is a situation which is not unique to Nigeria, but what does make the Nigerian situation concerning is the fact that Nigeria is a nation which has been under military rule in the past. The presidency of Buhari is supposed to be a civilian government, yet the world witnessed the Nigerian military being sent to massacre civilians under the leadership of a civilian government which was elected to represent the very civilians it was massacring.

In her speech about the 2020 massacre, Udeh mentioned a Nigerian phrase which goes, "wahala no dey finish." This means that problems are never done. The struggle for liberation is a continuous one. This is the main lesson that I took away from the End SARS movement in Nigeria. The movement to end SARS was a continuous one which took several years, just as the struggle for the end to military rule in Nigeria took several years. Those of us who are struggling for change in Nigeria and for change throughout Africa must recognize the continuous nature of this struggle. We must recognize that problems are never finished.

40

PAN-AFRICANISM AND THE QUESTION OF IDEOLOGY

Kwame Ture explained that Pan-Africanism is an objective, but that his ideology was Nkrumahism-Toureism. I start with this because the distinction which was made by Ture is an important one for understanding Pan-Africanism. Pan-Africanism does not represent any particular ideology. Pan-Africanism advocates for the unity of African people, but Pan-Africanists themselves have often disagreed on ideological approaches to achieving such a unity.

That Pan-Africanism does not represent any particular ideology should not be surprising. Pan movements are movements which seek to unify a particular group. As such, pan movements tend to encompass a diverse body of ideological beliefs within the collective group. This has certainly been true of the Pan-African movement. As Ture pointed out, some Pan-Africanists embraced Marxism-Leninism. Ture himself embraced Nkrumahism-Toureism. There have also been those who remained flexible in their ideology approach, such as Malcolm X.

Those who have expressed Pan-Africanism have often clashed with each other. Here I mention the ideological clash between W.E.B. Du Bois and Marcus Garvey. Both men advocated for a type of global Pan-African unity, but they differed over their approaches to achieving this unity. A deadlier example was the ideological clash between Walter Rodney and Forbes Burnham of Guyana. Burnham was a Pan-Africanist who supported liberation struggles in Africa. Rodney was a Pan-Africanist as well, but he opposed Burnham's government, which ultimately resulted in Rodney being assassinated.

The question of Pan-Africanism becomes more complex when one considers the question of unity and African identity itself. Is Pan-Africanism the unity of Africa or the unity of African people? And who is an African? Marcus Garvey clearly advocated for the

237

unity of all African people (black people) around the world. Robert Sobukwe, on the other hand, seemed to have viewed Pan-Africanism as narrowly confined to the unity of Africa, while excluding African Americans and West Indians. Then there is the previously mentioned matter of identity. Gamal Abdel Nasser was a Pan-Africanist, despite not being a black man. The same is true of Gaddafi. Is Pan-African unity one which includes the non-black people of North Africa or is Pan-Africanism the unity of black people specifically? This is also a question which is debated among Pan-Africanists.

The question of whether or not Pan-Africanism itself can be identified as an ideology is a difficult one. Ture saw Pan-Africanism as an objective and he saw ideology as something which informs how the objective is to be reached. I think Pan-Africanism perhaps can be identified as an ideology, although not a pure ideology. By this I mean to say that Pan-Africanism is such a broad movement that there has been little ideological consistency within the movement other than a call for some type of international unity among African people. For example, the first Pan-African Conference was organized by Henry Sylvester Williams in 1900. Williams did not conceive of Pan-Africanism as an anti-colonial movement which advocated for self-government for the colonized nations in Africa. This obviously differs from the approach of those such as Du Bois and Kwame Nkrumah who both clearly saw Pan-Africanism as being an important aspect of the anti-colonial movement.

To conclude, there is no singular Pan-African ideology. Rather, Pan-Africanists have often expressed different and at times conflicting ideologies. Thus, to speak of "the ideology of Pan-Africanism" can create confusion because, as noted before, Pan-Africanism by itself is not a pure ideology. Those who adhere to Pan-Africanism are those who advocate for the unity of African people. The method achieving this unity, the purpose of this unity, and what this unity looks like may differ depending on the ideological disposition of any particular Pan-Africanist or Pan-African organization.

41

IN DEFENSE OF THE AFRICAN RACE: THE LEGACY OF ANTÉNOR FIRMIN

Anténor Firmin was a Haitian lawyer, politician, historian, anthropologist, and revolutionary leader. He was a man with many different intellectual interests, but these interests were all utilized for the goal of advancing the African race. Firmin lived at a time when racism was not only enforced in the political policies and agendas of Western nations, but such racism was justified by the theories of anthropologists who argued that white people were the superior race. Firmin refused to accept the notion that black people were an inferior race of people and for this reason he dedicated his life to challenging these racist assertions.

The field of anthropology was one which has produced racist ideas which helped to justify the oppression of African people. One example of this is the Brazilian anthropologist Raimundo Nina Rodrigues who was a noted racist. These racist anthologists used the guise of science to promote the concept of white supremacy and black inferiority. It was this racism that Firmin intended to challenge with his book *On the Equality of Human Races*.[1] Firmin was not the first black man to point to the unity of human races. This was the argument that Martin Delany put forward when he wrote *Principia of Ethnology: The Origin of Races and Color with an Archaeological Compendium of Ethiopia and Egyptian Civilization*. Much like Firmin would later do, Delany cited Egypt and Ethiopia as examples of the capacity for black people to produce great civilizations.

The question is what is race? Race is not a scientific concept. Yet this does not mean that race does not exist as a biological phenomenon. This is to say that physical differences among humans do exist, but such differences alone do not indicate a difference in species. A white man is just as human as a black man. Race does not simply describe a physical difference, but a social difference as well. Thus, race is partly biological and partly social.

What this means is that race is a product of a person's ancestry and a product of the social group which a person identifies with.

In some instances, a person's racial identity is based more so on their social identity than their phenotypic appearance. The historian John Henrik Clarke spoke of his colleague John G. Jackson.[2] Jackson was a historian who wrote books on African history, such as *Introduction to African Civilization* and *Ethiopia and the Origin of Civilization*. Clarke explained that Jackson "looked whiter than most white people. He didn't have to walk down the black course. It was a choice, a conscious choice." Jackson consciously chose to identify as black, even though he was not always accepted as such because he did not look black. Clarke explained that in his hometown, Jackson was disrespected by black people who thought Jackson was a white man.

Some Marxists have argued that the working class, regardless of their racial background, have a common interest in joining together to fight against capitalist exploitation. Such a position is not necessarily incorrect, yet, as W.E.B. Du Bois explained in *Dusk of Dawn*, the communist "philosophy did not envisage a situation where instead of a horizontal division of classes, there was a vertical fissure, a complete separation of classes by race, cutting square across the economic layers." Du Bois also explained that "the split between white and black workers was greater than that between white workers and capitalists", which demonstrated the profound influence of race as a factor which shapes social relations.

For people of African descent, the question of race is especially important because race was used as a justification for slavery and colonialism. Race as a construct to divide humanity into different categories is unscientific, yet the impact that the concept of race has had on African people around the world has been very real. The impact of this racism is what Firmin was forced to confront in his day.

That Firmin was from Haiti was also significant to the work that he was engaged in. Haiti was the only nation in the Americas where enslaved Africans were able to successfully overthrow their slave masters to create a republic for themselves. Following this successful revolution, Haiti would struggle to deal with both external and internal pressures. The struggles which Haiti experienced were used by white supremacists as proof of the inferiority of the black race. For this reason, Firmin was especially sensitive to these racist theories.

Firmin was born in Haiti in 1850. As a young man, Firmin worked in different professions including as a teacher and a civil servant. Firmin also studied law and became a lawyer in 1875, at the age of 25. Firmin's early involvement in politics came as a supporter of the Liberal Party. The division between blacks and mulattos in Haitian society was one which went back to the days of the revolution. The division remained prevalent in Haitian society and influenced the politics in Haiti. As such, the National Party was a mostly black party, whereas the Liberal Party was a mostly mulatto party.

The Liberal Party advocated for a strong legislature and civil government rather than military rule. Their slogan was "government by the most competent". Jean Price-Mars[3] stated that Firmin "was already liberal before the formation of the Liberal Party." In support of the Liberal Party, Firmin created a journal called *The Message of the North* in 1878.

Firmin was not a mulatto, but he joined the Liberal Party. Firmin criticized the manner in which division between blacks and mulattos in Haiti was fostered for political purposes. Firmin experienced this himself. He noted that in the 1879 electoral campaign, his political opponents attempted to get the people of the countryside to unite against his candidacy by telling them that Firmin was a mulatto who was as clear-skinned as a white man.[4] Firmin would lose the election which he contested in 1879.

The problem of colorism in Haiti also impacted Firmin's domestic life. Firmin married Marie Louise Rosa Salnave in 1881. Together they had two children. Salnave was the daughter of President Sylvain Salnave. The union between Firmin and Salnave was initially opposed by their parents. There were rumors that the marriage was opposed because Firmin was black and Salnave was a mulatto[5]. Salnave would instead marry Gervais Piquion, but this marriage lasted for two years before Piquion died in 1878. The two did not have children together. Firmin and Rosa married a few years after Rosa's first marriage ended. That Firmin would choose to marry a light-skinned woman seems consistent with Firmin's remarks in *On the Equality of Human Races*, in which he expressed the view that mulattos are more beautiful than black and white people.[6]

Mrs. Firmin was apparently very defensive of her husband. Price-Mars recounted a particular incident which demonstrated this defensive nature.[7] Joseph Cadet Jérémie went to meet Mrs. Firmin. Jérémie recounted that Mrs. Firmin rejected his greeting. Her response was, "after all that you have done to my husband, you dare stretch out your hand to me." After this incident, Boisrond Canal remarked: "A man whose wife is such a woman cannot be President of Haiti." Far from reflecting poorly on Firmin, the incident demonstrated that his wife was very defensive of him and was not quick to forgive Firmin's political opponents. Price-Mars explained that Mrs. Firmin's behavior was that of a woman "who had suffered in her soul, in her heart, in her affection against the injustices and iniquities of which her husband had been the victim."

Firmin developed a relationship with President Lysius Salomon, who appointed Firmin as the sub-inspector of schools for the district of Cap-Haitien. Salomon also appointed Firmin to represent Haiti in Caracas, Venezuela, for an event to commemorate the centenary of the birth of Simon Bolivar. Price-Mars explained that Firmin and Salomon shared the same conception of the unity of the human species and that they both advocated the same objective, which was to "see that Haiti, the eldest daughter of Africa, emerged from slavery by the heroism of her children, should be a model, an example of the perfectibility of the black man and his ability to promote progress in all of the postulates of Western civilization." Where the two men differed was on the question of methods. Even with these differences, Firmin still remained sympathetic to Salomon and agreed to serve in Salomon's government in a non-political capacity. Eventually differences between the two men caused Firmin to sever his contact with Salomon. Firmin left Haiti in 1883 and went to Paris, France.

It was during Firmin's time in Paris that Firmin wrote and published what would become his most influential book, *On the Equality of Human Races*. This book was written as a response to

Joseph Arthur de Gobineau's work, which had argued for the inequality of the human races. Gobineau classified humanity into three categories: the Aryans, the Yellows, and the Negroes. Price-Mars described Gobineau's work as "science fiction" which created a stir in Germany. Gobineau's claim that Germans descended from the Aryan race would lay the foundations for the Nazi ideology years later. In his work, Gobineau also used Haiti as an example to support his argument for the inferiority of the black race. He argued that the history of democratic Haiti "is merely a long series of massacres" and that the black race belongs to "a branch of the human family that is incapable of civilization."

Firmin's work challenged this doctrine of racial inequality by asserting the equality of all human races. A major component of Firmin's argument was to explain why it was that the white race came to view itself as being a superior race to others. He wrote in *On the Equality of Human Races* that "the white race dominates everywhere. Proud of its unprecedented position, it must find it natural that all other races accept its laws and obey its will. Why should it be otherwise? It controls science, this science which has become the greatest authority, the least discussed, and the most respectable of those to which one can appeal." Firmin noted that this same science was used to discover and explain secret forces of the universe which seemed to ancients to be supernatural phenomena which were conjured by some invisible entity.

Firmin then praised the white race for producing men such as Newton, Shakespeare, Humboldt, Schiller, and others. Firmin conceded that the white race has every right to be prouder of these men than the Egyptians of all their pyramids and other Pharaonic constructions. Firmin also mentioned engineering wonders such as the building of the Suez Canal in Africa and the Panama Canal in the Americas. He saw the building of the Panama Canal as the physical separation between the Anglo-Saxons of North America and the Latins in South America.

Firmin explained that as Europeans behold their achievements—which he argued were more beautiful than anything that has preceded it—Europeans could be forgiven for believing that they were born to rule the world. Firmin's concern was how to bring Europeans back to reality. He noted that Europeans had not always been so advanced. He also challenged the notion that the black race was an inferior race. To demonstrate this, Firmin pointed to the achievements of black people throughout history.

Rather than challenging the premise of civilization as defined by European writers, Firmin conceded that at the present moment Europeans have a civilization which is more advanced than that which Africans have. Firmin was not wrong in the sense that he did recognize that scientific advancements in Europe resulted in Europeans acquiring a dominant position in the world. It is important to note that the scientific advancements of Europe were often achieved at the expense of Africans and other people who were conquered by Europeans. This was the point which Eric Williams would make in *Capitalism and Slavery* and the point which Walter Rodney would make in *How Europe Underdeveloped Africa.* Firmin's writings did not explore the relationship between Europe's scientific advancement and European colonialism, nor did he address the role of slavery and colonialism in Africa's underdevelopment. Even so, Firmin certainly did recognize that Africa at the time was underdeveloped when compared to Europe and concluded that Europe at the time had a more advanced civilization than Africa's.

Firmin argued that the source of Africa's comparative underdevelopment was the environment. He explained: "Whenever we have to consider the slowness that Africans take to emerge from their present state of inferiority, we must therefore be careful not to believe that this long incapacity is the sign of an organic and fatal inferiority. It will suffice to remember that if the men of the European race, left to their own efforts, deprived of the long experience of a civilization that is many years old and above all of the hereditary culture of a long succession of generations, were condemned to living under the depressive influences of the tropical climate, they could never overcome the difficulties against which black Africans have to struggle."

Firmin did not seek to challenge the idea that Western civilization was the most advanced civilization in the world. Firmin's argument was that the dominance of Europeans was not evidence that Africans and other races were inherently inferior or incapable of achieving what Europeans had achieved. Firmin conceded that Africa at the time was not as advanced as Europe, but he noted that in the past the Africans of Egypt had a more advanced civilization than Europe had and that the civilization of Egypt even influenced the development of Greece. Firmin noted that Thales of Miletus was the first Greek scientist who dealt with mathematics and that he had acquired the best part of his knowledge in Egypt. Firmin also raised the question of whether or not Pythagoras arrived at his ideas through Egyptian priests after studying under them in Thebes.

George M. James would also explore the idea that the Greeks owe the development of their civilization to Africans in a book titled *Stolen Legacy*. James argued that Greek philosophy was the product of the Egyptian mystery system. To support this argument, James pointed out that philosophers in Athens were treated very poorly: "Another point of considerable interest to be accounted for was the attitude of the Athenian government towards this so-called Greek philosophy, which it regarded as foreign in origin and treated it accordingly. Only a brief study of history is necessary to show that Greek philosophers were undesirable citizens, who throughout the period of their investigations were victims of relentless persecution, at the hands of the Athenian government. Anaxagoras was imprisoned and exiled; Socrates was executed; Plato was sold into slavery and Aristotle was indicted and exiled; while the earliest of them all, Pythagoras, was expelled from Croton in Italy." Years before James published *Stolen Legacy*, Firmin would declare that the black race was the oldest of all other races in the career of civilization and that white people who spoke of the inferiority of blacks were merely "ingrates".

Firmin maintained that Pharaonic Egypt was a black civilization. The racial identity of the ancient Egyptians is a topic which has been contested by scholars. Price-Mars himself concluded that "it would be somewhat risky to claim that the population of ancient Egypt was completely black or even Negroid. We would be much closer to reality by maintaining that it was, in large part, mixed race and that its mixing revealed a considerable contribution from black Africa." In Firmin's view, there was little doubt as to the racial identity of the ancient Egyptians.

Another topic which Firmin confronted in his book were the theories of Clémence Royer. Royer translated Darwin's *Origin of Species* into French. In Royer's view, Darwin's work supported the notion of racial inequality. She argued that the theory of natural selection was one which left no doubt that superior races emerge and that these superior races are destined to supplant the inferior races. Royer also believed that racial mixing had the effect of lowering the average level of the species. Royer's views on race can be demonstrated by an encounter she had with Firmin. Royer and Firmin were both members of the Paris Anthropology Society. On one occasion when Firmin challenged the racist theories being promoted by some of the members, Royer confronted Firmin and asked him if his intellectual ability was not the result of some white ancestry.[8]

In his response to Royer in *On the Equality of Human Races*, Firmin noted the fact that she was a woman. In his view only men have the education and temperament to study complex issues from all sides. Here, Firmin employed sexism as a response to Royer's ideas by suggesting that a woman would not be capable of fully understanding Darwin's theory. In a book which argued for the equality of races, it would appear that Firmin also suggested an inequality among the sexes. Firmin does not elaborate more on this point, so one is not sure if Firmin believed that these differences between men and women are biological, or if he is referring to the social conditioning of women. Whatever the case may have been, this remark by Firmin certainly stands out because it seems rather at odds with Firmin's mission of challenging unscientific ideas.

Firmin also challenged the notion that the white race had greater morality than the black race. Firmin explained that prostitution was so well-accepted in Greek and Roman antiquity that "it is impossible to understand how such institutions could coexist with the refinements of civilizations who tolerated them." Firmin also noted that such acts of immorality still persist in Europe. He noted that in certain large European cities, "acts of revolting immorality take place in the open air."

Aside from pointing to sexual immorality among the white race, Firmin also wrote about the behavior of the white race to other races of the world. He explained: "As for the relations of Europeans with men of another race, especially with blacks, there is nothing more dreadful, nothing more barbarous. The whole history of the slave trade is stained with bloody pages, where crimes of all kinds occur with such frequency that one would have to say that the owners of slaves were prey to cruel madness." This passage is important because the racism of white people was precisely the reason why it was necessary for Firmin to write *On the Equality of Human Races*.

Firmin presented the struggles and achievements of African people in the face of such racism as further evidence of the capacity of the black race. He particularly cited Toussaint Louverture, who was one of the leaders of the Haitian Revolution. Of Toussaint, Firmin wrote: "It echoes in my heart and comforts my faith in the future of my race, of the black race whose incomparable, eternal glory, is to have produced such a man, where so many other races would have offered only a brute with a human face." Toussaint was born a slave, but he overcame those conditions to become a brilliant revolutionary leader. Toussaint represented the ability of the black race to produce great leaders under adverse conditions, which is why Firmin wrote: "Certainly, when a race has produced an individuality as marvelously gifted as Toussaint-Louverture was, it is impossible to admit that it is inferior to others, without demonstrating an inconceivable blindness or absence of logic."

In Firmin's view, the black race would come to pursue justice more forcibly than other races have done. He wrote: "Splendid will be the role it will have to play in the world. Its great share of action, in the blossoming of progress, will be above all to develop the sense of justice with much more force and, at the same time, much more of delicacy than the jaded and dry-hearted races which arose in Europe or which grew in the plains of the Middle Kingdom and Tartary." In expressing this view, Firmin is not necessarily asserting that black people inherently have a superior morality to other races. Firmin expressed the view that the "races are equal; they are all capable of achieving the noblest intellectual development, as they are of falling into the most complete degradation." Firmin also noted that the Egyptians enslaved other races, including the children of Seth and Japheth—this was a reference to the Biblical enslavement of the Hebrews in Egypt. Firmin mentioned this to show that there was a period in time when black people had enslaved other races. The point that he made was that all races had been guilty of oppressing other races at some point in their history.

Firmin's treatment of religion in *On the Equality of Human Races* is interesting because it relates to a topic in Haitian history which Firmin would address in a later work. Firmin saw in Haiti's history a conflict between modernization and traditional African superstitions. In *Mr. Roosevelt, President of the United States and the Republic of Haiti,* he explained that Henri Christophe followed Toussaint and Jean-Jacques Dessalines in employing his energy to combat African superstitions. Firmin argued that Alexandre Pétion had taken the opposite view of Toussaint, Dessalines, and Christophe. Firmin explained that under Pétion's rule, those who wanted to be free abandoned cultivated land and lived in the woods where they were pushed back to ancestral savagery. Firmin does not elaborate on either of these points to define what he meant by African superstitions and ancestral savagery, but one could conclude that Firmin is referring to traditional African religious practices such as voodoo.[9]

Firmin's view of religion was that religions were superstitious beliefs which would lose their relevance as science progressed. In *On the Equality of Human Races*, Firmin wrote: "A fact that cannot be concealed is the serene indifference that all men of high intelligence, in all times and in all civilizations, have always shown towards religious practices." Firmin also expressed the view that "faith is dying." He noted that an increasing number of individuals were turning away from Christianity, though Firmin also recognized that the transition away from Christianity is not an easy one for white people. Firmin made the argument that it would be easier for black people to transition away from religion. He explained: "Never having conceived the religious fanaticism and the dogmatic spirit, in the shackles of which the Caucasian race painfully struggles, the Blacks find themselves quite ready to evolve towards rational and positive conceptions, in conformity with the system of the universe and the resulting moral order."

Firmin described African religions as being "fetishism and totemism" which he described as being the adoration of animals and stones, as well as the belief in charms accompanied by repugnant and bloodthirsty rites. Firmin did note that these practices are also found among several backward nations of other races. He explained that all the peoples of the white race also had a period in their existence in which they practiced fetishism, so that this practice is not limited only to African people alone.

Firmin is not totally dismissive of African religions for he also argued that the religion of African people was not wholly based on superstitious rituals. He described African religions as "a kind of practical rationalism" in which Africans believed that the greater deity is so far above humans that it is too great to worry about human affairs. Firmin made reference to Mungo Park's observation that the Mandinka people believe that God is so superior that they believe it was ridiculous to imagine that mortals could change the decrees or the aim of infallible wisdom through prayer.

Firmin rejected the notion that humanity can be divided into a racial hierarchy in which whites were the superior race, but he did not completely reject the concept of race itself. This may seem like a contradictory position, but Firmin understood that although race did not exist as a scientific reality, the social reality of race was real and had an effect on the lives of African people. Thus, by bringing attention to the achievements of great African civilizations and great individual leaders such as Toussaint, Firmin was demonstrating that African people were just as capable of contributing to human civilization as other races.

Firmin was also a Pan-Africanist who believed that Haiti had a role to play in the rehabilitation of Africa.[10] Not only did Firmin believe that Haiti had to serve in the rehabilitation of Africa, but he believed that the elevation of the black race would help Haiti. Firmin wrote in the preface to *Mr. Roosevelt:* "As long as black people continue to be an object of contempt by other men, whether white or yellow, Haiti will never be taken seriously..." Firmin recognized that the destiny of Haiti was linked to the destiny of other African people around the world. He demonstrated this link in *On the Equality of Human Races*, where he explained that the independence of Haiti "had a positive influence on the fate of the whole Ethiopian race, living outside Africa."

For Firmin, the question of unity is significant for understanding the European conquest of the world. In *On the Equality of Human Races*, Firmin expressed the observation that all the European nations, of the white race, are naturally inclined to unite in order to dominate the rest of the world and that "whenever a European power lends its ostensible or hidden assistance to a people of Asia or Africa, it is to better paralyze the progress of a rival, whose greatness it is jealous of or fears, than to favor this people to whom it comes to aid only with the ulterior motive of being able to exploit it in turn." Firmin also noted that the focus of European politics seemed to be Asia and Africa. He particularly focused on the European presence in Africa, where he noted that Europeans justified their colonial conquests on the basis that Europeans have a right to exterminate those who resist their invasion.

Whereas Europeans have been united in their efforts to conquer the world, Africans have had to face the challenge of disunity. This was particularly the case for Haiti. In *Mr. Roosevelt*, Firmin noted that the diversity of ethnic groups was one of the challenges which Haiti had to confront given that the Africans in Haiti were drawn from different parts of Africa and came from different ethnic groups. Firmin wrote that Haiti was populated by "strangers forced together from diverse places in Africa, often as distant as the space that extends from Portugal to the Ural Mountains..." Firmin continued to note that these Africans spoke very diverse languages, which was unlike European languages which have a common Latin influence and therefore share some words in common. Firmin argued that the invasion of Arabs improved the state of affairs by providing an Africanized language of the conquerors, but that the difficulty in understanding each other still remained an obstacle for Africans.

Firmin attended the Pan-African Conference in 1900 which was held in London. Carolyn Fluehr-Lobban explained: "Had he not been preoccupied with Haitian politics and a bid to become President as head of a Firminist movement, ending in his exile in St Thomas ordered by President Nord Alexis, Firmin might have continued to be involved on an international level with the nascent Pan-Africanist movement." Indeed, it would seem that Firmin's primary concern was Haitian politics. Firmin's view was that Haiti had to serve in the rehabilitation of Africa. It is not apparent what Firmin had in mind when he wrote this statement, however. One is not sure how Firmin envisioned Haiti assisting with the rehabilitation of Africa. What is apparent from this remark by Firmin is that he was concerned with the rehabilitation of Africa and believed that Haiti should play a role in this process.

Henry Sylvester Williams, who organized the Pan African Conference, did not conceptualize the Pan-African movement as an anti-colonial movement to liberate Africa from colonial domination. In Williams' view, the Pan-African movement was one which would secure the rights and business interests of Africans living in "civilized" countries of the world.[11] Firmin's view on this issue is difficult to ascertain. Firmin invoked Africa's ancient past to counter the claims of black inferiority, but he wrote very little about the contemporary situation in Africa. Fluehr-Lobban noted that "Firmin was largely ignorant of the contemporary African continent of his day, recalling that much of the African interior had yet to be fully explored and mapped at the time of the writing of *De l'égalité des races humaines*, in 1885. The Berlin Congress dividing the continent amongst the major European powers had occurred the year before, in 1884." The colonial powers of Europe partitioned Africa among themselves. By 1900, Africa had been colonized by various European nations. Firmin certainly recognized that this desire for global conquest on the part of Europeans was detrimental to the people of Africa, but it would appear that Firmin was more concerned with strengthening and protecting Haiti than with confronting colonialism in Africa.

Price-Mars, who was influenced by Firmin's work, expanded on the Pan-African work of Firmin. Firmin challenged racist theories about African people, but he seemed largely indifferent towards affirming the African cultural roots of the people of Haiti. Price-Mars, on the other hand, explored the African roots of Haitian culture in more depth than Firmin seemed interested in doing.

Price-Mars also went further than Firmin in challenging the manner in which the colonial legacy shaped the way that Haitians viewed their own identity. In his book *So Spoke the Uncle*, Price-Mars noted that some Haitians disassociated from their African ancestry and preferred to view themselves as colored Frenchman.[12] Massillion Coicou, a poet who was killed for his role in the Firminist rebellion, went so far as to write a poem in which he professed his love of France and expressed the view that Haiti was the "Black France."[13] This was an example of the type of mentality which Price-Mars referred to.

This type of thinking displayed that although Haiti was politically independent, many Haitians were still psychologically colonized. This psychological colonization led some Haitians to recoil from their African identity and seek to embrace the identity of the colonizer. It would appear that Firmin was proud of his African identity and did not view himself as a black Frenchman, although he did express the view that Haiti shared a common destiny with France. In *Mr. Roosevelt*, Firmin explained that Haitians had a tie of sympathy to France which could not be erased "from the heart of the Haitians, without erasing all the pages of our history, which prove that, even while fighting each other, in the great struggle for freedom and national independence, Haitians and French kept something in common, the generosity of the heart and the admiration of true courage wherever it comes from."

Firmin explained: "By language, Haiti is France..." He continued to note that although Haiti was proud of its political independence, Haiti was also proud of the ties that bind it to "the old mother country" and seeks to strengthen those ties by imitating whatever comes to Haiti from France. Firmin did not seem to question this connection to France in the way that Price-Mars would later do. In Firmin's view, the duty of France was to cooperate with the United States to help Haiti rise more and more in the ways of civilization.

At first glance, there seems to be a significant gap between the work of Price-Mars and Firmin. After all, whereas Price-Mars openly challenged Haiti's psychological attachment to France and pointed to Haiti's African roots, Firmin seemed to have unquestionably accepted the fact that Haiti remained culturally connected to France, despite having won its political independence from France through a bloody revolution. Where Firmin differs compared to some other Haitian intellectuals was that Firmin did not seek to disassociate himself from Africa. Firmin had declared in *On the Equality of Human Races* that there was no fundamental difference between the blacks of Africa and the blacks of Haiti. This alone was a profound remark which displayed Firmin's Pan-African worldview and his embrace of Africa.

France of Firmin's day was one of the colonial powers which was exploiting the people of Africa through colonialism. One would have hardly expected France to have done anything to contribute to Haiti's development, but Firmin was optimistic about the possibility that France and the United States would assist Haiti. Haiti's relationship to France, as Firmin pointed out, was based on a shared history and shared language, whereas Firmin saw Haiti's relationship to the United States as being based on a shared history of revolutionary struggle against the colonial forces of Europe.

One could argue that Firmin was perhaps too optimistic in viewing France and the United States as being nations which would serve to uplift Haiti, but Firmin was not alone in his optimism about France and the United States. Marcus Garvey had expressed a similar view. When Garvey noticed France's alarmed reaction to the work that his organization was doing in Africa, Garvey explained: "Why France should act in this manner I am unable to say, because it has always been the belief of a large number of us that France was friendly disposed toward the higher development of the Negro race, but recent happenings have proved to us that France is no better than the other colonial powers that have ravished and exploited Africa for hundreds of years." Regarding the American government, Garvey explained: "We believe that America's friendship for the Negro is unparalleled and that when the time comes America will do more for us as a race than any other government in the world." The American government, just like the French government, was alarmed by Garvey's work and endeavored to oppose what Garvey was doing.[14]

In *Mr. Roosevelt*, Firmin described George Washington as an "illustrious hero" in the War of Independence and as a man whose "immortal name" will always awaken respect and admiration. Despite his praise for the American Revolution, Firmin recognized that the United States was a nation which had not lived up to its ideals. Firmin was particularly concerned about racism in the United States. He argued that before the American people could assume the role of vanguard of the civilized nations, it must address the problem of Afro-Americans, "whose admission to citizenship and social equality is so hotly contested throughout the American South." Firmin explained that the "question of race or color prejudice" was also a topic of interest for Haitians in their relations with the United States.

Firmin's political vision was hemispheric. He was an early proponent of creating an Antillean confederation years before the formation of the short-lived West Indies Federation or the Caribbean Community (CARICOM). Firmin's interest in Caribbean unity led him to connect with a Puerto Rican nationalist named Ramón Emeterio Betances. Betances also advocated for the creation of a Caribbean federation as well. Firmin not only advocated for a unity of Caribbean nations, but he also believed that the United States and Haiti should form a partnership. Firmin recognized that the two nations shared a similar history, since both nations were born out of a revolutionary struggle against a colonial power from Europe. Firmin put forward this vision in *Mr. Roosevelt*.

That Firmin did not look to Africa as a potential political force for Haiti to align itself with is hardly surprising. Not only was Africa colonized, but, as noted before, Firmin's understanding of Africa was very limited. Firmin had never traveled to Africa, although Benito Sylvain, another Haitian Pan-Africanist who attended the 1900 Pan-African Conference, had traveled to Ethiopia where he met Menelik II. It would appear that Firmin's vision was one in which Haiti would become a strong and stable nation with the support of the United States and France, and then Haiti would work toward establishing a great civilization in Africa. Firmin did not write much about the topic of colonialism in Africa, so it is difficult to determine if Firmin recognized that there would eventually be a struggle against the colonial powers in Europe over Africa's liberation. Firmin certainly condemned the brutal methods which European nations had employed in Africa, but Firmin's immediate concern was the possibility that Haiti could once again be dominated by foreign forces.

In *Mr. Roosevelt*, Firmin addressed the Monroe Doctrine. Firmin expressed support for the Monroe Doctrine, even going so far as to quote the words of the President of the United States, who declared: "I believe with all my soul, in the Monroe Doctrine." Firmin did not oppose the Monroe Doctrine in theory, but he did take issue to the Monroe Doctrine being used to justify American imperialism in the Caribbean. He criticized the American intervention in Cuba under President McKinley. Firmin wrote that McKinley "must have sensed that it was indeed him, the loyal knight, the Lohengrin, protector of the weak, whom the poet called to the help of desperate Cuba."

A French economist named Pierre Leroy-Beaulieu argued that the United States had a right to expand itself by intervening in Haiti, since the "semi-barbarous individuals" do not have the right to prevent the development of their countries "by other countries more civilized than them." Firmin suggested that France should not listen to Leroy-Beaulieu's views. Firmin also questioned why an American president would attempt to seize Haiti given the costs that would be involved in such an endeavor. He wrote: "Besides, what American statesman, shrewd and wise, would want to undertake to seize Haitian territory or a part of it by force, by comparing the benefit of such an acquisition with the efforts and the considerable thoughts, in human lives and in money, that it would be necessary to deploy and carry out to bring its enterprise to a successful conclusion?" Firmin further noted that if Haiti's republic was threatened, Haiti should be determined to fight to preserve its independence. Firmin recognized the need for Haiti to defend itself, although he did not view President Theodore Roosevelt as a threat to Haiti's independence. He believed that Haiti had nothing to fear from Roosevelt. Firmin was correct as Roosevelt was not the president who would oversee the American invasion of Haiti in 1915.

America's imperial intentions towards Haiti became apparent in the affair over Môle St. Nicholas. The United States sought to secure control of Môle St. Nicholas to establish a naval base in the

Caribbean. The talks over this territory began in 1981. Frederick Douglass, who at the time was the American ambassador to Haiti, was sent to engage in negotiations. Price-Mars described Firmin as being trapped between Haitian public opinion and American public opinion. In the end, Firmin succeeded in staving off the American claims to Haitian land by citing the Haitian Constitution, which forbade cession of territory to foreigners. Firmin and Douglass both resigned from their positions at the end of the negotiations.[15] Price-Mars explained that from this resounding victory the ideology of "Firminism" was born. He compared Firminism to a religion which had its fanatics and its martyrs. Among those martyrs was the poet, Coicou.[16]

Firminism in Haiti developed into a revolutionary political movement which sought to transform Haiti. Throughout Firmin's life, he had been at the forefront of efforts to politically transform Haiti. When Firmin returned to Haiti in 1888, he joined a revolutionary committee which was organized against Salomon's government. This revolutionary movement managed to successfully remove Salomon from power and a provisional government was established. The provisional government drafted a new constitution for Haiti. Firmin and another lawyer named Léger Cauvin led the debates of the assembly over this new constitution. In the newly established government, Firmin was to serve as the Secretary of State for External Relations, Finance, and Trade. Firmin proved to be very effective at managing the nation's finances. In a short time, the credit of the state was enhanced and there was a gradual rise in the rating of the bonds of external debt on the Paris Stock Exchange.[17]

After another period of being overseas, Firmin returned to Haiti in 1902 to bury the remains of his daughter who died while they were living in France.[18] Now back in Haiti, Firmin decided to struggle against General Nord Alexis for power in Haiti. Alexis and Firmin worked together on the revolutionary committee which had overthrown President Salomon. Now the two men would become bitter political rivals. The wedge between the two men was partly due to the fact that when a new government was formed in 1902, Alexis was included in the government, but Firmin was excluded.[19] Alexis used his position in the new government to position himself into power, while also targeting Firmin and

Firmin's supporters.

The contest for power between Firmin and Alexis became a violent one. Firmin, who had opposed the militarism in Haiti, found himself in a situation where armed struggle was necessary to achieve his political aims in Haiti. In this struggle, Firmin relied on the services of his brother-in-law, Albert Salnave. Salnave and Alexis seemed to have held each other in high esteem. Price-Mars recalled that in 1903 he was brought to the National Palace where he met with Alexis. Papillion was at the meeting as well. Papillion was a former minister who was given the right to return from exile. Alexis asked Papillion about Albert Salnave's life in exile to which Papillion provided some information. Alexis responded by accusing Firmin of having involved his brother-in-law in the rebellion.[20]

Price-Mars attributed Firmin's defeat to Firmin's mistaken decision to order a man named Hammerton Killick to seize arms and ammunition from a German steamer. Rather than allowing his ship, the *Crête-à-Pierrot*, to be captured, Killick decided to destroy the ship. Killick went down along with the ship. Firmin praised Killick's actions, describing his conduct as being glorious. He compared Killick's sacrifice to that of Marcus Curtius of Rome and Louis Delgrès from Martinique. In his statement praising Killick, Firmin instructs Killick as follows:

> You say to Dessalines that contrary to his advice we have admitted the foreigner among us and that he has become the working machine of our troubles and our divisions.
>
> You will tell Christophe that certain Haitians have intentionally kept the people in ignorance, idleness, laziness, but that the descendants of the titans of 1804 are not yet prepared for slavery.[21]

Firmin ended the letter by declaring, "for God, save the black race, save the country, save Haiti." In Firmin's view, Killick had made a great sacrifice in defense of Haiti and the black race, but Price-Mars argued that this incident displayed Firmin's greatest weakness. Price-Mars noted that the decision to seize weapons from a German steamer was a poor one on the part of Firmin and that no one around Firmin was able to advise him properly. Price-Mars explained "Firmin's fault has been attributed to his infatuation. It seems that he had no one in his entourage who had enough authority to make him see to what calamity his decision was going to bring him."

Following his defeat, Firmin went into exile. Firmin continued his resistance to Alexis' government. In 1908, Firmin traveled to the United States, where he declared that with the support of the "sympathetic neutrality" of the American government, he would proceed to overturn Alexis' government in Haiti. A report on this comment by the *New York Times* noted that Firmin was known in diplomatic circles as "a professional revolutionist."[22] The United States expressed little interest in aiding Firmin. As the report noted, Firmin's opposition to granting America a naval base in Haiti was enough to prevent the existence of any kind of sympathy for Firmin. Alexis' government was not viewed as being an ideal government. Alexis faced pressure from the United States after he executed political prisoners, but America had no interest in intervening to help Firmin into power. America was more interested in maintaining Alexis' government in power. Alexis claimed to be pro-American and received American assistance in suppressing the Firminist rebellion in Haiti.[23] Alexis remained president of Haiti until 1908 when he was ousted from power. He left for Jamaica where he lived in exile.

Firmin sought America's help in his endeavor, but he was under no illusion about the fact that Haiti needed to be in control of its own destiny. In *Mr. Roosevelt*, Firmin concluded that even if France were to unite with the American Union to aid Haiti, it would be in vain if Haitians do not decide to take a retrospective look at their past and change their habits. He explained: "Our destiny, in the final analysis, must be our own work."

Firmin spent the last years of his life in exile. Firmin made an attempt to return to Haiti in 1911. He arrived on August 12, but was not allowed to get off the boat. Firmin's presence in Haiti remained a source of concern for the Haitian government. Firmin was allowed to greet friends who wished to see him aboard the steamer, however. After this brief return to Haiti, Firmin returned to St. Thomas, this time accompanied by his wife. Firmin initially went into exile to St. Thomas without his wife. Firmin had attempted to bring his wife with him to St. Thomas. He asked Captain Le Breton to ask the president for a passport to be issued to Rosa Firmin. The request was granted by President Antoine Simon, but this recommendation was ignored. Firmin, who was ailing, died that same year.[24]

Firmin recalled that America's decision to annex Puerto Rico was "like a fatal blow, aimed at the heart of Doctor Betances, with the irremediable failure of his long-cherished and patriotic hopes." Betances had lived in exile for almost thirty years. He swore to never set foot in Puerto Rico unless it was a free and independent nation, but he watched helplessly as his homeland passed from Spanish domination to American domination. Firmin explained that Betances was more wounded by the overthrow of his aspirations than he was by the disease from which he was suffering from at the time.[25] Firmin would not live to see Haiti suffer a similar fate, although he foretold that such a fate could be possible for Haiti. In the years following Firmin's death, his concerns would prove to be prophetic. Haiti did in fact fall under the foreign domination of the United States in 1915, only four years after Firmin's death.

Since Haiti became independent, Haiti struggled with political stability and military rule. Firmin pointed out in *Mr. Roosevelt* that the danger of national independence obtained by war is that power is concentrated in the hands of the military force, which is both an instrument of coercion and defense.[26] This was precisely the problem in Haiti. The American invasion of Haiti did little to resolve this problem of political instability in Haiti, however. Price-Mars noted that the tradition of having military men in power in Haiti ended following the 1915 invasion of Haiti, but the civilians who came to power were often inferior to their predecessors.[27]

The American occupation of Haiti lasted from 1915 until 1934, but America would continue to influence Haiti's politics even after the occupation ended. The corruption, abuse of power, and instability would continue as well. Firmin's hope and vision for Haiti was that Haiti would serve as a testament for the capability of the African race. This was not a vision which Firmin lived to see, but in the years that followed his passing, Firmin's vision remained just as relevant.

Notes:

1. *De l'égalité des races humaines* (*On the Equality of Human Races*) is one of the two books by Firmin which are referenced in this essay and translated from the original French text. The other book is *M. Roosevelt, Président des États-Unis et la République d'Haïti* (*Mr. Roosevelt, President of the United States and the Republic of Haiti*).
2. John Henrik Clarke's discussion on John G. Jackson here is quoted from "On My Journey Now: The Narrative and Works of Dr. John Henrik Clarke, the Knowledge Revolutionary" in *The Journal of Pan African Studies*, vol. 6, no. 7, February 2014.
3. Jean Price-Mars published a biography of Anténor Firmin titled *Antenor Firmin*. The quotes presented in this essay were translated into English from the original French version.
4. This incident is mentioned by Firmin in *Mr. Roosevelt*. Price-Mars mentioned it as well in *Antenor Firmin*.
5. The rumors surrounding the reason why Firmin was initially rejected when he expressed an interest in marrying Rosa Salnave is addressed by Price-Mars in chapter twelve of his biography.
6. In chapter seven of *On the Equality of Human Races*, Firmin compares physical beauty among the races. He concluded that the color of the white race enhances its beauty more than the Ethiopian race, but he also explained that he found the mulatto to be the most beautiful color of all.
7. This incident is recounted in chapter thirty-seven of Price-Mars' biography on Firmin. Price-Mars explained that it was unclear whether Firmin himself was aware of this incident or what his views on it were if he was aware.
8. This exchange between Firmin and Royer is mentioned by Carolyn Fluehr-Lobban in "Anténor Firmin and Haiti's contribution to anthropology" in *Gradhiva* 1, 2005.
9. Based on the remarks which Firmin made on religion in *On the Equality of Human Races* and in *Mr. Roosevelt*, it would seem that Firmin was not religious, but his writings would suggest that he

was not an atheist either.

10. Firmin writes this in the preface of *On the Equality of Human Races*.

11. For more information on Henry Sylvester Williams' role in the Pan-African movement see "The Historical Aspects of Pan-Africanism: A Personal Chronicle" by Rayford W. Logan.

12. Price-Mars addressed the negative attitude that Haitians had towards their African roots in the preface of *So Spoke the Uncle*.

13. This is a reference to a poem by Massillon Coicou titled "A Un Fraiçais" from a collection of Coicou's poems titled *Poésies Nationales*.

14. These quotes by Marcus Garvey are taken from *Selected Writings and Speeches of Marcus Garvey*.

15. Price-Mars provided a detailed account of the negotiations over Môle St. Nicholas in his biography of Firmin. Amy Reinsel also provides a brief summary of the incident in "Poetry of Revolution: Romanticism and National Projects in Nineteenth-century Haiti."

16. Coicou was killed for his role in participating in a Firminist rebellion in Haiti. Coicou's support of the Firminist movement and his execution are detailed by Reinsel in "Poetry of Revolution: Romanticism and National Projects in Nineteenth-century Haiti."

17. Price-Mars detailed Firmin's role in the government in his biography on Firmin.

18. The death of Firmin's daughter Anna is mentioned by Price-Mars in *Antenor Firmin*. Price-Mars explained that Firmin returned to Haiti to bury his daughter in 1902 to dismiss some claims which stated that Firmin returned to Haiti that year to disrupt the general elections. Price-Mars also recounted that in 1901, he was invited to have lunch with Firmin, his wife, and his daughter Anna. Price-Mars wrote: "It was the only time I had the opportunity to see a modest Firmin, mute with admiration, in a conversation in which his daughter displayed the liveliness and grace of her mind." Price-Mars had a lively dialogue with her about the difficulties of the German language and the English language. Anna died a year later.

19. Reinsel provided an account of the conflict between Firmin and Alexis in "Poetry of Revolution: Romanticism and National Projects in Nineteenth-century Haiti." In this account, Reinsel

mistakenly stated that General Tiresias Augustin Simon Sam became the president of Haiti in 1902. Sam actually left the office of the presidency in 1902.

20. This is mentioned in Price-Mars' biography. In 1903, Price-Mars had returned from Europe and was brought to the National Palace by the Minister of War to present his duties to Nord Alexis. Price-Mars concluded that Alexis and Albert Salnave had equal consideration for each other.

21. This statement by Firmin is quoted by Price-Mars in chapter thirty-five of his biography in Firmin. Price-Mars described Firmin as a "fierce doctrinaire" who opposed the domination of class and money oligarchies in Haiti.

22. This was reported in a *New York Times* article from June 22, 1908, titled "Ridicule Firmin's Boasts: State Officials Regard Haitian as a Professional Revolutionist."

23. In "Poetry of Revolution: Romanticism and National Projects in Nineteenth-century Haiti," Reinsel mentioned that in 1908, the United States intercepted an arms' shipment which was headed to Firmin supporters in Haiti.

24. In "Anténor Firmin and Haiti's contribution to anthropology," Fluehr-Lobban states that Firmin was 61 at the time of his death, whereas Price-Mars states that Firmin's age was 60.

25. Firmin's friendship with Doctor Betances and Firmin's views on Caribbean unity are addressed in Firmin's essay titled "Haiti and the Confederation of the Antilles" in *Inter America*, Volume 5.

26. Firmin addressed this topic in the section of *Mr. Roosevelt* which addressed the Haitian government during the reign of Jean-Jacques Dessalines.

27. Price-Mars addressed the American invasion of Haiti in chapter seventeen of his biography on Firmin.